CRIMINOLOGY
THE BASICS

'...book is a superb starting point and one I recommend to foundation and first year ...nts to enable them to grasp the complex subject that is criminology. Its beauty ... simplicity and accessibility, it covers a lot of ground and beginners are soon ...king like criminologists, exploring key issues around crime and criminals, from ...uring crime to hidden crimes of the powerful.'
...hard Peake, *University of Leeds, UK*

'[Sandra Walklate] has set out the subject matter of criminology in a reader-friendly manner but one in which the reader can question their own conventional notions about crime, crime causation, crime theorizing and crime control.'
David C. Perrier, *Saint Mary's University, Canada*

'...s text will be a welcome addition to many libraries, including my own!'
...ara Perry, *University of Ontario, Canada*

As crime continues to be a high-profile issue troubling politicians, the public and the media alike, the study of criminology has boomed. Providing an international and a comparative introduction to the discipline, *Criminology: The Basics* is an accessible guide to the theoretical and practical approaches to the phenomena of crime.

...ics covered in this new edition include:

- challenging myths about crime and offenders
- searching criminological explanation
- thinking about the victim of crime
- introducing critical criminology
- preventing crime and the future of crime control
- looking into the future, cultural criminology and terrorism.

Easy to read, concise and supported by a glossary of terms and pointers to further reading, *Criminology: The B...* ...ant and popular subject.

Sandra W... ...f Liverpool, UK. Her previc... *, Gender, Crime and Crimi...* ...

D0233926

The Basics

CRIMINOLOGY
THE BASICS
SECOND EDITION

Sandra Walklate

DUDLEY PUBLIC LIBRARIES	
000000476988	
Bertrams	15/06/2011
364	£11 99
	HA

Routledge
Taylor & Francis Group

LONDON AND NEW YORK

Second edition published 2011
by Routledge
2 Park Square, Milton Park, Abingdon, Oxon OX14 4RN

Simultaneously published in the USA and Canada
by Routledge
711 Third Avenue, New York, NY 10017

Routledge is an imprint of the Taylor & Francis Group, an informa business

© 2011 Sandra Walklate

The right of Sandra Walklate to be identified as author of this work has been
asserted by her in accordance with Sections 77 and 78 of the Copyright, Designs and
Patents Act 1988.

All rights reserved. No part of this book may be reprinted or reproduced or utilized
in any form or by any electronic, mechanical or other means, now known or
hereafter invented, including photocopying and recording, or in any information
storage or retrieval system, without permission in writing from the publishers.

Trademark notice: Product or corporate names may be trademarks or registered
trademarks, and are used only for identification and explanation without intent to
infringe.

First edition published by Routledge 2005

British Library Cataloguing in Publication Data
A catalogue record for this book is available from the British Library

Library of Congress Cataloging in Publication Data
Walklate, Sandra.
    Criminology: the basics/Sandra Walklate—2nd ed.
    p. cm.—(The basics)
    Includes bibliographical references.
    1. Criminology. I. Title.
    HV6025.W353 2011
    364—dc222010051283

ISBN: 978-0-415-57553-9 (hbk)
ISBN: 978-0-415-57554-6 (pbk)
ISBN: 978-0-203-81370-6 (ebk)

Typeset in Aldus and Scala Sans
by Book Now Ltd, London

MIX
Paper from
responsible sources
FSC
www.fsc.org   FSC® C004839

Printed and bound in Great Britain by
CPI Antony Rowe, Chippenham, Wiltshire

CONTENTS

ILLUSTRATIONS

Figures

Tables

PREFACE TO THE
SECOND EDITION

This book is intended to introduce both the lay reader and the prospective student to the issues and dilemmas that exist within the discipline of criminology. As the reader will discover, criminology is not an easy or a straightforward area of analysis to distil into one basic format. It is not like politics or sociology. They are disciplines whose basic concepts and ways of thinking (such as political institutions, concepts of justice or voting behaviour in the case of politics, or the structure of society, social class or questions of identity in the case of sociology) are agreed upon by those working within them. The debates that exist within those disciplines reflect how to make best sense of the polity on the one hand or society on the other. Criminology is different. It is an area of analysis that is not constituted by an agreed set of concepts or ways of thinking but is constituted by its subject matter: crime. As a result psychologists, sociologists, lawyers, politicians, all claim to have something to say about crime but they do not speak the same language or necessarily share in the same understanding of what counts as crime. So, trying to offer a 'basic' introduction to an area of analysis like this is neither easy nor straightforward.

There is, of course, another difficulty here, if the reader thinks about the question of what counts as crime. Although those interested in politics, sociology or psychology can talk to each other across cultures (language difficulties notwithstanding) because they share in a common understanding of their discipline, criminologists do not find that so easy. Since what might be criminal in one country is certainly not in another. As a result, the problems for the discipline and the policies that might flow from the discipline in different countries can vary enormously. A book like this cannot capture all of this diversity. This book is written by someone most familiar with the discipline of criminology as it has unfolded in the United Kingdom over the last 30 years, and as a consequence, it is inevitably Anglocentric. In addition, because the author works within a sociological frame of reference and has spent much of her time working with and on victims of crime, that too structures what has been included and excluded from what might be considered 'basic'. The reader should therefore read the pages that follow with these issues in mind.

Having said that, it is certainly hoped that the reader gets a sense of the challenge that criminology offers as a result of its diversity. A challenge that should at a minimum leave the reader with a sense that common sense and media presentations of crime, the criminal and the victim, are often misplaced but hopefully with much more than that too. The overall intention is to encourage the reader to think critically about what it is that the media and politicians have to say about crime and in thinking critically, to tempt you to read or study further about the issues that this book raises for you. If you are reading this book to look for answers then you will be disappointed!

My thanks go to the anonymous reviewers who offered comments on the first edition of this book and took the time and the patience to offer me valuable feedback on its strengths and weaknesses. Their independent comments have proved to be invaluable in putting this edition together. The faults that remain are my own.

Professor Sandra Walklate
Clawddnewydd
November 2010

ACKNOWLEDGEMENTS

Excerpts from *Home Office Statistical Bulletin* 16/10 © Crown Copyright 2010, public sector information licensed under the Open Government License v1.0.

Excerpts from *Race and The Criminal Justice System: an Overview of the Complete Statistics 2004–5* (2006) © Crown Copyright 2010, public sector information licensed under the Open Government License v1.0.

Excerpts from Walker *et al.* (Eds.) *Crime in England and Wales 2008–9* © Crown Copyright 2010, public sector information licensed under the Open Government License v1.0.

Diagram showing structure of the court system, © Crown Copyright 2010, public sector information licensed under the Open Government License v1.0.

Prison Service Statement of Purpose, © Crown Copyright 2004, public sector information licensed under the Open Government License v1.0.

Facts on female staff in the criminal justice system, reprinted by permission of the Fawcett Society.

While the publisher has made every effort to contact the copyright holders of the material used in this volume, they would be happy to hear from anyone they were unable to contact.

Diagram from Newburn, T. (2007) *Criminology*. Reprinted by permission of Routledge.

WHAT IS CRIMINOLOGY?

The purpose of this chapter is to get a sense of criminology as an academic subject. To do this we shall explore some features of the origins of the discipline and how those features still influence what it is that criminologists do and do not do. In particular this chapter will explore popular media images of crime and offer good reasons as to why those images are misplaced. To do this we shall explore the historical development of criminology, and its sister discipline, **victimology**. This exploration will help us understand how the boundaries of the discipline have been set and who is included and excluded by those boundaries. At the end of this chapter we shall use a case study, that of the UK serial murderer Harold Shipman, to establish the extent to which the boundaries of criminological and victimological knowledge can help us make sense of such behaviour.

INTRODUCTION

Before it is possible to say what criminology is, it is important to have some understanding of what it is not. Disciplines like politics, sociology, economics or psychoanalysis are held together by their adherence to the polity, the structure of society, the nature of economies or the individual psyche, as their central focus regardless of the social or legal context in which these disciplines are practised. Of course, that social or legal context may add variety to the kinds of analyses those various disciplines offer, but the conceptual and analytical framework in which the disciplines operate does not. The same cannot be said for criminology. Criminology is inevitably and inexorably a potentially different creature dependent on how crime itself is brought into being in different social and legal contexts. Thus what might be understood as crime, and as criminal, in France may vary from how that is understood in the United States. Appreciating and understanding the importance of differences like these is the central challenge of a book of this kind for both the author and the reader. There is, however, another challenge. That lies within contemporary media images of crime, the criminal and the criminologist, and the extent to which these images gel with what we think we 'know' about crime.

It has to be said that the subject matter of crime is a very popular source of entertainment. Indeed for many people what they see on the television or what they read in the newspapers is their only source of information about crime since, despite variable crime rates over the last 30 years or so, most people most of the time have no experience of their own of crime or the criminal justice process. This makes media images of crime potentially very powerful especially in equipping individuals with ideas about what it is that criminologists do. However the presence of Sherlock Holmes, Inspector Poirot, Crime Scene Investigators (CSI), other 'detective' stories and the forensic psychologists, popularized in the media notwithstanding, what these people claim to do and what criminologists actually spend their time doing, are two quite distinct activities. Criminology is not concerned with ways of catching criminals. That is the work on the one hand of a good police officer and on the other a good supply of information from the general public. Criminology is much more concerned to explain the cause(s) of crime, but how it does so will very much depend on what kind of criminologist you are.

Paul Rock (1986), a British sociologist, once described criminology as a 'rendezvous' subject. This was a way of trying to capture a sense of what, if anything, binds criminologists together. Put simply, the subject matter, crime, binds them together. Why make an issue of what seems to be fairly obvious? Of course criminologists are interested in crime. However exploring this obvious fact is what makes criminology as an area of investigation somewhat different than other areas of investigation. Psychologists, for example, explore how the mind works, sociologists are interested in social structures, economists in economic systems, historians in how what happened in the past can help us better understand the present, and so on. Each of these different disciplines are marked by the boundaries between them and how they go about their business in relation to what it is that they study: the past, society, the mind, the economy, and so on. However, within these boundaries they can all be interested in crime. So what binds criminologists together is that they share an interest in the same subject matter, but importantly they do not necessarily share the same way of thinking about how to study that subject matter. So criminology, as Rock said, is a meeting place for people coming from different ways of thinking about crime. It is multidisciplinary. So it is possible to find psychiatrists, historians, sociologists, psychologists, lawyers and economists who all claim the label 'criminologist' but might be looking at the question of crime through very different lenses. Criminology, as a consequence, is marked by debate. There are very few things that criminologists may agree on. One thing, however, that they may all share concerns about, is what it is that we understand by crime.

WHAT IS CRIME?

Again this seems an obvious question to ask. We 'all know' that crime is the behaviour that breaks the law. However, is it so straightforward? Even the Sage Dictionary of Criminology (2006) makes it clear that what we mean by 'crime' is highly contested. So what might that contest look like? If we take law-breaking behaviour as the starting point for our understanding of what we mean by crime, and thereby what it is that criminologists study, then this raises at least three issues.

- First, if it is the law that defines what it is that is criminal this clearly separates, what we mean by criminal from the rather more emotional use of the term. This in some respects is a useful starting point as the use of the term 'criminal', on the one hand prejudges the guilt or innocence of the offender, and on the other, taps into other kinds of views of 'wickedness' or 'evil' doing. So it may be more helpful to say that criminologists are interested in law-breaking behaviour. However, this definition is in itself problematic as it gives a status to the law as though this were above social processes of levels of tolerance and acceptability of different behaviours, that is clearly not the case.

- So, second, making what is and is not legal the defining characteristic of what it is that criminologists study places the law at centre of the criminological stage. The law defines what is and what is not a crime. However, it must be remembered that over time laws change. Some behaviours are newly defined as criminal (law breaking) others are decriminalized (defined as non-law breaking). (Think, for example, about the changing legal status of 'being gay' over time and in different places.) This being the case the key question that follows is, what are the processes that produce such changes? And moreover, who influences such changes and how are they implemented? Is it an understanding of these processes that produces an understanding of crime? This is quite a different question than a psychologist interested in crime might ask. They might be much more interested in what kinds of personality types predispose some individuals to engage in criminal behaviour. Such behaviour might occur, of course, regardless of the actual content of the law but may nevertheless be problematic (this is what sociologists call 'deviant' behaviour).

- However, there is a third difficulty in taking the law as defining what is crime. If this is taken as the defining characteristic of the criminal, does that mean that criminologists then can only legitimately study those that have been found guilty of transgressing the law? For many criminologists this kind of position would prove to be highly problematic given its inherently narrow focus on those individuals who have been caught and successfully prosecuted.

So from this discussion it can be seen that what counts as crime and thereby what criminologists study is neither consistent nor uniform and this will vary from country to country over time. Putting all of this together with the different ways in which people think about what counts as crime, we can identify at least five different understandings of what crime is.

Legal: Crime is that behaviour prohibited by the criminal code

Moral: Crime is that behaviour that offends the 'collective consciousness' and provokes punishment (usually, though not always, enshrined in the criminal law)

Social: Crime is that behaviour that violates social norms (including violation of the criminal law)

Humanistic: Crime is that behaviour of individuals, institutions or states that denies basic human rights (some of which is enshrined in human rights legislation and not necessarily criminal)

Social constructionist: Crime is that behaviour so defined as criminal by the agents and activities of the powerful (reflected in what is and what is not defined as criminal and what is and what is not acted on within the legal code more generally)

Figure 1.1: Different understandings of what crime is.

Figure 1.1 illustrates some of the different ways in which crime can be, and has been defined, by criminologists. As can be seen they each in their different ways take the law as a starting point for their understanding of crime but only the legal understanding takes the criminal code as the *definitive* start. Figure 1.1 also illustrates the way in which these different definitions harness different understandings of what Henry (2006: 78), a North American criminologist, has called the determining elements of crime. He suggests that there are three:

1. Harm (nature, severity, extent of the act committed, and/or the kind of victim the act has been committed against)
2. Social agreement or consensus (the extent to which there is social agreement that the victim has been harmed)
3. Official societal response (whether or not there is a law that specifies the act committed as a crime or not and how those laws are enforced)

So far from being straightforward, defining what crime is can be quite complex. This complexity arises as a result of a number of questions being muddled up; what crime is, who the criminal is, and what it is that criminologists study. (Moreover Henry's definition above introduces another dimension to what it is that criminologists study: the victim of crime, see also below.) Some of this complexity relates to the fact that this is a multidisciplinary area of concern and some of it reflects the historical focus that criminology has had in trying to formulate a general theory of crime. As a consequence, it is possible to define the subject matter of criminology in different ways. For example, Coleman and Norris (2000: 13–14) identify the subject matter of criminology in the following ways:

- an attempt to measure the extent of crime and offenders;
- an analysis of the causes of crime;
- understanding how laws are formed;
- understanding how laws are applied;
- understanding the issues around punishment;
- crime prevention;
- exploring the impact of crime on victims;
- exploring public attitudes and media presentations of crime.

As can be seen this is quite a wide-ranging list of topics. Newburn (2007: 6) focuses this list by defining criminology as:

- the study of crime;
- the study of those who commit crime;
- the study of the criminal justice and penal systems.

On the other hand, Walklate (2007: 14) defines the key features of criminology in a different way. She states criminology as a discipline is:

- held together by one substantive concern: crime;
- it is multidisciplinary so it is important to understand the conceptual apparatus with which a particular criminologist might be working;
- criminologists disagree with each other especially over how to 'solve' the crime problem, they nevertheless are concerned to offer some advice on policy.

- what criminologists do sometimes resonates with common sense thinking about crime but often challenges that thinking;
- all of these features of criminology need to be situated within societies increasingly preoccupied with crime, risk and insecurity.

If we put these lists together then it is clear to see that the discipline itself, if it has claims to such a title, is not only wide-ranging but also highly stimulating and frustrating in the debates that it creates.

In this book we shall be taking primarily a sociological orientation to understanding criminology and in so doing we will cover issues that include problems of measurement, understanding the victim of crime, looking at the relationship between criminology and crime prevention amongst other issues. However, there is one over-riding concern that is implicit to all of these lists and in much of criminology. That concern is with trying to identify and understand the causes of crime and the reasons why people commit crime.

As Figure 1.1 implies, the importance of formulating a general theory of crime has led different versions of criminology to resolve the question of what is crime in different ways, pointing to not only its multidisciplinarity but also its theoretical diversity. This emphasizes the highly contested nature of the discipline and what it is that criminologists study. In an effort to unravel some of this complexity a little more, we shall now consider the history of criminology in a little more detail. However, to do that it is important to appreciate and understand a central feature of much criminological work: positivism.

Positivism is defined as:

A theoretical approach that emerged in the early nineteenth century which argues that social relations and events (including crime) can be studied scientifically using methods derived from the natural sciences. Its aim is to search for, explain and predict future patterns of social behaviour. In criminology, it straddles biological, psychological and sociological disciplines in an attempt to identify key causes of crime — whether genetic, psychological, social or economic — which are thought to lie largely outside of the individual's control.

(Muncie 2006: 302)

In our exploration of the history of criminology the importance of positivism will become apparent.

THE EMERGENCE OF CRIMINOLOGY AS A DISCIPLINE: THE ITALIAN JOB

Criminology, like many other academic disciplines was driven by the concerns of the post Enlightenment period. This was a time in history when the natural sciences were embraced as constituting a better knowledge base than religion for understanding and controlling nature (which Bacon defined as female and a point which we shall return to in understanding criminology). In their wake the social sciences followed suit in looking for ways to better manage (read control) social problems. Post the French revolution and Industrial revolution; Auguste Comte, a French social theorist, was particularly influential in formulating an early version of sociology (that he called social physics) whose role he saw as exerting a positive influence on society. This is one way of understanding the term 'positivism' that was to have so much of an influence on the emergence of criminology as a discipline.

In criminology positivism has been, and still is, very powerful in defining what it is that criminologists do and do not study. Criminology embraced Comte's understanding of positivism and its historically significant links with policy in wanting to manage social problems. Criminology also embraced a more philosophical understanding of positivism in its efforts to model itself on the natural sciences. That understanding of positivism, a concern to measure the appearance of things and on the basis of that measurement formulate universal explanations of things, was to provide criminology with the evidential base on which to assert its influence on the policy-making process. This gave early criminology three central characteristics: **differentiation, pathology** and **determinism**.

- *Differentiation* refers to the desire to measure the differences between individuals and their behaviour.
- *Pathology* refers to the process of assigning abnormality to those differences.
- *Determinism* reflects a concern to understand how factors beyond the control of human beings affect their behaviour.

These ideas underpin the work of one of the most famous and influential criminologists of the nineteenth century, the Italian prison psychiatrist, Cesare Lombroso.

Lombroso is probably best described as a criminal anthropologist whose work was very much influenced by the ideas of Charles Darwin. Darwin's theory of evolution has one key law: the law of bio-genetics. This law states that every organism revisits the development of its own species within its own developmental history. Hence, the human embryo goes through various stages of development before reaching its humanoid state. However, not all organisms reach the state predicted by their biological origin; sometimes there are abnormalities. Darwin referred to this as a state of '**atavism**': a throwback to an earlier stage of development. These ideas in general, but the notion of atavism in particular, appealed to Lombroso in his efforts to understand and explain the criminal.

While working in the prison environment, Lomboso made systematic observations of prisoners. He noted that criminals shared a number of common physical attributes: sloping foreheads, receding chins, excessively long arms, are a few of them. On the basis of these observations he constructed four criminal types: the insane, the opportunist, the passionate and the born criminal, all of whom shared differently in the characteristics he observed but only one of them, the born criminal, constituted the true atavistic type. In other words what Lombroso was doing was borrowing Darwin's ideas and applying them to his observations in order to offer a general explanation of criminal behaviour. Criminals were criminals because they were throwbacks to earlier biological forms that were manifested in physical or mental attributes and resulted in criminal behaviour.

However odd these ideas might sound in contemporary terms (and it should be noted that some people would still agree with them), it should also be remembered that these ideas led to rather more liberal interpretations of punishment. These criminals may be different (*differentiation*), may be abnormal (*pathology*) but they were subject to forces outside of their control (in this case determined by their biology) and therefore imprisonment might be a more appropriate punishment than execution, for example. Moreover, Lombroso's work set an important agenda for criminology the legacy of which can still be felt contemporarily in two ways: first in the continuing presence of **biological positivism** and second in ideas around who is, and who is not, likely to be criminal: the **Criminal Other**. They were particularly pertinent in constructing understandings of female criminal behaviour as we shall see.

Looking to biological explanations of human behaviour is, of course, not peculiar to criminology and much work through the early part of the twentieth century took biology as its general starting point for the explanation of all kinds of behavioural and mental abilities. Indeed, other criminologists, following Lombroso produced a range of different understandings of the relationship between biology and crime. For example, some focused on body type and criminal behaviour, some on the relationship between chromosomal abnormalities and propensity for criminal behaviour (especially violent crime), others on understandings of the relationship between personality type (as an innate feature of a human being) and criminal behaviour, and more recently some have made observations on the variations in brain wave imaging available from neuroscience and criminal behaviour. All of which share in common with Lombroso the three concerns of differentiation, pathology and determinism.

Perhaps one of the most influential expositions of this kind of work, in the policy arena in recent years, has been the work of the North Americans Wilson and Herrnstein. Their book *Crime and Human Nature* published in 1985 argued that there were three factors that contributed to criminality: an individual's constitution (i.e. their biological make-up), the social and psychological reinforcers they were or were not exposed to (reflecting a particular understanding of the process of socialization) and their conscience (how guilty they felt or did not feel in relation to their behaviour). Whilst more complex than the ideas of Lombroso of a century before, biology is still clearly present and some have argued that the work of Wilson and Herrnstein provided the intellectual support for the rise in the use of imprisonment as a punishment in the United States from the late 1980s onwards. The importance of this biological legacy, however, lies in our understanding of who is assumed to be criminal and who is not. Put another way, biological positivism puts some crimes and criminals at the centre of the criminological agenda and ignores others. This is sometimes referred to as the construction of the 'Criminological Other'. We shall explore this more fully.

On the face of it biological positivism tells us quite clearly that the criminal is different than us, and that those differences are observable and measurable. However, there is a deeper understanding of this (different) criminal that is clearly derivable from the work of Lombroso. That understanding can be constructed if we re-visit the ideas of Darwin for a moment. The bio-genetic law referred to earlier has some assumptions deeply embedded within it. Put simply, for Darwin the pinnacle of evolutionary development is the white, Caucasian, heterosexual male. Women for Darwin, for example, were closer to nature (because of their child-bearing capabilities) and were therefore less advanced than men. He went so far as to say that they suffered from 'arrested development' because of their biology. So when Lombroso came to study the female offender with his colleague Ferraro, they took this presumption as their starting point, that is, that women were arrested in their development in some way. So if the male criminal was a throwback (i.e. atavistic) in Lombrosian theory, the female criminal suffered a double biological blow. Already suffering from arrested development through being female she was also a throwback (atavistic) as an offender: a real monster! The female offender then is doubly deviant. This is part of the deeper structure of the Criminal Other that has left its mark on criminology as a discipline and suggests boundaries around about who can and cannot be criminal.

Of course, what is also embedded in the work of Darwin and Lombroso are wider anxieties associated with the intellectual climate of the nineteenth century, a time of huge social, economic and political upheaval. However, the assumptions rooted in these anxieties are still to be found in our current everyday thinking. That thinking reflects a tendency to divide the world into two: male/female, normal/abnormal, rational/irrational and culture/nature. These are some of the divides familiar to us. In the context of biological positivism within criminology this kind of divide presumes that the differences between men and women, for example, are natural differences; given by nature and that women, by definition, are less well-developed than men. As a result, women form part of the Criminological Other, that is marginal to the concerns of the discipline and outside of its understanding. Biological positivism reflects a deeply rooted assumption that the criminal is always male. However, this is not the only version of positivism to have had a profound effect on the discipline. **Sociological positivism**, which we shall discuss next, substitutes the social for the biological and creates a different, though connected image of who is and who is not likely to be a criminal and therefore a focus of concern for the discipline.

THE DEVELOPMENT OF CRIMINOLOGY AS A DISCIPLINE: THE AMERICAN STORY

If biological positivism has its origins in European anxieties of the nineteenth century, sociological positivism (as developed within criminology) has its origins in North American anxieties at the turn of the twentieth century. In that setting it would be difficult to deny the importance of the Chicago School of Sociology in setting this differently oriented agenda for criminology.

For the first three decades or so of the twentieth century the United States experienced massive social and economic change that was particularly marked by immigration. During this time the larger towns in the United States, and in this respect Chicago was no different than many others, grew rapidly both in terms of population and in terms of their local economies. Sociologists at the University of Chicago, influenced by the work of Comte and Durkheim, another French social theorist, were concerned to understand the pattern and impact of that social change and also to develop policies to manage the worst effects of it. Two of them, Park and Burgess, sociologists working at the University of Chicago, developed a social–ecological model of the growth and development of Chicago as a way of making sense of what they observed taking place. This model became known as the **concentric zone theory** of the city. These theorists argued that just as it was possible to identify patterns in the processes of adaptation made to the environment by animals, so it was possible to identify patterns in relation to the growth and development of the city. In this way they identified a series of circles radiating from the city centre with each circular zone having different social and economic characteristics and the people living in those areas adapting differently to those social circumstances.

So different patterns of statistical data gathered from the different zones of the city demonstrated the different modes of adaptation to the social and economic circumstances that people were presented with. From this kind of analysis particular attention was focused on the **zone of transition**, the one nearest the city centre. This was the area in which new immigrants to the city settled (as it was inexpensive and near to places of work) but it was also the area that seemed to manifest the most social problems (according to official statistics) from incidences of ill health to crime. The existence of these problems in this area was explained by the social ecologists as being the result of the highly mobile and transitory nature of social life there that in itself bred impersonal and fragmentary social relationships. In this way all kinds of social problems including crime were given a social origin. This social origin was called 'social disorganization'. Herein lie the beginnings of sociological positivism within criminology.

According to the Chicago School social disorganization was the root of all social problems including crime. This term was intended to reflect the ways in which the problems of immigration and migration produced communities in which there were competing social values. This competition led to the breakdown of accepted ways of behaving making way for different ones, and in the process of change, produced abnormal (pathological) social conditions. This was especially the case in the 'zone of transition' that in more contemporary times came to be known as the 'inner city'. Concern over the relationship between living in the 'inner city' and crime has continued from the 1930s until the present. The labels people have used to demonstrate this concern have changed, sometimes talking about disadvantaged communities or frightened communities, or socially excluded communities. All of these labels are bound together by one presumption; that it is the structure of the local community (or more precisely the lack of structure) that shapes the local crime rate rather than the propensity or otherwise of any individual to commit crime.

This view of Crime, its location and explanation, offers us a different picture of the Criminological Other. In this view the middle classes are the other, outside of the discipline and outside of its understanding. The criminal is always working class, or perhaps more accurately, part of the underclass, and most likely not only male but also a member of an ethnic minority. These are the people who live in and comprise the problematic communities for both policy and politics. Though such communities are not as socially disorganized as the Chicago School would have us believe, they are, and have been, nevertheless defined as problematic. These groups are separated out in this version of positivism from the rest of society on the basis of their culture not their nature.

Summary

So it can be seen from these two different stories of the emergence of criminology as a discipline, positivism, both biological and sociological has had a profound effect on not only how the discipline conducts its business, but also by implication what the discipline has been concerned with in the conduct of that business. Taking these influences together criminology, as a discipline, has been historically defined by its concern with young, male, working-class criminal activity. This does not mean the there have not been criminologists who have concerned themselves with middle-class crime (or more generally the 'crimes of the powerful'; this issue is taken up later in this book) or who have been keen to address female criminal behaviour. They have. It does mean, however, that the way in which much of that concern has been constructed has to be understood in the light of the central focus of the discipline as outlined here. This is a theme that we shall return to on more than one occasion as we endeavour to uncover an understanding of what criminology is about.

However, it should also be noted that much contemporary criminological, policy and political debate in and around crime and the crime problem have been much more concerned to address the victim of crime. Indeed to appreciate the contemporary nature of criminology it is just as important to understand some of the features of its sister discipline, victimology, as it is to understand the more mainstream discipline of criminology itself. So we shall now pay some attention to the story of the emergence of victimology as an arena of academic and policy debate.

VICTIMOLOGY: THE HOLOCAUST CONNECTION?

The origins of victimology are usually located in the work of Von Hentig and Mendelsohn. They were two émigré lawyers cum criminologists who worked in the United States in the late 1940s. As with many other like-minded intellectuals of the late 1940s and the 1950s who found themselves in the United States as a consequence of the Second World War, they were perplexed by the events that had happened in Germany. This led Von Hentig and Mendelsohn to think about the dynamics of victimization, though being lawyers how they understood those dynamics was very much at the level of the individual and very much informed by their legal training. It is also possible to see the influence of early criminological thought reflected in their work.

Both of these theorists were concerned to develop ways of thinking about the victim that would enable the victim to be differentiated from the non-victim. In other words both were clearly suggesting that there is a normal person who, when the victim is measured against them, the victim falls short. To achieve this kind of understanding they each developed victim typologies. Von Hentig's typology worked with a notion of **victim proneness**. He argued that there were some people, by virtue of their structural characteristics who were much more likely to be victims (in this case of crime) than other people. These he identified as being women, children, the elderly, the mentally subnormal and so on. (He had 13 categories in all.) Thinking about this categorization critically, it is possible to see that Von Hentig thought that the normal person was the white, heterosexual male. Similar presumptions to those of Lombroso discussed earlier, though Von Hentig does not suggest that there is a 'born victim' that parallels the idea of a 'born criminal'. Von Hentig's ideas have been influential and are most keenly identified in the concept of 'lifestyle' that has informed much **criminal victimization survey work**. (See below.)

Mendelsohn adopted a more legalistic framework in developing his typology. His underlying concept was the notion of **victim culpability**. Using this concept he developed a six-fold typology from the victim who could be shown to be completely innocent, to the victim who started as a perpetrator and during the course of an incident ends as the victim. Arguably his typology is guided by what might be considered a reasonable or rational way of making sense of any particular incident in the context of the law. Given the law as the starting point it is possible to suggest that his understanding of reasonable also equates with that which the white, heterosexual male would consider to be reasonable. This is especially demonstrated in the later work that was generated from Mendelsohn's ideas, in which victim culpability is translated into **victim precipitation** as we shall see with the work of Amir (1971) discussed below.

From these beginnings the concepts of lifestyle and victim precipitation have formed the core of much traditional victimological work and illustrate what Miers (1989: 3) has called a positivistic victimology.

Positivistic victimology is defined as:

The identification of factors which contribute to a non-random pattern of victimization, a focus on interpersonal crimes of violence, and a concern to identify victims who may have contributed to their own victimization.

The parallels with criminology are clear. Within positivistic victimology there is a similar emphasis on measuring differences, seeing those differences as being somehow abnormal, and looking for explanations of those differences that lie outside of individual choice.

It is interesting to note that during the 1980s and since, both in the United Kingdom and North America, the victim of crime became much more 'politicized' (see for example the work of Miers, 1978; Williams, 1999). In others words, the victim of crime has been used increasingly as a symbolic reference point for policy makers and politicians in justifying criminal justice policy and usually policy of the more punitive kind. Part of this process has also involved the recognition within each of these criminal justice systems that they could not solve the crime problem, but what they could do was make people feel better about what had happened to them. In this way, the victim of crime, and associated victim movements, have achieved quite an important and powerful influence within the policy arena. But who are these victims of crime?

The development of the criminal victimization survey in the United States in the late 1960s and used in the United Kingdom since the first British Crime Survey conducted in 1982, and internationally since 1989, has been an important tool in both measuring the nature and extent of criminal victimization, and going some way towards identifying who the victims of crime are. The criminal victimization survey, derived initially from the lifestyle model of understanding the likelihood of becoming a crime victim, asks a general sample of the populations questions about how they spend their time, their experiences of crime, their attitudes towards the police, where and when they are afraid of crime, amongst, other issues. On the basis of the data sets that this process provides, it is possible to say that the group of people most likely to be criminally victimized is the young adult male who goes out drinking two or three times a week, and those least likely to be criminally victimized are elderly females. (Some of these issues are discussed in greater detail in Chapter 5.)

There are a number of conundrums hidden within general findings of this kind not least of which is the fact that young males are the least likely to express fear of crime and elderly females are the most likely to express such fears. Much criminological effort has been put into unwrapping this equation which is not of central concern here (see Chapter 2), but suffice it to say that issues such as exposure to risk on the one hand and levels of **vulnerability** on the other play a part in understanding findings such as these. However, the role of the media in portraying pictures of criminally victimized elderly women, as though these were the most likely targets of criminal victimization, is not helpful. A clear example of the way in which criminological (or more accurately in this case, victimological), knowledge, stands in stark contrast to media images. Contradictions such as these offer us one way of exploring the question of who comprises the **Victimological Other** along the same lines as we explored the Criminological Other discussed above.

THE VICTIMOLOGICAL OTHER

Given that much of contemporary criminal justice policy within what we might call the Western Anglo speaking nexus (i.e. North America, Australia, New Zealand and the United Kingdom) appears to be preoccupied with images of the crime victim, it will be useful to develop our understanding of the assumptions that frequently underpin such images. Victimology, like its sister discipline, criminology, has played its part in contributing to those assumptions and it is these that it is important to unpick.

As the previous discussion has intimated, early victimologists followed a similar line of thinking to that of the early criminologists. They tried to find ways of marking out the differences between victims and non-victims. In doing this, both Von Hentig and Mendelsohn used different kinds of measuring sticks but each in their different ways drew implicitly on the idea that the white, heterosexual male was the norm (i.e. the non-victim) against which victims were to be measured. For example, nowhere in Von Hentig's classification of 13 victim types is the white, heterosexual male mentioned, thus reflecting the assumptions from which he was working. These assumptions went largely unchallenged until the 1970s and the publication of Amir's work Patterns of Forcible Rape. In this work Amir applied the concept of victim precipitation, derived from the work of Mendelsohn, to the crime of rape, and came to the conclusion, that 19 per cent of recorded rapes that formed part of his study could be deemed 'victim precipitated'. This conclusion did not go down well with the growing feminist movement of the 1970s who were vociferous in their criticism of Amir's work arguing that his use of the concept of 'victim precipitation' was not too far removed from saying that 'women asked for it'.

This critique of Amir, of course, connected with the wider discomfort that many feminists also felt (and still do feel) with the use of the term 'victim' in relation to women in general. The concept of **survivor** is much preferred by feminists as this captures the positive strategies women employ to live their day-to-day lives given their inherent structural powerlessness rather than the passive acceptance implied in the concept of victim. (This concept is discussed in more detail in Chapter 5.) Here began a relationship between feminism and victimology that has always been one full of tension. However, the incursion of the feminist challenge to victimology (and it has to be said criminology) has also been an important source for the development of both disciplines.

What feminist work did was, not only to offer a different conceptual apparatus with which to understand women's lives in general, it applied that apparatus to the crimes that affected women's lives: mainly rape and 'domestic' violence. Of course, in the 1970s the understanding of 'domestic' violence looked somewhat different than it does contemporarily, and it has to be said that both criminology and victimology as academic areas of study have benefited greatly as a result of feminist work that clearly put both of these issues on these respective academic agendas. There have, however, also been other gains and losses in this process. A clear gain has been that, in addition to putting particular crimes on the academic agenda, feminism also contributed to making visible the extent to which crime was predominantly a male occupation. And moreover, that much of that male crime was committed against women. Herein lies a loss. This equation, male = criminal, female = victim, became a double-edged sword resulting in hiding male victimization and to a certain extent female criminality. Arguably the end result being the construction of the white, heterosexual male as the Victimological Other: that which cannot be spoken.

Summary

The increasing policy interest in the victim of crime has widened the agenda for how criminologists spend their time and the kinds of questions they might be interested in. From the discussion above it can be seen that feminism has played its part in extending this agenda significantly. So much so, that In the contemporary context It would be difficult for any academic criminologists to deny the importance of **gender** as a key factor in predicting engagement in criminal behaviour and in understanding response to victimization. Though as the previous paragraph suggests, the question of understanding men's reaction to victimization is not as central to criminological concerns as their propensity to engage in crime. In conclusion then it might be fair to say that whilst the (working class) male, and given the likelihood that people from ethnic minorities are much more likely to find themselves at the lower end of the social hierarchy, this also invariably means the working class, ethnic minority male is highly visible as the criminal, he is much less visible as the victim. Hence, in the terms of this chapter, the Criminological Other is for the most part middle class and female, the Victimological Other is the white and ethnic minority, heterosexual male.

The purpose of this book is, of course, to unpick the implications of the last statement in much more detail, but it is hoped that this last statement has also introduced the reader to another important aspect of academic criminological work that makes it very different from media images constructed of crime, the criminal and the victim. That is, its commitment to exploring, in a critical, and sometimes provocative manner, common sense knowledge about crime. The importance of critical analysis is perhaps best demonstrated through the use of a case study and we shall do this here by considering the case of the UK serial killer Harold Shipman. This case study will help us think about what criminologists from different disciplinary backgrounds might offer as an explanation of Shipman's behaviour and it will also help us think about the criminological and Victimological Other that we have discussed in this chapter so far.

CRIMINOLOGY, CRIMINOLOGICAL PERSPECTIVES AND HAROLD SHIPMAN

Harold Shipman was a general medical practitioner in Hyde, a suburb of Greater Manchester, England. In January 2000 he was convicted of the murder of 15 of his patients though it is clear that the inquiry that was set-up to investigate how that could have happened believed that they had evidence that he had murdered somewhere in the region of 200 patients throughout his medical career. By far the majority of his victims were elderly females. He was found dead in his prison cell, having committed suicide, in January 2004 never having admitted to the acts of which he had been found guilty. Shipman's case raises all kinds of interesting questions for the criminologist and lay person alike and much of that interest lies with the question of motivation: why did he do it? After all, he certainly did not fit the usual criminological type; far from being poor, and a member of an ethnic minority, he was a well-established medical practitioner, in a well-respected and well-rewarded job, who appeared, for the most part, to solicit good opinions from his patients. Before we go on to explore this question of motivation it will be useful to define a serial killer.

Serial killers are predominantly male. Whilst there have been some historically notorious female serial killers from Lucretia Borgia to Eileen Wuornos, 95 per cent of known serial killers are male. It is also often assumed that sex is a key driver for the male serial killer. This does not necessarily mean a desire for conventional sexual activity, but serial killers are known to have, either in the act of killing, or before, or after, used this as a means of expressing their particular sexual proclivities. In addition, to qualify as a serial killer, there must be three or more victims. This makes them different from spree or mass murderers, who may kill more than three people but who tend to do so all at the same time. Serial killers usually have a 'cooling-off' period between murders, which obviously makes the question of motivation all the more interesting. Lastly, it is often the case that serial killers become more and more adventurous in their killing activities, often resulting in a killing in which it seems apparent that they 'wanted' to get caught.

Much of what is known about serial killers, some of which is embedded in the statements in the previous paragraph, has come from the killers themselves. In the course of them being caught, arrested and incarcerated, and then subject to interrogation and psychiatric investigation, much has been learned about the motivation for this kind of criminal behaviour; so first of all we shall consider the relevance of psychiatry to the case of Shipman.

PSYCHIATRY AND CRIME: INSIDE THE SUBCONSCIOUS MIND

Holmes and Holmes (1998) have put a good deal of that data together in such a way that they have been able to construct a typology of serial killing (Figure 1.2).

Based on this typology it is possible to suggest that Harold Shipman fits into the last type. The problem here is, however, that he never admitted to any of his crimes and never allowed himself to be subjected to psychiatric investigation, so this conclusion has to be pure guess work. Nevertheless psychiatry is often considered to be the best place to start with serial killers, and following this tradition the inquiry that was set-up to investigate how he managed to commit so many murders invited a team of psychiatrists to offer some analysis of him. So we shall draw on some of their observations here.

Many of Shipman's patients report him as having a very good 'bedside manner', especially with the elderly. However the inquiry report also comments that he was aggressive, conceited and arrogant as well as dishonest. In the words of the inquiry report, 'he was a consummate and an inveterate liar'. The psychiatrists consulted by the inquiry team suggest that these personality traits may be indicative of someone who is rigid and obsessive, who may have difficulty in expressing their emotions and may also suffer from low self-esteem. They also suggest that he may have felt threatened when unable to control events so reacted in such a way as to assert control. They also go on to hypothesize that he may have gained a 'buzz' from the association with death, and, given the addictive pleasure of this may have

---

Visionary: Responding to voices/hallucinations. Probably psychotic

Missionary: Rid the world of particular problem groups

Hedonistic: This group covers those who kill for lust, thrills or comfort. The sexual dimension is most obvious in this group though not necessarily absent in the others.

Power and control: To have the power over life and death

Figure 1.2: A typology of serial killing: based on the work of Holmes and Holmes (1998).

had a 'need' to kill with his final act of forging the will of his last victim (the only case in which there was any obvious indication of a possible financial reward), representing a 'subconscious' desire to be caught.

The reader can get a good feel from this summary of responses to the Shipman case both as to how a psychiatrist might begin to make sense of his criminal behaviour and the extent to which that sense fits, or does not fit with the typology, outlined above. The question of control and hedonism both feature in these opinions but, as has been said before, the puzzle remains because Shipman refused to talk. Other psychiatric approaches have made much of his relationship with his mother: he watched her die from cancer as a 17-year-old youth, and of his relationship with his wife, who remained loyal to him throughout. However again, nothing can be said definitively on either count, with his wife also, so far, having refused to talk about their relationship. So psychiatry, in this case, can offer us some clues, but no answers. But what might a different discipline do with Harold Shipman?

PSYCHOLOGY AND CRIME: THE SEARCH FOR INDIVIDUAL DIFFERENCES

Psychologists are generally concerned to search for explanations through an understanding of particular factors that might predispose one individual to commit a crime rather than another individual. Such factors can vary from establishing the presence of a mental disorder, a particular personality type, having suffered some physical or mental trauma in childhood, or other 'triggers' like job loss, the break-up of a relationship and other stressful situational factors. However, one branch of psychology that has become increasingly popular in recent years is **evolutionary psychology** and it is that way of thinking about murder that we shall use here to illustrate how a psychologist might approach the Shipman case.

Evolutionary psychology suggests to us that human beings not only adapt to their environment as biological beings (i.e. they evolve) but that such adaptations also occur at a psychological level. Such psychological adaptations reflect the importance of the processes of natural selection, perhaps put more simply, the survival of the species. As such survival processes are highly dependent on continued propagation, sex constitutes a key motivator for human action in general, but male action in particular. So, for the evolutionary psychologist two processes drive male behaviour: sexual jealousy and sexual rivalry. Both are seen to be the mechanisms whereby access to women is secured and male power is maintained both over women and between men themselves. It must be remembered that this analysis is not arguing that men choose rationally to behave in this way but that these drivers reflect ancestral adaptation of the psyche to both biological and social conditions. How might this kind of approach apply to Shipman?

If you consider the patterning of the murder statistics, they indicate that the majority of murderers are male, and that the overwhelming majority of serial killers are male, with their victim likely to be a female intimate or another male friend in the case or murder and in the case of serial killing most likely to be female. As a result it is possible to see that the over-riding principle of 'male sexual propriety' can make some sense. But how does that apply to individual cases? It has to be said that there have been some notorious male serial killers to whom the sexual motive can clearly be applied, albeit the expression of that sexuality might be considered distorted. Dennis Nielson, Peter Sutcliffe in the United Kingdom and Ted Bundy in the United States are just a few names to whom the sexual motive might be assigned and in each of these cases the issue of male sexual propriety might also make some sense. However, in the case of Harold Shipman there has been no obvious evidence of a sexual motive nor was there any evidence of sexual expression unless that was in the form of some deep-seated necrophilia. Yet, by far the majority of his victims were female. So there remains something to be understood here in relation to sex but what that looks like the evolutionary psychologist does not seem to be able to help us with very much. At this juncture it might be useful to consider how a sociologist might understand him.

SOCIOLOGY: OUTSIDE THE CRIMINAL MIND

It might be odd to consider how a discipline like sociology, concerned as it is to understand the nature and impact of social structures in society, helps us to understand pathological behaviour like serial killing, yet it is important to remember that individual behaviour is not constructed in a vacuum: it takes place within particular social and cultural contexts. Coleman and Norris (2000: 108) suggest that sociology can cast some light on serial killing by asking questions such as:

- Why do there seem to be more serial killers in one society than in another?

- If the incidence of serial murder is changing over time, why is this?

- Why do particular societies at particular times focus on particular problems (such as serial murder) and see those problems in particular ways?

These are good questions for a sociologist, but a sociologist will also think about how the particular socio-cultural setting in which a serial killer has found themselves might have contributed to the kind of crime they committed and who the victim of such crime might be.

In the case of Harold Shipman such a view would pay just as much attention to the social characteristics associated with the position in which he found himself as much as seeing those characteristics as part of his individual personality. So, if we revisit the comments made about his personality above, for example, his arrogance, this might have been given particular expression to as a result of his training in the medical profession and the social characteristics more generally associated with that profession. Moreover, his desire to play 'master of ceremonies' at the scene of some of the murders he committed could also be attributed to the social expectations associated with the role of the medical profession in which being *in control* and *taking control* are divided by a fine line. Of course his access to his murder 'weapon', drugs, is wholly explicable by reference to his profession, and the effectiveness with which he remained free from suspicion for so long is again totally explicable by reference to his chosen profession. If we turn to his choice of victim, mostly elderly females living on their own, this too can be explained by reference to his profession. The doctor/patient relationship is one that is not only confidential, but also rooted in trust: another concept around which there are all kinds of social expectations. The fact that people commented on his 'bedside manner' in relation to the elderly in particular, adds to the importance of understanding the social processes that both facilitated his activities and enabled him to remain above suspicion. Of course, they do not explain his individual motivation, but they do help us understand the processes whereby his activities could take place.

FEMINISM, SERIAL KILLERS AND MASCULINITY

The last perspective we shall consider with respect to Harold Shipman derives from feminism. As this chapter has already suggested, feminism has asked many hard questions of criminology and victimology, and in asking those questions has had some influence on encouraging both areas of analysis to think differently about the problems they are concerned with. In the context of criminal behaviour it has encouraged criminology to think about the maleness of the crime problem. This has led some analysts to think about the question of masculinity.

In a well-noted piece of work Cameron and Fraser (1987) were concerned to make sense of Peter Sutcliffe: known in the early 1980s in the United Kingdom as the Yorkshire Ripper. In this analysis they argue that the central project of masculinity is the search for transcendence; the struggle to master and control nature. This expresses itself in masculine sexuality in three ways: through performance, penetration and conquest. These expressions do not necessarily have to be present in the actuality of the sex act, nor do they have to be expressed in the acts of serial killers (though for some all elements are present in both settings) but in the context of murder they can be understood as part of the ultimate act of transcendence: the holding of another person's life in the balance. In Cameron and Fraser's analysis the thrill of this kind of control is the ultimate achievement of the masculine project: the ultimate sign of masculinity. This understanding of the nature of masculinity leads us to think about the thrill, control and excitement that Harold Shipman might have associated with his behaviour, not as a pathological expression of himself as a man, but more as an extension of what we might call normal forms of masculinity in modern society. In this view Shipman's behaviour is 'merely' an extension of the (masculine) search for control in a rapidly changing social world.

Summary: What have we learned?

Discipline	Focus	Helpful on Shipman?
Psychiatry	The subconscious mind	Maybe
Psychology	Mental differences and psychological evolution	No
Sociology	Structural conditions social expectations	Yes
Feminism	Masculinity	Yes

(Continued)

(Continued)

This table highlights the author's assessment of the contribution that each of these different ways of thinking about crime might make in helping us understand the case of Shipman. The reader may come to a different conclusion. However, in the absence of Shipman now being able to cooperate with any psychiatrist, and so far the unwillingness of any of his family to engage in the same kind of cooperation, there is little else left for us to work with. However, the importance of exploring this case study was to:

- Demonstrate the diversity within criminology and between criminologists.
- Illustrate the way in which that diversity leads to different ways of thinking about crime and criminals.
- Highlight the importance of understanding not only the criminal but also the relevance of thinking about the victim in the commission of crime.
- Show the differences between criminological approaches to crime and the criminal and more journalistic and/or media analyses of crime and the criminal.

The last point should be particularly noted. In none of the analyses offered above have the terms 'villain' or 'Dr. Death', or 'evil fiend' been used. It might be that individual criminologists might have such opinions about Shipman as an individual, but such terms do not constitute part of how a criminologist might make sense of Shipman's behaviour. Such opinions are left to others. However, and perhaps of most value in terms of the project of this book, the Shipman case does illustrate for us some of the conventional boundaries of both criminology and victimology, and the importance, in studying this subject, to challenge those boundaries.

CONCLUSION: THINKING CRITICALLY

This chapter has been concerned to introduce the reader to some basic features of criminology as a discipline, to be aware of the historical development of those features and their contemporary relevance. In the process of doing this the reader has been introduced to two important ideas: the Criminological Other and the Victimological Other. These ideas are intended to encourage the reader to think critically about the traditional foci and boundaries associated with each of these areas of analysis. For example, in our discussion of the Criminological Other, it was argued that criminology has spent much of its time and effort on thinking, researching and writing about the lower class, predominantly ethnic minority male, leaving the white middle-class male and virtually all women free from the criminological gaze. These latter two groups and women in particular constituting the Criminological Other: outside of the discipline's gaze and also for the most part outside of the policy gaze. This does not mean that women do not commit crime (we all know they do) or that middle-class men do not commit crime (again we all know they do and Shipman constitutes a very good case in point). Moreover there are criminologists who study both. However it does mean that these groups, and their behaviours, are in the background, not quite wallpaper but certainly not constituted as the criminological problem. In the same way in the discussion of the Victimological Other, it was argued that men were outside of our understanding of victimization, and women, especially elderly women, were quite central to the conventional victimological gaze. As it happens, the centrality of elderly women fits very well with the Shipman case, but it should be remembered that they were not victims of reckless, young, working-class males as media images might suggest, but victims of a well-respected, white, middle-class male whom they trusted.

So, in conclusion, it is just as important for the prospective student of crime and criminology, not only to think critically about the media presentations of crime, but also to think critically about how criminologists and policy makers make sense of such behaviour, by always asking who is included here, who is excluded and why. These are themes that we shall return to in the chapters to follow. In the next chapter we shall consider the different sources of knowledge available to criminologists about crime.

EXERCISE

As a way of encouraging the reader to 'test out' your own critical thinking, read the following resume of a recent case in France (presented below) and make a note of your answers to the questions that follow. How well do you think you have done?

In January 2008 the Societe Generale Bank in France announced a trading loss of 4.9 billion euros (6.8 billion dollars) attributed to the activities of one trader, Jerome Kerviel. In October 2010, Jerome was found guilty of breach of trust, forging documents and computer hacking and was ordered to serve 3 years imprisonment and to repay the losses to the bank. At the time of writing he is appealing this decision. In his defence it is reported that, in taking bets on the future direction of the markets, he took no money for himself but was motivated to boost his bonus and to make money for the bank. His defence also suggested that the bank turned a 'blind eye' towards his activities.

You can use the Internet to search more information about this case should you wish to, but in the light of the above:

1. What do you think:

    i)   a psychiatrist would make of this behaviour
    ii) a psychologist
    iii) a sociologist
    iv) a feminist?

Reflect in the different ways these perspectives have been used in relation to the Shipman case to inform your answers.

2. In what ways, if at all, does this case challenge or confirm the idea of the Criminological Other?
3. Who, if at all, is the victim here?
4. What other issues does this case lead us to think about in terms of what counts as crime and what criminologists might be interested in studying?

RECOMMENDATIONS FOR FURTHER READING

Soothill, Peelo and Taylor (2002) *Making Sense of Criminology* (Oxford: Polity) is written in an accessible style and uses media images to develop a deeper criminological understanding of the nature of crime, its commission, as well as people's experiences of the criminal justice process. Wayne Morrison's chapter, 'What is crime? Contrasting and competing definitions' is a really interesting read and offers some challenging thinking on what is understood as crime. You will find this in the book edited by Hale, C., Hayward, K., Wahidin, A., and Wincup, E. (2005) *Criminology* (Oxford: Oxford University Press). Similarly, the introductory textbook by Tim Newburn (2007) *Criminology* (London: Routledge–Willan) affords a useful overview of the issues (and others) discussed in this chapter.

2

COUNTING CRIME

This chapter will explore the different ways criminologists know things about crime. We shall consider the various sources of information available to criminologists and their strengths and weaknesses as sources of information. We shall also consider some of the other main ways that criminologists attempt to know things about crime as they conduct their research. The central purpose of this chapter is to encourage and develop the critical thinking that we ended with in Chapter 1 and at different points in this chapter you will be asked to engage in exercises that are intended to facilitate this.

INTRODUCTION

Clearly there are different ways in which we can know things about crime: personal experience, as an offender, a worker in the criminal justice system or as a victim of crime all are sources of knowledge. What we know of the experiences of members of our family or friends is another. The information provided by the media, whether as news or fiction, is yet another. Indeed, this latter source of information, given the apparent entertainment value and range of crime-related television programmes available to us is, contemporarily, probably the most likely source of our knowledge. In addition to these sources of information there are two other important sources of information about crime. First, there are the official statistics on crime, punishment and victims. Second, there are the research findings of criminologists. Soothill *et al.* (2002: 24) list these different sources of information in the following way:

- direct experience of crime
- mediated experience
- official information
- research knowledge.

All these, they are keen to point out are partial sources of information. Our experiences will tap different aspects of the crime problem; the media tend to work with particular stereotypes, official information only addresses those aspects of the crime problem that have come to the attention of the criminal justice system, and criminological research tends to be focused around specific crimes or specific problems. However, if we are to understand what criminology and criminologists do, then it is important that we put aside what we think we know about crime from our direct experience or our mediated experience and focus attention on official information and research knowledge. This chapter, then, will first of all focus its attention on the strengths and weaknesses of these two sources of information.

OFFICIAL INFORMATION ABOUT CRIME: CRIMINAL STATISTICS

The first country to gather national statistics on crime was France. This started in 1826 with the first published analysis of those statistics being presented by Adolphe Quetelet in 1842. Crimes recorded by the police have been published in England and Wales since 1876 and in the United States since 1930. So although some official data about crime has been available for some time now, some of the problems that are associated with 'official' information remain the same. As Quetelet himself commented 'our observations can only refer to a certain number of known and tried offences, out of the unknown sum total of crimes committed'. This is often referred to as the **dark figure of crime**: all those criminal events that are unknown to anyone except the offender and the victim. However, before we go on to explore the implications of this comment, we need to think about what kinds of data sources are considered 'official' and how can we get hold of them.

A publication entitled *Criminal Statistics in England and Wales* is produced every year and these statistics are more often than not the starting point for anyone trying to construct a picture of the nature and extent of crime. They are not, however, the only source of official information. The Prison Service, the Probation Service and Her Majesty's Inspectorate's of Constabulary, Probation and Prisons also produce statistics on a quarterly and yearly basis. Each police force produces its own annual report and since the 1998 Crime and Disorder Act local authorities in England and Wales are now required to produce reports on crime and **crime reduction**. All these sources of information (and this list is not exhaustive) are publicly available either from places such as Her Majesty's Stationery Office or, more easily and readily for many people, over the Internet. A good place to start for information about crime is the Home Office's own website: www.homeoffice.gov.uk and its associated research and statistics department. More recently the Ministry of Justice (www.justice.gov. uk) has also become an important source of data on prisons and probation. However, these sources of information take as their starting point, incidents that have been reported to the police and are recorded as crime by them, and take as their finishing point what has happened to the offender should they have been caught. There are other policing organizations, for example, the British Transport Police, the Ministry of Defence Police and the UK Atomic Energy Authority Police. These agencies also record offences, but their records will not necessarily be included in the *Criminal Statistics* unless there has been a prosecution. The same could be said about the Inland Revenue in respect of tax evasion and the work of the Customs and Excise departments in respect of failure to pay Value Added Tax. So it is already possible to see that the comment made by Quetelet in 1842 is still pertinent today.

Similar data sources exist in the United States and Europe. In the United States, Uniform Crime Reporting (UCR) was introduced in 1929, and the Federal Bureau of Investigation was given the responsibility of collecting, publishing and archiving these statistics across all 17,000 policing jurisdictions in 1930. Now a visit to www.fbi.gov offers access to a wide range of reports on crime and policing in the United

States. There are annual reports of Crime in the United States (CIUS), Hate Crime Statistics, reports on Law Enforcement Officers Killing and Assaults, Bank Crime Reports and terrorist incidents. Moreover, it is possible to get statistical information on crime in Europe through the European Community (EUROSTAT) and the Council of Europe. The majority of countries in Europe also collate their own information on crime reported to the police, the resources allocated to the criminal justice system and their respective prison populations. Indeed, the UCR of the FBI comes with the following 'health' warning.

It is incumbent upon all data users to become as well educated as possible about how to understand and quantify the nature and extent of crime in the United States and in any of the nearly 18,000 jurisdictions represented by law enforcement contributors to the Uniform Crime Reporting (UCR) Program. Valid assessments are possible only with careful study and analysis of the various unique conditions affecting each local law enforcement jurisdiction.

Historically, the causes and origins of crime have been the subjects of investigation by many disciplines. Some factors that are known to affect the volume and type of crime occurring from place to place are:

- Population density and degree of urbanization.
- Variations in composition of the population, particularly youth concentration.
- Stability of the population with respect to residents' mobility, commuting patterns, and transient factors.
- Modes of transportation and highway system.
- Economic conditions, including median income, poverty level, and job availability.
- Cultural factors and educational, recreational, and religious characteristics.
- Family conditions with respect to divorce and family cohesiveness.
- Climate.
- Effective strength of law enforcement agencies.
- Administrative and investigative emphases of law enforcement.
- Policies of other components of the criminal justice system (i.e. prosecutorial, judicial, correctional, and probational).
- Citizens' attitudes toward crime.
- Crime reporting practices of the citizenry.

Crime in the United States provides a nationwide view of crime based on statistics contributed by local, state, tribal, and federal law enforcement agencies. Population size and student enrollment are the only correlates of crime presented in this publication. Although many of the listed factors equally affect the crime of a particular area, the UCR Program makes no attempt to relate them to the data presented. *The data user is, therefore, cautioned against comparing statistical data of individual reporting units from cities, counties, metropolitan areas, states, or colleges or universities solely on the basis of their population coverage or student enrollment.* Until data users examine all the variables that affect crime in a town, city, county, state, region or other jurisdiction, they can make no meaningful comparisons.

(Extracted from Crime in the United States, 2009. US Department of Justice, Federal Bureau of Investigation, September 2010. www.fbi.gov)

You might like to reflect on this statement and consider why the FBI felt it necessary to release it. What do you think it is saying about crime statistics, the nature of crime, and to be discussed more fully in Chapter 4, how we might explain it?

In all these data sources it is important to note that there is a difference between the number of offences recorded and the number of offenders recorded. For example, a burglar (one offender) may have been tried and convicted for burglary (and will therefore count as one statistic probably in the prison system) but may have admitted to 20 or 30 burglaries (offences) which will appear as 20 or 30 different offences in the crimes known to the police statistics. Recognizing this helps to understand the important features of all the data sources mentioned earlier:

- Not all recorded offences have an identifiable offender.
- Not all offenders who are assigned to an offence are tried and convicted.

In other words, all criminal justice systems 'suffer' from what is called an **attrition rate**. It is sometimes useful to think of these statistical records as being the end product of something like the London or the New York marathon: a lot of people start but they do not all finish!

So it would certainly be fair to conclude that there is a good deal of official information readily available, especially over the Internet, about crime although not all of this information may necessarily be presented in the same way. *The Criminal Statistics in England and*

Wales, for example, offers a raw picture of the numbers of incidents, whereas other jurisdictions, such as Canada, offer figures calculated to represent the likely rate of something happening per 100,000 adults and children in the population. Each method of presentation can be used to convey different messages about the nature and extent of crime that needs to be thought about fairly carefully. This is an issue we shall come across again when we look at the problems of measuring different kinds of crimes in Chapter 3 and in making comparisons at the end of this chapter. The question at this juncture is then: how useful is this information? Quetelet was quick to observe the partiality of the information available to him in the 1840s. Has the situation improved at all? What do official statistics actually tell us?

THE THREE 'R'S: RECOGNIZING, REPORTING AND RECORDING

All the statistics referred to above, whilst numerical in their form, are the end product of fairly complex social processes. As Chapter 1 highlighted, for an act to be labelled criminal then there has to be a law that prohibits that behaviour. So, the first stage in this process might arguably be the country in which the act was performed since what is considered criminal (unlawful) in one country may not be the same in another country. So, from a point of view the first issue of recognition is that the act or behaviour must be defined as unlawful. However, this is not the full story of the problem of recognition. Behaviour may be unlawful, but the person who witnesses the behaviour may not recognize it as such. There are different reasons for this. It might be as a result of lack of knowledge of the law on the part of the witness or the victim, or it may be as a result of them being so used to certain things happening (such as violence in the home or racial harassment) that they do not define the behaviour as criminal, or they may recognize the act as criminal but consider it not serious enough to report (e.g. petty vandalism). However, having recognized an act as criminal and decided upon its seriousness, the next stage for the witness or the victim is to report the incident to the police. Approximately 80 per cent of incidents recorded by the police in England and Wales are reported by members of the public. So again it is important to understand reporting behaviour.

There are a number of reasons why individuals may or may not report criminal behaviour to the police. As an exercise you might like to consider the following scenario and think about whether or not you would report what you have witnessed to the police and the reasons for your reaction.

Your next-door neighbour is a young woman with three children. You know her partner to be out of work but actively seeking employment and he also has a reputation for getting violent. You happen to see her one day in your local supermarket out shopping though she does not see you. As you move closer to her, you observe her put a packet of meat containing two pork chops underneath the baby's blanket in the pram. She goes to the checkout and pays for the other items she has in her basket but does not pay for the pork chops. What do you do?

So what would you do? What do you think the issues are here, in addition to the law-breaking behaviour?

Some of the things that stop people reporting incidents, like the one above are:

- They think it is too trivial an offence.
- They do not think there is a victim.
- They do not want to get involved.
- They would not want to go to court to give evidence against a neighbour and suffer the possible recriminations and/or threats that might result.
- They do not trust the police to do anything.

In addition, of course, some people would report this to the store with the result that the police would be involved. Hopefully, what this has illustrated, however, is that reporting crime is not a simple or a straightforward process and the willingness to report does seem to vary on the kind of crime under consideration. For example, people are much more likely to report a burglary or a car theft (especially if they want to make an insurance claim) than they are violence or theft from the person. Having reported an offence to the police, the next issue is whether or not it is recorded as an offence.

Not all offences that are reported to the police end up as recorded crime, that is, become part of the crime that is counted within the official statistics under discussion here. Variation in recording behaviour can, again, be the product of a number of different processes. Although the police have a statutory duty to record criminal behaviour, they also have considerable discretion over whether or not a particular incident is serious enough to demand more detailed attention, and as a consequence have resources allocated to it. So, for example, a dispute between neighbours may have involved some criminal damage on the part of one party to the dispute that could be resolved by the police officer noting that 'advice was given' rather than necessarily pursuing a charge of criminal damage. Such an outcome obviously depends, to a certain extent, on how the aggrieved party wants to pursue such an incident. A good deal of the time people report incidents to the police wanting the police to stop what is happening rather than necessarily wanting to pursue criminal charges. On other occasions, of course, it may be that the police have targeted particular behaviour, like drinking after hours in licensed premises. In these circumstances, the police may apply discretion in the interests of meeting the target of clamping down on this kind of activity. Moreover different police forces may have different targets and this is another ingredient in understanding the different patterns of recorded criminal behaviour across different jurisdictions.

The potential importance of understanding differences in recording behaviour is especially important if you are trying to use official statistics to say something about whether crime is rising or falling, that is, crime trends. There are (at least) two issues to think about here. The first is about understanding the law at the time at which the crimes were being recorded and whether or not, over time, the legal definition of a crime has changed or remained the same: some behaviour may be newly defined as criminal and other may be decriminalized, that is, may become legal. This in and of itself will feed into the statistics. The second concerns whether or not there have been any recommended changes in how an offence is to be defined, and acted on, over time. For example, the introduction of the Final Warning scheme for young offenders under the 1998 Crime and Disorder Act (in England and Wales) removed from the police the potential of using informal warnings, which may have taken place as a way of dealing with the same behaviour, with the result that some things are now recorded that once may not have been.

In addition, there are factors external to the recognizing, reporting and recording process that feed into the official statistics on crime. Inflation, for example, can result in many more offences of criminal damage as the value of property increases, but the monetary value attached to the offence of criminal damage remains the same. Hence, there will be more offences of criminal damage. Moreover if we continue with this line of thinking and apply it to the statistics relating to the later stages of the criminal justice process; how many offenders are caught, how many cases prosecuted, how many found guilty, what are they sentenced to and how many people go to prison; it is possible to see that there is both a problem of attrition (the numbers get smaller) and a problem of discretion (which behaviours get chased and which do not) at potentially every stage in the process. The reasons for this may look different at different points in the criminal justice system, but given that it is a system with limited resources, even if it was possible it would be very unlikely that all cases would be pursued with the same vigour or with the same success.

The picture of crime presented by official statistics is therefore never a complete picture of the crime problem. This lack of completeness is well known and well recognized by criminologists and as a consequence encourages a very careful reading of such statistics. Historically, criminologists have referred to this as the problem of the dark figure of crime. Put another way; what about all that criminal behaviour that we do not know about? All that behaviour that is not recognized, not reported and not recorded? How might we find out about the dark figure of crime?

OFFICIAL INFORMATION ABOUT CRIME: CRIMINAL VICTIMIZATION STATISTICS

Criminal victimization statistics are generated by conducting a sample survey of the general population (whether or not they have been a victim of crime or reported a crime etc.) and asking this sample of people about their experiences of crime and the criminal justice system. The first survey of this kind was conducted in the United States in the late 1960s and since that time this way of gathering information about the dark figure of crime has proved to be increasingly popular. The use of the sample survey to uncover people's experiences of crime, aided by the statistical techniques that make possible generalizations from a sample of the population, assumes that this method can actually count people's experiences of criminal victimization. So, it is important to examine this assumption to begin with.

The criminal victimization survey concerns itself with measuring criminal incidents for which there are clearly identifiable victims. As a consequence it focuses attention on asking people questions about crimes against them as individuals and crimes against their property. So, because of the need to identify the victim and the difficulties of doing so, for example, of say, Inland Revenue returns, it tends to ignore this kind of criminal activity. A more accurate representation of the criminal victimization survey would be to say that they provide an additional source of information about those kinds of crimes most likely to be reported to the police and recorded by them. They are therefore useful for making comparisons with police statistics in estimating the extent of specific incidents. However, that comparison is not necessarily a perfect one. Although criminal victimization surveys tend to work with definitions of incidents that are close to the legal definition, in other words they work with understandings of events that could be defined as illegal and thereby punished; these are not necessarily those events that actually have been defined as illegal and thereby punished. As a result there is always some slippage between the evidence that the criminal victimization survey operates with and that contained within the statistics of crimes known to the police.

Despite this kind of inherent difficulty criminal victimization surveys have proved to be very popular for policy makers and politicians in making assessments about the nature and extent of what we might call conventional crime: crimes against the person and crimes against property. The first criminal victimization survey was conducted by the Home Office in England and Wales in 1982. They are now conducted every year. In addition such surveys are conducted in the United States, Canada and Australia. They are not so popular in continental Europe but international criminal victimization surveys have been conducted in Europe in addition to other countries across the world. However, as sources of data criminal victimization surveys face the problem of the fourth 'R': the respondent.

THE FOURTH 'R': THE RESPONDENT

The social survey as a research instrument generally has problems with respondents; summed up simply as the problems of getting people to talk to you. However, criminal victimization surveys suffer from particular problems above and beyond this because of their interest in wanting to match people's experiences of crime with the records of the criminal justice system. Empirical testing has shown that it cannot always be assumed that while crime might be seen as an important and impactive event as far as politicians and policy makers are concerned, the same cannot be said for members of the general public. People do not always remember what has happened to them and may, of course, not always want to tell an interviewer about their experiences. The following are some of the respondent problems associated with the criminal victimization survey:

- People 'forget' especially when an event involves someone they know.
- People may not 'know' that is, recognize what has happened to them as criminal (same problem as earlier).
- People remember inaccurately.
- People remember incompletely.
- People include events not relevant to the time period of the survey. (This is referred to as the problem of telescoping.)
- People may not share in the same definition of an event as the survey. (This problem is probably at its most acute with respect to questions around violence.)

Given that the criminal victimization survey is intended to offer us a more complete picture of the nature and extent of crime it is important to be aware of how and under what circumstances these respondent problems have a greater or a lesser effect on the kind of data these surveys produce. For example, some of these problems have been shown to have their greatest impact on understanding the nature and extent of 'domestic' violence, which has resulted in the development of more sensitive data gathering techniques and questions. Such respondent difficulties notwithstanding, criminal victimization surveys have become a very important source of information for criminologists and others concerned to map the changing nature of the crime problem.

From the discussion so far, the reader should be aware that making sense of 'official' data on crime is a very subtle process with two inherent problems.

1. There is a big difference between crimes known to the police and the dark figure of crime.
2. There is a big difference between crimes made visible in these counting processes and those that remain invisible (e.g. offences associated with defrauding the tax system or health and safety at work legislation).

Nevertheless these sources of data, provided that we are aware of their limitations, do provide criminologists and policy makers with a 'good enough' picture of the kinds of crimes that people routinely worry about especially crimes against their property. There is, however, another source of information about crime. That is the information produced by criminologists themselves as part of their research.

CRIMINOLOGICAL RESEARCH KNOWLEDGE

Criminologists, like other social scientists use a whole range of different methods to explore the issues that interest them. It is usual to divide these methods into two broad categories: quantitative and qualitative. Quantitative methods encompass using the official statistics discussed above and subjecting them to further, often more in-depth, statistical analysis as a well as social surveys. Qualitative methods encompass those kinds of research techniques that do not led themselves so readily to statistical analysis such as in-depth interviewing or a range of different observational methods. This is not the place to explore the strengths and weaknesses of these different methods of investigation since those strengths and weaknesses are not peculiar to the criminological use of them. What is important to understand about the production of criminological research knowledge is whether or not there is a match between what it is that a criminologist is trying to find out and the method they have chosen to investigate this. Put in more abstract words, this is the question of understanding the relationship between criminological theory and criminological method. In understanding the importance of this and its relationship with what it is that we know about crime we shall discuss two issues here:

meaning and understanding. Each of these will be explored through the example of making sense of the 'fear' of crime.

MAKING SENSE OF THE 'FEAR OF CRIME': MEANING AND UNDERSTANDING

Criminal victimization surveys discussed earlier have, since their inception, asked all kinds of questions about people's experiences of crime. In addition, those questions have also covered such issues as what people will and will not do in the evening and whether or not they feel safe in their own homes after dark because of crime. Questions such as these have become the fairly standard and routine way in which official statistics have attempted to measure the changing nature of the fear of crime. These statistics have repeatedly produced the finding that although elderly females are the least at risk from criminal victimization they are the most fearful of it, and although young males who go out drinking two or three times a week are the most at risk from criminal victimization they express the least fear of it. There are different ways to make sense of these findings. Those different ways highlight the problem of meaning. The two figures that follow illustrate a number of different hypotheses all of which might make sense of why elderly women are fearful and young males are not. Take a look at these and think about them.

The reader might like to consider which of these ways presented in Figures 2.1 and 2.2 (and the lists are not exhaustive) make sense and

---

1. Elderly women are irrational: their levels of expressed fear do not match the known risk.
2. Elderly women's expressed fear reveals their exposure to and the impact of media images of criminal victimization.
3. Elderly women's expressed fear is an expression of their vulnerability rather than a measure of their fear.
4. Elderly women's expressed fear is a way of them talking about other things that worry them more: money, health and so on.

Figure 2.1: How to make sense of findings on the fear of crime: elderly women.

1. Young males are irrational: their expressed levels of fearlessness do not match the known risk.
2. Young males' expressed fearlessness is an expression of their bravado rather than a measure of their fear.
3. Young males' expressed fearlessness is a way of talking about themselves as young men and their masculinity rather than being a measure of fear or anything else.
4. Young males are rational: they know the risks but marginalize the consequences (such as feelings of fear) to carry on with what they do on a routine basis.

Figure 2.2: How to make sense of findings on the fear of crime: young males.

which do not. However, the important point about the lists is that they each make sense of the same data in different ways. This is the problem of meaning. The way in which a criminologist might choose between these different ways of making sense of this data would be related to the theoretical perspective and/or concepts they think are the most helpful to them in this process. This is the problem of understanding.

In each of the lists above there are clues as to how the problem of meaning and the problem of understanding are connected to each other. For example, if we take propositions 3 and 4 from Figure 2.1, both of these propositions shift the meaning of the statistics by introducing a new concept. In other words, they ask us to think about how fear might be connected to something called **vulnerability**. Of course, to understand whether or not this is a meaningful thing to do, we would need to do some more research that takes us beyond these statistics. We would need to do some qualitative work, that is, spend some time talking in-depth with elderly females as a way of trying to establish whether or not when they talk of the fear of crime, that is, what they are talking about or whether they are talking about something else. In a similar way, if we consider propositions 3 and 4 in Figure 2.2, these shift the meaning of the statistics by introducing the concept of masculinity. (We shall discuss this concept more fully in Chapter 4.) So, in the same way, it would be necessary to do some more empirical work to establish whether or not this was a more meaningful way of making sense (understanding) of the statistical evidence available from official statistics.

Criminological research, then, introduces another dimension to what it is that we know (and do not know) about crime and its impact. That dimension stresses the importance of thinking about the different ways it is possible to make sense of the findings that are made available to us: back to the importance of thinking critically. Such critical thinking about the relationship between theory, data and meaning raises at least four questions that the reader might like to think about when considering any research findings:

- What theory or concept is being applied here? Is there an alternative that might be useful?
- How has the data been gathered, by whom and what are its strengths and limitations?
- How close have the researchers been to the issue they are investigating?
- How has the data and the theory been connected, by whom and for what purpose?

Criminological research then offers the opportunity to think more theoretically and more critically about what the various sources of official statistics say about crime and its impact. However, before we move on it will be useful to say something briefly about two other ways of getting some information about criminal behaviour: self report studies and other records.

SELF-REPORT STUDIES

The self-report study is the technique of asking samples of the general population to report, in confidence, whether or not they have committed any offences. This method has been used particularly as a way of trying to measure the nature and extent of young people's offending behaviour and it has been used, in particular, to access an understanding of the kinds of things young people who are still at school get up to. These studies are one way of getting a picture of the estimated 97 per cent of offending behaviours that never secure a conviction or a caution from the criminal justice system and as a consequence do not feature in those statistics at all. Researchers who use this method find that young people do admit to offending behaviour with boys more likely to report violent behaviour than girls, but girls too reporting more offences that would appear to come to the attention of the criminal justice system. However, one of the main problems with this method of accessing information about crime is whether or not what is being measured, and as a consequence what is being reported, would actually qualify as a crime if it had been reported to the police. Therefore, some care should be taken in making sense of the findings of such work. However, it is nevertheless the case that the self-report method does give us some limited information about the nature and extent of offending behaviour.

OTHER RECORDS

Criminologists interested in the kinds of crime that often remain hidden from the criminal justice system, such as white-collar crime that is discussed in Chapter 6, frequently resort to various other data sources that might help them draw a picture of the kind of crime they are interested in. Under this heading, it is possible to list records such as those of the health and safety at work executive, businesses' private records on theft at work, the records of private security firms and so on. These records will suffer from many of the same problems as more 'official' statistics, but they can nevertheless prove to be a very useful data gathering starting point. As Chapter 6 will illustrate, and as is discussed below, accessing information about this kind of criminal behaviour is difficult and sometimes requires quite imaginative thinking in order to explore the kinds of behaviours that might be equally criminal as that recorded in police statistics.

Summary

So, official sources of information about crime and criminological knowledge are not perfect but what makes them different from personal experience and mediated experience is their efforts to offer a consistent and systematic picture of the crime problem. Some of that picture will resonate with our personal experiences some of the time and some of which will resonate with what we learn through newspapers and television representations of crime. However, despite the problems that are inherent in official statistics and the problem of grasping the meaning of those statistics and thereby being able to understand them, to be a criminologist it is important to move beyond personal anecdotes and media representations. Having said that it is apparent from the discussion here that it is much easier to count some crime more than others. In other words, some crimes are much more visible than others. So to complete the picture on counting crime, we shall now consider some of the problems associated with crimes that are not so visible to us.

COUNTING 'INVISIBLE' CRIMES

According to Victor Jupp *et al.* (1998), all criminologists in the United Kingdom identify what they call 'seven features of invisibility' associated with particular kinds of criminal behaviour. To understand what kind of crime is counted and what kind of crime is difficult to count, it will be useful to consider the features that these authors identify.

Some of the features identified in Figure 2.3 have already been mentioned in this chapter; for example, the relative absence of statistics on tax evasion in official statistics on crime is largely accounted for by the fact that such incidents are only recorded in

| No knowledge |
| No statistics |
| No theory |
| No research |
| No control |
| No politics |
| No panic |

Figure 2.3: Seven features of invisibility.
Source: Jupp *et al.*, 1998: 6–23.

the official statistics if a prosecution has been proceeded with. In other words, the criminal offence of tax evasion can, depending on the nature and extent of it, be dealt with by agreement between a tax inspector and the offender. There are, however, other offences that occur on a routine daily basis that are also never recorded in official statistics on crime.

Perhaps the reader might like to think about all that behaviour related to the work place, the taking of stationery for personal use, making personal telephone calls from the office, the use of building supplies and materials in one's own home, insider dealing in the finance world and so on. All these activities are theft in different forms but because some behaviour is seen to be 'acceptable' in some working environments it rarely features as part of criminological knowledge and certainly never becomes part of the criminal statistics. Much of this kind of criminal activity has not been a main cause of concern of criminology or criminologists (though some criminologists do specialize in trying to explore this kind of criminality despite the difficulties involved). This has resulted in little theoretical interest in it and, as a consequence, little research. Add to these problems the difficulties of controlling such behaviour (if that were possible), and if it was controllable, the lack of political will to address it as a problem (the 'banking crisis' of 2008–9 might be worth considering here), there is, as a consequence no panic, that is, no public awareness or concern about such behaviour as a social problem. All these factors then contribute to the crimes that are seen, measured and thereby become the focus of politics and policy and, of course, conversely contribute to those crimes that are not seen, not measured and are not the central focus of the work of the criminal justice system. Hence, the issues pointed to in Figure 2.3. The questions that such invisibility raises for criminology are returned to in detail in Chapter 6. However, before we go on to review the key issues of this chapter, one problem remains. That problem is the problem of comparison. If there are so many caveats associated with the general information available about crime and criminal victimization, how is it possible to compare the rate of crime now with say 10 or 20 years ago which newspapers frequently do? Moreover, how is it possible to compare crime rates in different countries?

THE PROBLEM OF COMPARISON

Much political rhetoric when talking about crime frequently assumes that there is some 'golden age' of the past when things were different which is usually taken to mean better. We are all used to newspaper headlines that report crime as 'soaring out of control' and even when there is some statistical evidence that the incidence of some kinds of crime is actually falling, effort is usually made to highlight those criminal behaviours on the increase. Violent crime is a useful example to consider when thinking about the question of whether or not there was some 'golden age' in which things were better.

Thinking about whether or not things were better in the past depends on how far back in time you want to go. Historians of crime tell us that in the eighteenth and nineteenth centuries the world was a much more violent place given the relative absence of policing and an acceptance of the rule of law. This is probably epitomized by the fact that responses to crime were also much more violent with capital punishment being used much more often for a wide range of criminal offences. However, when people talk of a time when things were better, they are often not thinking about 200 years ago but about how they think things used to be in their area when they were younger. Some of this is, of course, about seeing the past through 'rose-tinted spectacles' but some of it is also about people's levels of tolerance of different behaviours changing during a time when social life has changed very rapidly. For example, Internet crime did not exist 20 years ago, yet now fraudulently accessing people's bank accounts over the Internet is something that worries people who use such services. So as social life changes tolerances may change, the things that people worry about may change; making the past look very attractive. All of which can be compounded by what the evidence may or may not be saying. This, of course, is the point at which making sense of what the evidence might be further complicated not only by the four 'R's discussed earlier but also by the law itself.

Changes in the law and practices associated with how the law may or may not be enforced make any meaningful discussion of whether or not crime has gone up or gone down very difficult if not impossible unless a way is found to 'factor in' the likely impact of such changes. Little of this kind of 'factoring in', however, takes place in media coverage of crime statistics or political rhetoric and sometimes not in criminological work either, yet awareness of its importance does mean that comparing the present with the past has to be done with caution. That said, the myth of a 'golden age' is significant as it taps into social and individual nostalgia reminding us of the importance of cultural processes and their contribution to our understanding of what constitutes the problem of crime. The importance of culture also features in some of the difficulties in trying to compare the problem of crime across different societies.

Some time ago David Nelken (1994), a criminologist, argued that the future potential of criminology lay within the importance of being able to conduct comparative research. His argument pointed to the increasing impact of trans-national crime and in seeking to combat it more needed to be known about how different countries operated legally, politically and culturally, before any preventive agenda might be put in place. In raising the importance of this kind of crime, not only for criminology but also for national political and economic policies, he drew attention to what might be learned from such comparative work and the problems inherent in engaging in it. These problems can be summarized in one question: what do we compare? Thus, subsuming a wide range of possible 'levels' of comparison designed to seek out similarities, differences, the value of concepts, the applicability of explanations, the working of criminal justice systems, an understanding of cultures, to name a few. There is considerable debate within the criminological literature as to the appropriateness of focusing on the similar or the different, but what shall be evident to the reader, as the rest of this book unfolds, is just how difficult it is to make those comparisons and as a consequence just how difficult it might be to 'borrow' policies from one socio-cultural context and apply them in another.

Summary and conclusion

What is known and not known about crime and criminal victimization comes from a number of different sources: our own knowledge and experiences, what we learn from the media, what we can find in official statistics of various kinds and what can be found in criminological research. Each of these different sources of information are useful and important, but for the criminologist of central importance is to establish a systematic and meaningful understanding of the nature of the crime problem. This means being sensitive to and critical of the strengths and the weaknesses of the various data sources that are available to count crime. In being sensitive and critical, a criminologist is also concerned to be aware of what is made visible and invisible in those data sources and how different theories or concepts might lead to a better understanding of both the nature and impact of criminal victimization. For the criminologist, it is important to test their theories and understandings against the data to ensure that they make sense, that is, are meaningful. The importance of this will become apparent when in the next chapter we go on to explore what it is that we know and do not know about the nature and extent of crime and which offenders are made visible by the processes of data collection that we have discussed here.

EXERCISE

In September 2010, the FBI, reporting on CIUS for 2009 reports that:

In 2009, the estimated number of violent crime offences was 1,318,398, a decrease of 5.3% over the 2008 estimate.

All violent crime offence estimates decreased in 2009 when compared with the 2008 estimates. Robberies decreased 8.0%, murders decreased 7.3%, aggravated assaults decreased 4.2% and forcible rapes decreased 2.6%.

The 2009 violent crime rate was 429.4 per 100,000 inhabitants, a decrease of 6.1% when compared with the 2008 violent crime rate.

When compared with 2008 rates, violent crime rates in 2009 declined in all offence categories.

In 2009, the murder rate was 5 per 100,000 inhabitants, an 8.1% decrease when compared with the rate for 2008.

The estimated number of property crimes in 2009 was 9,320,971, a 4.6% decrease from the 2008 estimate. The 2009 property crime rate, 3,036.1, was down 5.5% when compared with the 2008 figure.

The estimated number of motor vehicle thefts decreased 17.1% and larceny theft and burglary decreased 4.0% and 1.3%, respectively.

(Crime in the United States, 2009, Overview: www.fbi.gov)

In October 2010, the quarterly report from the British Crime Survey (BCS) states that:

Based on BCS interviews in the year June 2010, there was a decrease of 4% in the number of incidents of BCS crime compared with the year ending June 2009. The number of crimes recorded by the police fell by 8% in the year ending June 2010 compared with a year earlier.

- BCS interviews showed that the risk of being a victim of crime (21.5%) has decreased compared with the year ending June 2009 (22.4%).
- In the year ending June 2010, there were no increases in any of the police-recorded crime offence groups compared with the previous year, with the exception of sexual offences (which increased by 8%). The largest percentage falls were for criminal damage (down 17%) and offences against vehicles (down 16%).
- Levels of BCS violent crime showed no statistically significant change compared with the previous year. In contrast, violence against the person offences recorded by the police fell by 4% and robberies by 7%.
- Numbers of BCS household crimes showed a decrease of 4% compared with the previous year, mainly due to falls of 12% in vehicle-related theft and 6% in vandalism. There was no statistically significant change in the overall levels of BCS personal crime over the same period.
- BCS burglaries showed no statistically significant change compared with the previous year. In contrast, police-recorded domestic burglaries fell by 8% and other burglaries by 11%.

(*Home Office Statistical Bulletin*, 16/10: 1; www.homeoffice.gov.uk)

Comment on each of these data sets in the light of the issues that we have discussed in this chapter:

- recognizing
- reporting
- recording
- respondent
- comparison.

How would you make sense of the reported decline in violent crime pointed to by both sets of data?

RECOMMENDATIONS FOR FURTHER READING

Excellent coverage of the problems of measurement within criminology is offered by Coleman and Moynihan (1997) *Understanding Crime Data* (Buckingham: Open University Press). This is written in an easy and accessible style without oversimplifying the issues involved. See also Mike Maguire's chapter 'Crime data and statistics', in Maguire, M. *et al.* (eds) (2007) *The Oxford Handbook of Criminology* (fourth edition) (Oxford: Oxford University Press). For a different take on these issues see Tim Hope (2005) 'What do crime statistics tell us?' In Hale, C. *et al.* (eds) *Criminology* (Oxford: Oxford University Press). Above and beyond this the reader, if they have access to the Internet, would do well to explore for themselves the wealth of data that is now made available on various governmental websites in relations to crime. Much of this information can either be read on those websites and/or downloaded free of charge. In particular, in the United Kingdom, go to www.homeoffice.gov.uk where access to the Home Office's own research and statistics department can be found. In the United States, www.fbi.gov covers much the same territory and in Europe, the Council of Europe gives access to some, though rather more limited information.

HOW MUCH CRIME?

Challenging myths about crime and offenders

This chapter will build on what we have learned from Chapter 2 by taking a look at what the various data sources that were discussed tell us about how much crime there is. It is hoped that having read Chapter 2 the reader will be well aware of the difficulties involved in trying to assess the nature and extent of crime. However, you will remember from Chapter 1 that criminology is a 'modern' discipline and that means that part of its intent as a discipline is to provide the kind of information that might better inform how to deal with the problem of crime. So, it is necessary to form some picture of the problem of crime despite the inherent difficulties in trying to do this. It is also important to remember that part of the role of criminology is to offer a critical assessment of what is understood as crime. In this chapter, we shall be taking our understanding of this critical role further by thinking about the nature and extent of crime under three general headings; crimes of the streets, crimes behind closed doors and crimes of the suites. As with Chapter 2, the reader will be asked to think about different questions as they become appropriate in our exploration of the question: how much crime?

INTRODUCTION

In Chapter 2, it was acknowledged that people have different kinds of information about crime. In that chapter, the reader was encouraged to compare and contrast the information they had about crime with the kinds of information that criminologists might work with in putting together their understanding of the crime problem. In this chapter, the reader is going to be encouraged to compare and contrast their own information with criminological knowledge a little further through trying to put together an answer to the question: how much crime? Answering this question, hopefully, will also involve challenging some of the myths that we all possess about crime, victims and offenders. So, by the end of this chapter the reader should have an understanding of the problems of trying to assess how much crime there is and as a result should also (hopefully) have a better understanding of who the offenders and victims are. In addition, building on the problems of comparison discussed at the end of Chapter 2, the reader should also have a picture of what the problems are for criminologists trying to understand what these issues look like in different societies. However, before we take any of this any further it will be useful to have a sense of some of the common myths around the problem of crime. One place to start is to try and dispel mass media images of crime and offenders.

DISPELLING MYTHS ABOUT CRIME

On 18 May 1964, in Margate, a seaside resort in the United Kingdom, 'mods' and 'rockers', two clearly identifiable (through dress, mode of transport and general self-presentation) teenage groups clashed on the beach. The nature and extent of that clash was subject to considerable debate, however, what was clear was that the media played an important role in contributing to how people thought about what went on that day and what might ensue on subsequent public holidays. Stan Cohen, a UK criminologist, was later to describe this response as a 'moral panic'. The notion of a 'moral panic' was first used by Howard Becker, a North American sociologist, who used it to refer to the concern and response to the use of drugs in the United States, but as an idea it was developed in much more detail in Stan Cohen's book *Folk Devils and Moral Panics* (which was a detailed study of the response to the 'mods' and rockers' in the 1960s) and was published in 1972. In this study, Cohen describes a moral panic as the way in which the police, politicians, but especially the media, respond to a problem in such a way that the nature of a problem is so exaggerated that it has the effect of generating concern and anxiety out of proportion with the actual nature of the problem itself. In Cohen's view, this is what happened in the United Kingdom in the 1960s in relation to the 'mods' and rockers'. The concept of 'moral panic' as he developed it and the role of the media in generating such panics, have become a central feature of much sociological and criminological research.

How the media influences our understandings of crime is a highly debated topic but can be thought about by asking at least three different questions:

1. Does exposure to media images of crime and violence cause people to engage in similar behaviour? (The ill effects debate.)
2. Does the media work with unfair stereotypes about offenders and victims and so heighten fears and anxieties? (The moral panic debate.)
3. What role does the media play in how crime is consumed as popular culture? (The cultural criminology debate.)

Whilst there are different answers to each of these questions, they all assume that the media does have a role to play in contributing to the kinds of perceptions that the general public may, or may not have, about crime, how much of it there might be, the impact on the victim, the appropriateness of the response of the criminal justice system, the discovery of 'new' crimes, and so on. The precise nature of this role is unclear but given the powerful images that the media has at its disposal, to deny its importance would be foolhardy. However, how accurate these portrayals are in comparison with what it is that is known about crime (the facts), as opposed to that which is interpreted, constructed as a story, or considered newsworthy (the narratives) is a moot point. Much criminological work is concerned to bridge the gap between these different kinds of knowledge. One way of bridging this gap and challenging some of the myths and images of crime, victims and offenders, is to consider a current and widely accepted view that crime is a real problem for people.

CRIME AND EVERYDAY LIFE

Marcus Felson is an influential North American criminologist whose book *Crime and Everyday Life* was first published in 1994. This work is very much concerned to convey the ordinary, everyday nature the experience of crime and has come to be known as the 'routine activity approach' to understanding criminal behaviour. (We shall be discussing the importance of this work again in Chapter 4.) However, to establish his case for accepting that much crime and criminal behaviour is routine, mundane and ordinary, he suggests that challenging mass media images is a good place to start. In so doing in the fourth edition of his book, he identifies nine fallacies about crime. We shall start with a brief review of four of them as they are the most relevant to our discussion.

FELSON'S FALLACIES

THE DRAMATIC FALLACY

Media images of crime lead us to believe that crime and its impact is far more dramatic than it really is. Portrayals of murder are a good example of this. In media representations, murders are frequently constructed as highly complex affairs, perhaps driven by jealously in responses to some domestic outrage. Indeed some murders are like this but this is by no means commonplace. As Felson and Boba (2010) point out most murders result from a petty quarrel and in the United States in particular are a product of a 'gun to near' and a 'hospital too far'. You might also like to reflect on the discussion of Harold Shipman in Chapter 1 and in the light of this 'dramatic fallacy'. But it is not only the portrayals of particular kinds of crime that are given dramatic license. The same drama is attributed to the role played by the criminal justice professionals from the Sherlock Holmes factor in detective stories to the drama of the crown court and the 'comedy' of prison life. As we shall see, and as Felson contends, most crime and most of the work done within the criminal justice system is not like this. It is very ordinary and mundane.

THE INGENUITY FALLACY

This fallacy presumes that the criminals are far cleverer than they really are. Felson argues that much crime that comes to the attention of the criminal justice system is not committed through daring or ingenuity but as a result of opportunity and/or petty vandalism.

For example, a burglar tends to commit crimes in circumstances that offer them relatively easy access and little chance of getting caught. Shoplifting is made more or less easy, depending upon the design and layout of the store. Criminal damage does not take intelligence. Someone involved in email-based Internet fraud is ultimately reliant on the recipient giving them the information with which to complete their criminal act. Though it is a moot point as to the extent to which ingenuity is a prerequisite for some aspects of financial fraud for example.

Felson goes on to argue that assuming that criminals are clever leads people to think that there is more organized and centrally controlled criminal activity than there really is, though this is an issue to which we shall return. However, the central message might be that whilst the victim of a crime might want to make sense of what has happened to them by attributing ingenuity to the criminal, and that this might make good media copy, again most crime is ordinary and committed by ordinary people.

THE AGE FALLACY

Felson suggests that most media images leave people with the impression that victims and offenders are much older than they actually are. In the United Kingdom, this is especially the case in relation to street crime and/or burglary. Newspapers frequently make headline stories from particularly violent attacks on the elderly, especially elderly females. Such things do, of course, happen, but as we shall see most offenders and most victims of petty theft, robbery and acts of violence are young people, more often than not young males.

THE CONSTABULARY FALLACY

This fallacy assumes that the police in the first instance, and other branches of the criminal justice system in the second, know more about crime and can do more about crime than they actually do. Again it is a view of the criminal justice process, often driven by media constructions, that creates an image of crimes being solved and of the wrong doers being brought to justice. As the previous chapter has demonstrated, the criminal justice system only becomes aware of those crimes that have been reported, or are the result of some police pro-activity. In addition, not all crimes get solved!

Having considered some of Felson's fallacies, the reader might like to think about the following questions:

1. To what extent do some of the fallacies discussed above match with your own views of crime, victims and offenders?
2. What do you think has influenced your views?
3. Does what you read in the newspapers and see on the television influence your views? If so why, if not why?

As has already been said, some criminologists have spent a good deal of time trying to work out what kind of influence the media has on people's ideas about crime; asking questions, for example, as to whether or not the media make people worry about crime more or not. That kind of question is not of central importance here. What is important to appreciate is that the information we get from the media is one source of information about crime for all of us, and in the absence of being a victim of crime or an offender or working within the criminal justice system, it is an important source of information. It is that kind of information that is often translated into 'common sense' (what we all 'know') as opposed to 'good' sense (what is actually the case). One of the tasks of criminology and the criminologist, as has been stated elsewhere in this book, is to subject such 'common sense', and the influences on it, to theoretical and empirical investigation. So, in the rest of this chapter we shall be concerned to compare the fallacies discussed above with what it is that the data sources that were discussed in the previous chapter tell us about crime.

HOW MUCH CRIME?

Those of you who have already read Chapters 1 and 2 should be aware of some of the problems in trying to answer this question. Nevertheless, politicians and policy makers regularly make decisions on the assumption that such a question can be answered. To make this assumption it is necessary to do three things:

1. Use the same data source consistently.
2. Be aware of any shortcomings within the data-production process.
3. Suspend any doubts about the possibilities of measurement!

However, the extent to which policy makers and politicians do any of these things is a moot point. Moreover, it is important to remember that such data sources make some crimes more visible than others, and as a consequence, some criminal behaviour is much more visible than others. Thus, in trying to offer a picture of how much crime, it is also important to think about what kind of crime is being talked about. For our purposes, we shall pay attention first of all to the kind of crime that Felson assumes informs the fallacies discussed above: the routine crime. This might loosely be referred to as 'crime of the streets'. Later in this chapter, we shall consider other dimensions to the crime problem by discussing what might be called 'crime behind closed doors' and 'crimes of the suites', a distinction that will be used in subsequent chapters in this book.

ORDINARY CRIME OR 'CRIME OF THE STREETS'

THE NATURE AND EXTENT OF CRIME AND OFFENDERS IN ENGLAND AND WALES

A common starting point for criminologists trying to answer this questions is the British Crime Survey (BCS), more accurately described as a criminal victimization survey as discussed in Chapter 2. The first point to make here is that despite the fact that these surveys are conducted in the same way using the same central stock of questions, the findings from these surveys are not always presented in the same way. These differences in presentation sometimes reflect what is considered to be politically appropriate and sometimes what are considered to be the key policy issues. However, the interested reader might like to access a number of the summary statements of the findings from the BCS from different years and think about how and why those findings have been presented in the way that they have. This should more than illustrate one of the problems of comparison discussed in Chapter 2.

Interestingly, the report on *Crime in England and Wales 2008–9* begins by asking the question: is there more crime than last year? As that report states, and I quote:

The BCS and police recorded crime differ in their coverage of crime. Overall, crime as measured by the BCS shows no change compared with the 2007/08 BCS with no change in most crime types. Crimes recorded by the police show a five per cent decrease compared with 2007/08, with decreases in most crime types.

(*Crime in England and Wales 2008–9*: 1,
Walker *et al.* (eds) London: Home Office)

The report then proceeds to offer this comparative analysis of crime survey data with police recorded data.

BCS CRIME

→ All BCS crime stable (10.7 million crimes in 2008/09)

→ Violent crime – stable

→ With injury – stable

→ Domestic burglary – stable

› Vehicle-related theft – stable

↑ Theft from the person up 25 per cent

→ Vandalism – stable

↑ Risk of being a victim of crime up from 22 per cent to 23 per cent

---

POLICE-RECORDED CRIME

↓ All police-recorded crime down 5 per cent to 4.7 million crimes

↓ Violence against the person down 6 per cent

↓ with injury down 7 per cent

↑ Domestic burglary up 1 per cent

↓ Offences against vehicles down 10 per cent

↓ Theft from the person down 12 per cent

↓ Criminal damage down 10 per cent

↓ Robbery down 5 per cent

↑ Drugs offences up 6 per cent

The BCS reports are available free from the Home Office and are downloadable from their website and offer a wealth of detailed statistical data: far too detailed to make interesting to the reader! However, having offered this overview of the data from the 2008–9 report, the reader might like to:

1. Make a list of the ways in which this data supports your own knowledge about crime, victims and offenders.
2. Make a list of the ways in which this data does not support your own knowledge about crime, victims and offenders.
3. Think about these lists and the questions that were raised in Chapter 2 about the problems associated with gathering data about crime and make a few notes on what problems there might be (if any) with the findings cited above.
4. Make a list of what you think is particularly striking about the differences between these two tables and think about what those differences might actually mean.

If we accept the accuracy of the data above, it generates a number of interesting questions for the criminologist. For example:

- Why is some crime falling?
- Why is some crime stable?
- Why are there differences and how might they be explained?
- Is there a relationship between the confidence of the public in the police and different reporting behaviours that might be reflected in this data?

This list of questions is obviously not complete but they are the kinds of questions a criminologist might ask. However, in addition, the criminologist is interested in who the offenders are and the data above does not help with that kind of question.

Knowledge about offenders is clearly dependent on what we know about those people who are caught and admit to committing crime, and this accounts for a small proportion of all offending behaviour. Detailed knowledge about offenders in England and Wales is not so easily available as the detailed knowledge of criminal victimization outlined above. It is possible to find out how many people are in prison for what kind of offences and it is possible to find about those offenders and offences broken down either by the sex of the offender or the ethnicity of the offender. Since 1991 it has been a legal requirement that such statistics for England and Wales are produced on an annual basis, but it is often up to the researcher to establish the way in which these figures may or may not be related to each other. They are certainly not produced in the same readily available and easily accessible format as the criminal victimization figures. The following data is taken from a publication produced by the Home Office, *Race and the Criminal Justice System: An Overview of the Complete Statistics 2004–2005*: iv–v, published in 2006 as required by the 1991 Criminal Justice Act.

Main findings

- The 2004/05 British Crime Survey (BCS) shows that people from mixed ethnic groups face significantly higher risks of being a victim of crime than White people. However, there were no other statistically significant differences between people from different ethnic backgrounds
- The 2004/05 BCS shows that people in BME groups were significantly more likely than White people to be worried about burglary, car crime and violent crime.
- Racist incidents recorded by the police have continued to rise with about 58,000 incidents recorded in 2004/05, although the latest information from the BCS (self-reported crime) estimates that actual numbers of racist incidents fell from 206,000 in 2003/04 to 179,000 in 2004/05. This difference may reflect the encouragement given by the police to the reporting and recording of such incidents.
- There were 37,000 racially aggravated offences recorded by the police in 2004/05. Just over a third of these offences were cleared up – a similar proportion to previous years.
- In the three years, 2002/03, 2003/04 and 2004/05, the police recorded 2,653 homicides of which 545 were known to be from BME groups. Wide disparities in risks exist for different ethnic groups. Black people were 5.5 times more likely and Asian people nearly twice as likely to be homicide victims as White people (excluding Shipman and Morecambe Bay cases).

Experience as suspects, defendants and prisoners

- There were 839,977 stop and searches recorded by the police under Section 1 of the Police and Criminal Evidence Act 1984 and other legislation in 2004/05, a 14 per cent increase on the previous year.

This rise may be partly explained by an increased level of recording following the increased profile of stop and search arising from the implementation of Recommendation 61 of the report of the Stephen Lawrence Inquiry (Recording of Stops).

- Black people were six times more likely to be stopped and searched under Section 1 compared with White people, Asian people were twice as likely to be stopped and searched. These rates are similar to previous years.
- In 2004/05, 41,301 searches were recorded by the police under Section 60 of the Criminal Justice and Public Order Act 1994 in 30 police force areas. 56% of searches were on White people, 24% on Black people, 17% on Asians and 2% on those of 'Other' ethnic origin. However, this will be partly explained by the high BME population in areas where such searches were carried out.
- In 2004/05, 32,062 searches were recorded by the police under Section 44(1) and Section 44(2) of the Terrorism Act 2000. 73% on White people, 8% on Black people, 11% on Asians and 5% on those of 'Other' ethnic origin. These proportions reflect a high number of searches in London.
- In 2004/5 of an estimated 1.3 million arrests for notifiable offences (those included in the police returns to the Home Office), 9% were recorded as being of Black people, 5% of Asian people and 1.5% of 'Other' ethnic groups.
- The police cautioned 237,337 persons for notifiable offences in 2004. Relative to the number of persons arrested, Black people were less likely to be cautioned than White and Asian people.
- For those courts considered, BME groups were more likely than White people to be committed at magistrates' court to be tried by a jury at the Crown Court (20% for Black people, 30% for Asians and 15% for White people). BME defendants were substantially more likely to be acquitted at the Crown Court than White defendants (29% for Black people, 30% for Asians and 22% for White people).
- Black young offenders and those in the Mixed ethnic group were more likely to receive a community sentence compared with White offenders but less likely to be discharged or given a referral order.
- Black and Asian offenders accounted for 6% and 4% of persons starting court order supervision between October and December 2004.

You might think that this is an incredible amount of fairly dense data, but there are some interesting questions to think about here, for example:

- How might a criminologist explain the differences between the experiences of people from ethnic minorities as compared with white people with the criminal justice system?
- How might some of the statistics discussed here be a reflection of high profile policy changes?
- How does the experience of being a victim of crime relate to ethnic group?
- Do victims and offenders come from different ethnic groups or the same groups?
- Any more?

The disproportionate representation of people from ethnic minorities, especially black people, in the figures above is a source of constant concern for criminologists. As Maguire (2002: 363) states, drawing on data such as this and other criminological studies:

> Taken overall . . . the social characteristics of people who are arrested and processed by the criminal justice system – and particularly offenders who are eventually sent to prison – present a very different pattern from that found in the general population. There are many more males, young people, black people, poor people, poorly educated people, and people with disturbed childhoods than one would find in a random sample.

Taking all of these findings together, it is possible to concur with Felson's view that much crime is ordinary, mundane and exaggerated by the media. It is also possible to see that most of the offenders that come to the attention of the criminal justice system having committed this rather ordinary crime are male, poor, from ethnic minorities and from disturbed backgrounds. As we shall go on to consider in Chapter 4 one of the issues for criminology is to explain why this is the case but as we shall see this pattern in relation to ordinary crime or street crime is not unusual to England and Wales.

THE NATURE AND EXTENT OF CRIME AND OFFENDERS IN THE UNITED STATES

The United States Department of Justice produces annual bulletin reports of criminal victimization in the United States using data

from the National Criminal Victimization Survey (NCVS). Its report
for 2009, published in 2010, offers the following highlights:

> An estimated 4.3 million violent crimes, 15.6 million property crimes,
> and 133,000 personal thefts were committed against U.S. residents age
> 12 or older in 2009.

> Rates of violent (down 39%) and property (down 29%) crimes decreased
> between 2000 and 2009.

> The overall rate of firearm violence declined from 2.4 to 1.4 victimizations
> per 1,000 persons age 12 or older between 2000 and 2009.

> Armed offenders committed 22% of all violent crime incidents in 2009,
> including 8% by offenders with a firearm.

> Violence against males, blacks and persons age 24 or younger occurred
> at higher or somewhat higher rates than the rates of violence against
> females, whites, and persons age 25 or older in 2009.

> Females knew their offenders in almost 70% of violent crimes commit-
> ted against them; males knew their offenders in 45% of violent crimes
> committed against them.

> About half (49%) of all violent crimes and about 40% of all property
> crimes were reported to the police in 2009. Violent crimes against
> females (53%) were more likely to be reported than violent crimes
> against males (45%).

So, by implication, some of the questions that could be asked about
the nature and extent of crime in England and Wales might also
apply to the United States. Yet the reader should also be sensitive to
the problems of comparison and think about the following questions:

- Are the time periods being referred to the same and does
  this matter?
- Are the crimes being referred to the same and does this
  matter?
- Are the legal frameworks being referred to the same and
  does this matter?
- Is crime perceived to be the same kind of social problem? If
  so, where and for whom? If not, why not?
- Are there any similarities in these figures (between England
  and Wales and the United States)? Are they worth commenting
  on? How would we make sense of them?

There may be other questions to think about too when we consider what is known about offenders in the United States.

As an example of information about offenders in the United States, in 2004, the United States Bureau of Statistics produced a special report on the profile of jail inmates in 2002. This was a follow-on study from one conducted in 1996 and covers all those people held in local jails in 2002. Local jails in the United States hold all kinds of offenders, some who have been convicted, some who are awaiting adjudication and sometimes those who are awaiting a new trial. So, it is important to note that not all of these people have necessarily been found guilty of an offence (so this is the first difficulty we have in making comparisons); but it is a useful source of information about offenders and those arrested for offences. The findings of this report reveal that:

- More than six out of ten persons in local jails were from racial or ethnic minorities. An estimated 40 per cent were black, 19 per cent Hispanic, 1 per cent American Indian, 1 per cent Asian and 3 per cent of more than one race/ethnicity.
- Females made up 12 per cent of the inmate population and were more likely than males to be drug offenders.
- 46 per cent of jail inmates were on probation or parole at the time of arrest and 39 per cent had served three or more prior sentences.
- 55 per cent said they grew up in a single-parent household or with a guardian with one in nine having lived in a foster home or an institution.
- 31 per cent grew up with a parent who abused drugs or alcohol and 46 per cent had a family member who had been in jail.
- Over half the women in jail said that they had been physically or sexually abused in the past.

These figures paint a very similar picture of offenders to those discussed in relation to England and Wales (despite the problems of comparison), though the reader might like to reflect on one area of significant difference; that is the significant higher proportion of inmates from ethnic minorities in the United States. For example, the mid-year jail inmate statistics for 2009 indicate that 9 out of 10 inmates were male with 42.5 per cent of them being white, 39.3 per cent being Black and 16.2 per cent being Hispanic. This ethnic differential is far higher than that in England and Wales and is similarly far higher than would be expected given the proportion of people from ethnic minorities in the general population. One task for criminology is to devise explanations that help to understand both the differences and the similarities in such statistics. Pre-empting some of the discussion that we shall have in Chapter 4 on explaining crime and Chapter 8 in relation to crime prevention, the reader might like to consider the extent to which the differences and similarities that we have identified so far in trying to assess 'how much crime' can be explained by any of the propositions below offered by Pease (2002), a UK specialist in crime prevention:

1. Psyche: offenders have different way of thinking and relating to the world.
2. Opportunity: offenders offend because the opportunity presents itself.
3. Structure: offending behaviour is a result of people's different experiences and life chances as a result of where they find themselves in relation to the social hierarchy.

List the reasons you have for agreeing or disagreeing with any of the propositions above and keep your list on one side until you have finished reading this chapter. You might also want to revisit this list when you have read Chapters 4 and 6.

THE NATURE AND EXTENT OF CRIME AND OFFENDERS IN CONTINENTAL EUROPE

Gauging the nature and extent of crime across the member states of the European community is even more difficult than doing so in the United States or England and Wales. Problems of comparison, as was discussed in Chapter 2 are compounded by the differences *between* different European jurisdictions leading to offences being differently categorized and measured. In addition, not all European countries conduct criminal victimization surveys so that source of data is not always available for the purposes of comparison. However, Eurostat, a Europe-based statistical organization gathers all kinds of information across European countries including crime. Their *Statistics in Focus* report 36/2009 reports on crime reported to the police across Europe up to 2007. Its main findings suggest:

- It is possible to compare trends in total crime over the period 1998–2007 for only about half of the EU Member States. Crime rose from 1999 to reach a peak about 2002 but has fallen consistently in the last 5 years.
- The types of crime that have featured increasingly in the police records include violent crime (up 3 per cent), drug trafficking and robbery (both up 1 per cent) in the period 1998–2007.
- Types of crime that have become less prevalent include property offences such as theft of motor vehicles (down 7 per cent) and domestic burglary (down 3 per cent) over the period 1998–2007.
- The annual rate for homicides as recorded by the police in the period 2005–2007 was about 1.4 per 100,000 population, but rather higher in capital cities (average 1.9).
- The prison population has been rising by about 1 per cent annually over the period 1998–2007 to reach an average rate in EU Member States of 123 prisoners per 100,000 population for the years 2005–2007.
- The number of police officers in Member States remained almost unchanged over the period 1998–2007.

This data of course reveals nothing about who the offenders might be and who the victim of this crime might be, neither do these figures reveal anything about the likely chances of being an offender or criminally victimized in these different countries. Such data would require additional information on the composition of the population in these different countries as well as statistics on offenders and victims. There is some information on victims available in the international criminal victimization surveys that have been conducted on a number of occasions since 1989, but using this data source alongside recorded statistics is difficult since they frequently do not refer to the same time period. So, when criminologists want to compare and contrast the nature and extent of crime in different countries in Europe (language differences notwithstanding), their ability to do this is often tempered by the kind of data that is available to them.

This discussion has so far focused on the nature and extent of what might be called street crime or that kind of crime that comes most readily to mind when thinking about Felson's fallacies with which this chapter began. However, to complete our answer to the question, how much crime, we need to look at other ways of thinking about and defining the crime problem: what we have rather loosely called here, crime behind closed doors and crime of the suites. First of all we shall consider some of the issue relating to crime behind closed doors.

HOW MUCH CRIME? CRIME BEHIND CLOSED DOORS

This heading is one way of trying to capture all the potentially criminal behaviour that goes on in the home or within institutions that because of its location, and the fact that it is the kind of behaviour that frequently occurs between people who are well known to each other, is not very often reported to the police or anyone else. As a consequence this kind of crime is relatively invisible and as a result constitutes part of the dark figure of crime discussed in the previous chapter. In more recent years there has been an increasing awareness of this kind of crime and as a result more and more criminologists now consider this kind of crime to be an important topic on which criminology should have something to say. However, before reading this section you might like to think about the following issues:

- Think about the idea of the home as a safe haven? How accurate is this idea? What kinds of myths does this idea help perpetuate about where and when crime occurs and by whom?
- What kind of crime would you include as being 'crime behind closed doors'? (Make a list of the kinds of behaviours that you would fit under this heading.)
- Who do you think is the most likely victim of this kind of crime and why?
- Who do you think is the most likely perpetrator of this kind of crime and why?
- To what extent do your answers to the last three questions fit or fail to fit with the idea of the home as a safe haven?

Much of the contemporary criminological interest in 'crime behind closed doors' owes a great deal to the influence of the feminist movement. Whilst much feminist work was conducted outside of the discipline of criminology, especially in the 1960s and 1970s, and was concerned to campaign for women's rights, that work also played its part in drawing attention to the amount of violence perpetrated by men against women. Feminism and feminists did not necessarily put this level of violence within the framework of the law, (i.e. they were not concerned with it as crime, but as a manifestation of **patriarchy**), the documentation of the extent of such violence coined here as 'crime behind closed doors', played its part in putting such violence on the criminological agenda. So, the phrase 'behind closed doors' is intended to capture that kind of criminal behaviour that is less likely to be recognized as such, by the victim in particular, and as a consequence less likely to come to the attention of the criminal justice system. The kinds of crimes that might be included under this heading that criminologists have paid attention to are rape, domestic violence, child abuse and elder abuse. Space dictates that it is not possible to cover all of theses issues in great detail, however, it is important to say something about each of them. But first a note on understanding the data associated with the kinds of crime under discussion here.

To assess how much crime there is behind closed doors it is important to appreciate that different studies use different ways of measuring this kind of crime and as a consequence paint a different picture of the extent of it. Feminist informed studies, because their central concern is with women's experiences of patriarchy, often use what is referred to as prevalence measures. In other words they ask questions about women's experiences over their lifetime. Studies concerned with measuring the nature and extent of crime, for example, criminal victimization studies, use what is referred to as incidence measures. In other words they measure how many incidents of particular crimes have happened to individuals during a particular specified time period. This is so that victimization findings can be more accurately compared with the number of crimes that are actually recorded. In addition, prevalence studies sometimes let the victim define their own experiences as being criminal or not, incidence studies frequently use definitions informed by what the law would say was criminal or not. These different ways of measuring the same kinds of events produce very different pictures of the nature and extent of these kinds of crimes. For example, consider some of the findings below relating to rape and/or sexual assault:

- In a prevalence study conducted in London and published in 1985, Hall reported that one in six women had experienced rape and one in three women had experienced sexual assault in their lifetime.

- Myhill and Allen, two UK Home Office researchers, reported in 2002 using BCS data, an incidence of rape for the year 2000 of 61,000 women in England and Wales and a prevalence rate of 754,000 women since the age of 16.
- The international criminal victimization survey of 2000 measuring incidents over the previous 5 years suggests that about one in a hundred women in Sweden, Finland, Australia and England and Wales reported sexual assaults with women in Japan, Northern Ireland, Poland and Portugal being least at risk.
- The International Violence Against Women survey sponsored by The European Institute for Crime Prevention and Control affiliated with the United Nations and conducted in 2003 across 30 different countries reports that between 35 per cent and 60 per cent of women in the surveyed countries have experienced violence by a man during their lifetime, between 22 per cent and 40 per cent have experienced intimate partner violence during their lifetime, less than one-third of women reported their experience of violence to the police, and women are more likely to report stranger violence than intimate partner violence, about one-fourth of victimized women did not talk to anyone about their experiences.

Each of these findings conveys very different pictures of the nature and extent of sexual assault but they are all agreed on one common finding:

- Most rapes and sexual assaults are perpetrated by people known to the victim: partners, ex-partners, relatives or friends, and they are perpetrated by men.

(You might like to revisit your thoughts on the home as a safe haven at this point; you might also like to consider the legitimacy of some of the myths around rape, e.g. 'a woman runs faster with her knickers up than a man with his trousers down', when a woman says no she really means yes; prostitutes cannot be raped; real rape is stranger rape; rape can only occur outdoors; women cry rape etc.) And whilst all the findings above relate to women as victims of sexual assault, this does not mean that men cannot be victims of such crimes too; for example:

- In reviewing the literature on the rape of men in prison, a Human Rights Watch Report indicates that 21 per cent of male inmates had experienced at least one episode of pressured or forced sex since they had been in prison. (No Escape: www.hrw.org/reports/2001/prison.)
- In addition, an earlier study conducted by McMullen (1990) on male rape in the United Kingdom challenges the view that this kind of crime is purely a homosexual crime.

If all of these findings are put together they clearly put men but especially men known to their victims at the centre of our understanding of sexually motivated crime. If we add to this some brief findings on domestic violence, for example:

- Mooney (2000), a British criminologist, reports that one in three women, surveyed from a sample of the general population in north London during the early 1990s, had experienced some form of 'domestic' violence during their lifetime.
- A report produced by the Economic and Social Research Council in the United Kingdom on the nature and extent of violence in the United Kingdom published in 2002 reported that half the young men interviewed aged 14–21 thought that it could be acceptable to hit a woman or force her to have sex, as did one-third of young women in the same age groups.

Our picture and understanding of the nature and extent of crime behind closed doors becomes a little more complicated. Add to this, the family and gender dynamics that underpin child abuse, in which child physical abuse seems to be equally perpetrated by men and women on male and female children, but child sexual abuse appears to be something that primarily men do to female children, then the criminological problem of understanding and explaining 'crime behind closed doors' is compounded. Add to this, the family and institutional bases to abuse of the elderly and the crime agenda 'behind closed doors' is substantial indeed!

The impact that these kinds of questions have on criminology is usefully summarized in the following way:

- The study of crime incorporates much more than common images of the crime problem.
- If the findings presented here are taken seriously much of that study involved asking questions about things that are fairly ordinary experiences for a lot of people.
- Many of those ordinary experiences are hidden from view and as a consequence never come to the attention of the criminal justice system.
- Many of those ordinary experiences, though by no means all, are a product of men's behaviour towards women.
- The problem for criminology is how to incorporate findings such as these into explanations of crime and criminality.
- These are not the ordinary experience discussed by Felson.

In some respects it is possible to argue that one of the underlying mechanisms of crime behind closed doors is the question of power. In many of the examples cited above, particular incidents can be understood in part as a product of the personal power that one individual exerts over another with that power, sometimes having more influence and impact as a result of age and/or other factors. (At this juncture the reader might like to think again about the relevance of the three different kinds of explanation of criminal behaviour referred to earlier to this kind of crime, namely psyche, opportunity and structure.) Power, however, is not only exerted at an individual level. It is also part and parcel of structural relationships of society. Those structural relationships also feed into our understanding of the nature and extent of crime. Appreciation of the structural dimension to power relationships is central to the concern that some criminologists have with a further area of criminal activity also often hidden from view. This is referred to here as 'crime of the suites'.

THE NATURE AND EXTENT OF CRIME: 'CRIME OF THE SUITES'

Crime of the suites is used here to refer to a wide range of criminal and potentially criminal activity relating to the world of big business. Sutherland (1949), an American social scientist, first coined the term 'white-collar crime' to draw attention to the kinds of behaviour that may be considered routine practice in the world of work, like using the Internet in the office for personal purposes or taking a few extra pens home, as being suitable subject matter for the criminologists. However, the term 'crime of the suites' is intended to broaden our understanding of these kinds of routine practices to include the kinds of practices that business corporations may engage in against each other or just as a way of doing business. Put simply, we are here concerned with the rather fine line between sharp business practice and criminal practice whether that be in the form of flouting health and safety regulations, fraud or 'insider dealing'. Chapter 2 documented some of the problems associated with counting this kind of crime given its 'invisibility' most of the time, and of course those same problems feed into the extent to which criminology can paint a picture of the nature and extent of crime of this kind. It is very difficult to offer anything like an accurate statistical insight into these issues. Frequently when this kind of criminal activity does come to the attention of the public it tends to do so in a rather dramatic fashion. The examples that follow illustrate some of the drama that can be associated with 'crime of the suites'.

EXAMPLE 1: THE BHOPAL DISASTER 1984

On Sunday 2 December 1984 in Bhopal, India, at the Union Carbide Company of India (a subsidiary of the Union Carbide Corporation) water leaked into a storage tank filled with methyl-isocyanate, resulting in a chemical reaction and subsequent gas escape. Estimates vary on how many died on that day from 1,754 to upwards of 5,000 people. Sources report that two people have died every week since the accident as a result of exposure to that gas. The Indian Government has acknowledged 3,329 deaths for compensation purposes.

EXAMPLE 2: THE CHALLENGER DISASTER 1986

Messerschmidt (1997: 89–90), a North American sociologist reports:

> It has been over 10 years since the space shuttle Challenger exploded in midair, just 73 second into flight, killing all seven crew members. The President's Commission (1986) investigating the explosion concluded that the loss of Challenger was due to failure in the joint between two

segments of the right solid rocket booster (SRB). O-rings, intended to prevent hot gases from escaping through the joint during the propellant burn of the rocket engine, failed to seal properly because of the extremely cold temperature at launch time (29°F). More specifically, the cold temperature impaired O-ring resiliency, allowing hot gases to escape, ignite and within seconds penetrate the external tank.

The President's Commission (1986) further concluded that problems with O-ring design were well documented, and therefore well-known, by both government (NASA) and corporate (Morton Thiokol Inc.) officials before that fateful day. Indeed, the Commission concluded that the explosion was 'rooted in history' and that a 'flawed decision making process' led to the launch (ibid.: 82).

EXAMPLE 3: ABU GHRAIB

The following extract is taken from a report produced by the International Red Cross in February 2004 on 'The Treatment by the Coalition Forces of Prisoners of War and other Protected Persons by the Geneva Convention in Iraq during Arrest, Internment and Interrogation'. You can get the full report at www.globalsecurity.org.

25. The methods of ill-treatment most frequently alleged during interrogation included

- Hooding, used to prevent people from seeing and to disorient them, and also to prevent them from breathing freely. One or sometimes two bags, sometimes with an elastic blindfold over the eyes which, when slipped down, further impeded proper breathing. Hooding was sometimes used in conjunction with beatings thus increasing anxiety as to when blows would came. The practice of hooding also allowed the interrogators to remain anonymous and thus to act with impunity. Hooding could last for periods from a few hours to up to 2 to 4 consecutive days, during which hoods were lifted only for drinking, eating or going to the toilets;

- Handcuffing with flexi-cuffs, which were sometimes made so tight and used for extended periods that they caused skin lesions and long term after effects on the hands (nerve damage), as observed by the ICRC;

- Beatings with hard objects (including pistols and rifles), slapping, punching, kicking with knees or feet on various parts of the body (legs, sides, lower back, groin);
- Pressing the face into the ground with boots;
- Threats (of ill-treatment, reprisals against family members, imminent execution or transfer to Guantanamo);
- Being stripped naked for several days while held in solitary confinement in an empty and completely dark cell that included a latrine;
- Being held in solitary confinement combined with threats (to intern the individual indefinitely, to arrest other family members, to transfer the individual to Guantanamo), insufficient sleep, food or water deprivation, minimal access to showers (twice a week), denial of access to open air and prohibition of contacts with other persons deprived of their liberty;
- Being paraded naked outside cells in front of other persons deprived of their liberty, and guards, sometimes hooded or with women's underwear over the head;
- Acts of humiliation such as being made to stand naked against the wall of the cell with arms raised or with women's underwear over the head for prolonged periods while being laughed at by guards, including female guards, and sometimes photographed in this position;
- Being attacked repeatedly over several days, for several hours each time, with handcuffs to the bars of their cell door in humiliating (i.e. naked or in underwear) and/or uncomfortable position causing physical pain;
- Exposure while hooded to loud noise or music, prolonged exposure while hooded to the sun over several hours, including during the hottest time of the day when temperatures could reach 50 degrees Celsius (122 degrees Fahrenheit) or higher;
- Being forced to remain for prolonged periods in stress positions such as squatting or standing with or without the arms lifted.

26. These methods of physical and psychological coercion were used by the military intelligence in a systematic way to gain confessions and extract information or other forms of co-operation from persons who had been arrested in connection with suspected security offences or deemed to have an "intelligence value".

In this final example, that has been widely covered in the media and the subject of legal proceedings, I am asking you to think about a much broader conceptualized of 'crimes of the suites' to including crimes committed by the state and/or on behalf of the state. What crimes do you think are being committed here, if any, by whom, against whom and in whose interests? What kinds of laws are being transgressed? How does this example in particular relate to questions of justice? (see also Chapter 7).

All of the examples above touch on different dimensions of crime of the suites and as illustrations are not only dramatic in their reporting and impact but also allude, in a very real way, to the problems of trying to offer an estimate as to their nature and extent. However, the reader might like to revisit the seven features of invisibility identified by Jupp, Francis and Davies (1999) discussed in the previous chapter (no knowledge, no statistics, no theory, no research, no control, no politics and no panic) and to think about how each of these features apply to each of the examples above. The reader might also like to reflect on their presentation as 'disasters' or 'scandals' rather than crimes. (We shall discuss this again in Chapter 6.)

Needless to say but there have always been some criminologists who have concerned themselves with the kinds of crime problems illustrated above and we shall discuss that strand of criminology in more detail in Chapter 6. What the examples presented here illustrate is not only the potential nature and extent of 'crimes of the suites' (we only need to add to these examples like, tax evasion, offences against health and safety legislation and offences against financial regulatory agencies to get an added feel of that), but they also illustrate the wide variety of behaviours that might be included here as well as the difficulties associated with them being labelled as criminal. Some of those difficulties, as with crime behind closed doors are connected with the reluctance and/or inability of the victim to identify things that happen to them as criminal (and as a consequence they are not reported to anyone) and some of the difficulties lie with the powerful position that some of the organizations involved in such activities occupy. (Interesting enough, many of those individuals occupying the top positions in such organizations are also male, endorsing the need for criminological explanation to take account of gender in explaining crime. This is discussed in the next chapter. At this juncture, the reader might also like to think again about the relevance of psyche, opportunity and structure to this kind of criminal behaviour.) Leading some criminologists to conclude that 'the rich get richer and the poor get prison' aptly the sub-title to Chapter 6.

Summary and conclusion

This chapter began by stressing the importance of thinking critically about the kinds of images of crime, victims and offenders that are perpetuated by the media. In thinking critically about these images, we went on to consider some of the currently available data there was on the nature and extent of crime in the United Kingdom, the United States and continental Europe. In conducting this review, it has become clear that different data sources can offer us different answers to this question and that as a criminologist it is important to think fairly carefully about what such information does and does not tell us. In trying to extend our criminological imagination about the nature and extent of crime, we went on to think about different kinds of crime that occur in structurally different locations (crime behind closed doors and crimes of the suites) and to consider what that extended understanding had to offer us. There are a number of themes that this review has put to the fore for us. In summary, for the criminologist, the issues look something like this:

1. The importance of challenging media and common sense images of what counts as crime, and who the criminals are.
2. The importance of thinking about the problems of making comparisons from society to society about the nature of crime and offenders.
3. If there are problems in making comparisons about the nature of the crime problem in different societies then there must be additional problems in borrowing policies from one society and trying to make them work in another, without thinking critically about those differences as well as the similarities.
4. The importance of power in defining what we see as being criminal and what we do not see as criminal; whether that be personal power (men over women); institutional power (carers over the elderly); or economic power (big business corporations over all of us).
5. The maleness of much offending behaviour.

The reader is encouraged to think about the extent to which the different kinds of explanations of criminal behaviour to be addressed in the next chapter account, or fail to account, for the kinds of crime evidenced here.

EXERCISE

When politicians talk about the 'war on crime',

- What kind of crime are they talking about?
- Why?
- How might we construct a different answer to this question?
- What kinds of problems would this raise for policy makers?
- What kinds of problems would this raise for politicians?

RECOMMENDATIONS FOR FURTHER READING

A very accessible read is Marcus Felson's *Crime in Everyday Life* (London: Sage). This was first published in 1994 and is now in its fourth edition, which was published in 2010. This is a useful book for not only challenging some of the myths about crime, offenders and victims, but it is also one that will be of interest in following up some of the themes addressed in Chapters 4 and 7. Accessing the Home Office website for the United Kingdom (www.homeoffice.gov.uk) or the Bureau of Justice website for the United States (www.ojp.usdoj.gov) will also give you access to a whole range of different reports on the nature of offenders and criminal victimization. For those wanting a more advanced discussion on the nature and extent of crime in England and Wales a good starting point would be Mike Maguire's chapter 'Crime data and statistics and its implications' in Maguire, M., Morgan, R. and Reiner, R. (2007) *The Oxford Handbook of Criminology* (fourth edition). This is quite a technical overview but if you are serious about either, understanding the nature and extent of crime or serious about criminology, or both, then it is the kind of material that you will need to understand.

4

THE SEARCH FOR CRIMINOLOGICAL EXPLANATION

In this chapter we shall be considering the different ways in which criminologists attempt to explain criminal behaviour. The reader is reminded that in Chapter 1 we have already discussed two historically important ways in which criminologists have tried to explain criminal behaviour: biological positivism and sociological positivism. Here, we shall be considering some important sociological ideas that have been used over the last 25 years to explain crime. You might also recall from Chapter 1 that criminology was established as a 'modern' discipline. This means that its growth and development as a social science is parallel with the growth and development of modern society. One of the central aims of the discipline was, and still is, to look for ways in which the problem of crime, as a social problem, could be better managed in the interests of society as a whole. So that criminologists could offer information about the kinds of policies that would have this effect, they are concerned with understanding the cause(s) of crime. This means that much criminological endeavour is focused on searching for the explanation of criminal behaviour. In this chapter, we will be considering the relevance of four different kinds of criminological explanation: rational choice theory, social control theory, relative deprivation and hegemonic masculinity. At all times the reader will be encouraged to think about the extent to which these theories match with the evidence we have discussed in Chapter 3.

INTRODUCTION

Chapter 1 highlighted the importance of positivism to criminology and the way that positivism is manifested in both biological and socio-logical representations of the discipline. The purpose of this chapter is to develop a more finely tuned understanding of criminological expla-nation by considering the relative value of four different ways that criminologists have used in recent times to explain criminal behaviour: rational choice theory and its relative the routine activity approach, social control theory, the concept of relative deprivation and the con-cept of hegemonic masculinity. These four different ways of theoriz-ing about crime have also been chosen because they have each been differently deployed in informing policy-making decisions and they each make different assumptions about the importance of the role of the victim, or potential victim, in the perpetration of crime. They also offer us one way of taking our threefold concern with the psyche, opportunity and structure, introduced in the previous chapter a little further. However, we need to make sure first of all that we understand what is meant by theory and what is meant by explanation.

A WORD ON THEORY AND EXPLANATION

Thinking about theory tends to worry students. Yet, all of us work with 'theory' all of the time. Put at its simplest 'theory' refers to the ideas we have about the world. Our 'theories', or ideas, equip us with sets of assumptions that enable us to make sense of the world we live in. In the context of crime, each of us will have our own theories as to why some people commit crime and others do not. We sometimes call this 'com-mon sense'. What makes criminological theory a little more different than 'common sense' is that it attempts to offer ideas, assumptions and/or hypotheses to help us make sense of criminal behaviour that can be applied generally. In other words, criminological theory tries to work with ideas that enable us to make sense of the world above and beyond what we know based on our own experiences and/or anec-dotes. It seeks to make sense of the world beyond individual experience. This can be expressed as the difference between the theories we all have based on common sense from theories that can be generated on the basis of good sense. So, in the search for an explanation of crime, common sense is often not sufficient on its own to explain why some people engage in criminal behaviour and others do not. Common sense may work in some specific circumstances but it will not necessarily be applicable generally. Criminologists look for theories that can offer general explanations of crime. Only in this way can the link between theory and policy be seen to make sense.

A brief look at the range of books available on criminological theory offers a clue as to the variety and complexity that can be associated with this search for explanation. This should be expected. After all, human beings can be fairly complex creatures! However, in making sense of criminological theory, it is useful to ask a number of questions. Soothill *et al.* (2002: 98–9) list these as being:

1. What is the theory trying to explain, and therefore what aspects of the crime-criminal problem does it ignore?
2. How might we categorize this theory in relation to:

   - Schools of thought
   - Key concepts and ideas
   - Main theorists?

3. When and where was the theory written? What was the potential influence of the social context at that time?

To this list I would add two more questions:

4. What are the policy implications that flow from a theory?
5. How do those implications resonate with the political climate of the time?

So, put simply, it must be remembered that theory is not constructed or applied in a social vacuum. It is always important to have some sense of who the protagonists of a particular theory are and what their influence is likely to be. It is also important to remember that in order for criminological theory to work it has to make sense of what it is that we know about crime, criminals and criminal victimization. In other words, the theory is there to help us make sense of the evidence.

Some time ago, John Braithwaite (1989: 44–9), an influential Australian criminologist, stated that there are 13 facts about crime that criminology needs to explain that common sense knowledge can sometimes fail to appreciate:

1. Crime is committed disproportionately by males.
2. Crime is perpetrated disproportionately by 15–25 year olds.
3. Crime is committed disproportionately by unmarried people.
4. Crime is committed disproportionately by people living in large cities.
5. Crime is committed disproportionately by people who have experienced high residential mobility and who live in areas characterized by high residential mobility.
6. Young people who are strongly attached to their school are less likely to engage in crime.
7. Young people who have high educational and occupational aspirations are less likely to engage in crime.
8. Young people who do poorly at school are more likely to engage in crime.
9. Young people who are strongly attached to their parents are less likely to engage in crime.
10. Young people who have friendships with criminals are more likely to engage in crime themselves.
11. People who believe strongly in complying with the law are less likely to violate the law.
12. For both men and women, being at the bottom of the class structure – whether measured by personal socio-economic status, socio-economic status of the areas of residence, being unemployed or belonging to an oppressed racial minority – increases rates of offending for all types of crime apart from those for which opportunities are systematically less available to the poor.
13. Crime rates have been increasing since the Second World War in most developed and developing countries. The only case of a country which has been clearly shown to have had a falling crime rate in this period is Japan.

So, think about the extent to which these 'facts':

- fit with all kinds of crime;
- are produced as a result of the database they are derived from;

- fit or do not fit with your own common sense knowledge about crime;
- say anything about criminal victimization;
- relate to the data discussed in Chapter 3.

And, for the purposes of this chapter in particular:

- The ways of making sense of crime that are discussed below fit these 'facts'.

So, we now have five questions with which to evaluate any criminological theory:

1. What kind of crime is it concerned to explain?
2. Where does it fit in relation to the ideas of the time?
3. When and where was it written?
4. What policies flow from it?
5. How does it relate to the evidence?

Each of these questions will be considered in the light of the four different criminological explanations to be considered here: rational choice theory, social control theory, relative deprivation and hegemonic masculinity. These theories have been chosen largely because of their contemporary resonance and largely because they highlight the different policy possibilities that flow from them by way of illustrating how theory, evidence and policy can be connected in different ways.

RATIONAL CHOICE THEORY

Ken Pease (2006), a UK criminologist writing in *The Sage Dictionary of Criminology*, defines rational choice theory in the following way:

> The starting point of rational choice theory is that offenders seek advantage to themselves by their criminal behaviour. This entails making decisions among alternatives. These decisions are rational within the constraints of time, ability, and the availability of relevant information.

(339)

This definition offers an understanding of rational choice theory at its most general level and as a result encompasses another set of ideas that emphasise the rationality of the criminal actor: routine activity theory. These ideas are discussed in detail in a later section. The idea that the criminal is a rational actor has its origins in what is referred to as **classical criminology**. In classical theory the individual human being is seen as someone whose interests lie in maximizing pleasure and minimizing pain. Put in more economic terms, individuals weigh up the costs and the benefits of their actions and make choices on the basis of the benefits that they think will accrue from them. Thus, classical criminology puts great store by the deterrent effect of punishment. Despite the inherent problems with this view of human beings and assuming that deterrence works (for example, it disregards the problem that different things might work with different individuals), since the 1980s, there has been a considerable revival of interest in thinking about the criminal as a rational actor making decisions in the way suggested earlier.

Some would argue that rational choice theory does not comprise an independent theory at all because there are elements of the idea of the criminal as a rational choice maker in a range of criminological theories. However, it can be argued that the revival of interest in emphasizing the criminal as a rational actor was as much a reflection of looking for innovative policies of crime prevention (given the rising crime rates of the 1980s) as it was a concern to search for an explanation of criminal behaviour itself. Cornish and Clark (1986: 1) emphasize the value of rationality in the context of crime prevention policy in the following way:

> offenders seek to benefit themselves by their criminal behaviour; . . . that this involves the making of decisions and choices, however rudimentary on occasion these processes might be; and . . . these processes exhibit a measure of rationality, albeit constrained by the limits of time and the availability of information

So, by implication, this rational process of decision-making is used to account for not only the decision to commit crime but also the time and the place in which such crime is committed. Furthermore, this view of the criminal presumes that the harder the target of criminal behaviour, the more likely the criminal is to choose another target. Of course, as Cornish and Clarke (2006) recognize themselves, offenders (like all of us) are rarely in possession of all the information to make a perfectly informed rational decision. What offenders do is to engage in patterns of behaviour that have worked before rather than necessarily being able to make finely tuned, highly informed decisions. Their rationality is therefore *'bounded'*. However, the key to understanding offending behaviour is that while the quality of the decision-making process may be variable, the actions offenders engage in are always *purposive*, that is committed with the intention of benefiting the offender. Thus, crime is never senseless. Vandalism might reap the reward of esteem amongst peers. Violence in the home may secure the authority of the person committing the violence. So even in examples like these where other factors may be present, the behaviour of the offender is always seen to have a purpose.

However, this theory lends itself very readily to a range of policy initiatives referred to as **situational crime prevention** (see also Chapter 8). Put simply, if the opportunities for criminal behaviour are removed then the costs of committing crime will outweigh the benefits. However, the reader might like to consider whether or not this is the case after completing the following exercise.

- Make a list of all the crimes in which you think offenders weigh up the costs and benefits of committing crime.
- For each of the crimes in your list, do the costs and benefits look the same for each crime?
- For each of the crimes in your list, what practical intervention would you introduce to increase the opportunity costs of offending?
- What do you think would happen to the potential for criminal behaviour as a consequence of your intervention measures?

Hopefully what this exercise has led you to think about are some of the problems inherent in rational choice theory. It should have at least made you aware of some of the complexities of not only assuming that criminals are rational actors but also some of the other factors this emphasis on the rationality of the criminal leaves out. In particular, it might have led you to consider the problem of 'displacement'. The extent to which, making it harder to commit particular crimes in particular places, results in different kinds of crime being committed at different times and in different places. This suggests that target hardening (a key policy intervention that is derived from this theory which is discussed in detail in Chapter 8) in and of itself may only constitute a partial answer to crime as it taps into only part of the crime production equation. Cohen and Felson (1979), two North American criminologists, tried to develop the complexity of the crime equation a little more in detail by exploring the relationship between the offender and the opportunity to commit crime a little further. This they called the 'routine activity approach'.

The routine activity approach to understanding the choices made by offenders to commit crime at particular times in particular places against particular targets argues that crime is the product of three factors coming together: a motivated offender, a potential victim and the absence of a capable guardian. The way in which these factors come together can be identified in the daily, routine patterns of people's everyday lives. This view of crime, rather like rational choice theory, focuses attention on crime as an event, with the idea of understanding people's routine activity adding a predictive element to where, when and against whom crime might occur because of the attention that it gives to the *patterning* of activities. This way of thinking about the commission of crime has also been used to understand the patterning of victimization. Using the concept of lifestyle rather than routine activity, Hindelang, Gottfredson and Garofalo (1978: 250), three North American social scientists interested in criminal victimization, used this idea to understand the patterning of personal victimization. They state that for such victimization to occur:

> First, the prime actors – the offender and the victim – must have occasion to intersect in time and space. Second, some source of dispute or claim must arise between the actors in which the victim is perceived by the offender as an appropriate object of victimisation. Third the offender must be willing and able to threaten or use force (or stealth) in order to achieve the desired end. Fourth the circumstances must be such that the offender views it as advantageous to use or threaten force (or stealth) to achieve the desired end. The probability of these conditions being met is related to the life circumstances of members of society.

From this starting point, these authors then go on to list eight propositions as to why some individuals are much more likely to be subjected to personal victimization than others drawing on such variables as age, sex, ethnicity and so on. This way of thinking about the likelihood or otherwise of criminal victimization proved to be highly influential in the way in which the criminal victimization survey was developed. (The relevance of this work is discussed in detail in the next chapter.)

Rational choice theory along with the routine activity approach were harnessed by governments both in the United States and the United Kingdom during the late 1970s and early 1980s when the crime rate was rising rapidly as they offered opportunities for policy intervention. Governments could be seen to be doing something about crime. Indeed, the popularity of closed circuit television in city centres, for example, stands as testimony to the commitment to, and perceived value of, this approach. Moreover, within this explanation of crime, it should be noted that criminals are viewed as people just like us: offenders are ordinary people who commit ordinary crimes dependent on the supply of criminal opportunities presented to them. They are not 'pathological monstrosities' as Lombroso suggested in Chapter 1.

The influence of these ideas and the policies and politics associated with them came to be known during the 1980s as **right realism**. This term was intended to highlight the inherent political conservatism of these ideas and the implicit assumption that crime was a problem of individuals but not social structures. Lilly *et al.* (1995: 223) make the following observation:

> The 1980s saw a return to ways of thinking about crime that although packaged in different language, revitalised the old idea that the sources of lawlessness reside in individuals, not within the social fabric. The rekindling of this type of theorising, we believe, was no coincidence. Like other theories before it, conservative theory drew its power and popularity from the prevailing social context.

Thus, highlighting the importance of factors outside the sense of the theory that may or may not contribute to its success and influence. More recently, closely aligned to rational choice theory, routine activity theory and situational crime prevention has been **crime science**.

Gloria Laycock (2006), a UK criminologist defines crime science in *The Sage Dictionary of Criminology* in the following way:

> Crime science was launched in April 2001 as a new discipline directed at the prevention and detection of crime and the reduction of disorder in ethically acceptable ways. It involves the application of scientific principles – including the formulation of explanatory theory, the application of logic, the use of rational argument, and the empirical testing of hypotheses through the collection and analysis of data – to the problems of crime and disorder. The precise contours of crime science, however, are still evolving.
>
> (89)

Claiming to embrace the traditional principles of scientific practice, including experimentation, crime science makes the case for focusing on the immediate circumstances that surround criminal behaviour from the environment, to the rewards for crime, to how crime is committed and to the opportunities that permit crime to happen. This focus affords the opportunity to map crime or identify crime 'hotspots' and to test out what kinds of measures can be put in place to prevent criminal behaviour. In many ways, this approach to criminal behaviour is an extension of, and attempts to pull together, the other conceptual ideas we have discussed so far. For many criminologists, it is a contentious approach to crime because of its emphasis on a very circumscribed understanding of what affects individual behaviour. (For an interesting comparison between crime science and criminology more generally see the table produced by Tim Newburn in his book *Criminology*, on page 295.) Our next criminological theory takes a different direction.

SOCIAL CONTROL THEORY

The focus of social control theory is different than rational choice theory in two key respects. First, it is concerned with the effect that society and its various institutions has on individuals so its attention is on social processes rather than on individual ones. Second, it is concerned to understand how it is that people are encouraged to conform so its attention is on how law-abiding behaviour is achieved rather than law-breaking behaviour. Some would argue that its concerns are directly derivable from the famous quote of the social philosopher Hobbes (1651) that without control life would be a 'war of every man against every man'. Put simply, if rational choice theory puts at the centre of human motivation the maximization of pleasure and the minimization of pain, social control theory puts fear at the centre of such motivation because it is fear of the consequences that keeps people restrained. As Hobbes is reported as saying in Hopkins-Burke (2001: 201):

> Why do men obey the rules of society? . . . Fear . . . it is the only thing, when there is appearance of profit or pleasure by breaking the laws that makes men keep them.

There are many varieties of sociological theorizing that have put the processes of social control at the centre of their concerns and a number of different variations on these have appeared in criminological work. However, the most well-known proponent of social control is to be found in the work of Hirschi (1969), a North American social scientist, who developed what he called the 'social bond' thesis of social control.

For Hirschi there were four components to the social bonds that sustained or threatened social relationships: attachment, commitment, involvement and belief. Hirschi saw these as social relationships not psychological ones. In other words, they needed to be understood as a product of the extent to which the norms and values of any society or social relationship had become embedded within an individual. It will be useful to say something about each of these social bonds in turn.

- *Attachment.* This refers to the level of strength or weakness of relationships that an individual forms with others. In particular, it is concerned to identify the relative power of the social expectations that relationships with others have over an individual. The stronger the social expectations, the stronger the attachment, the more likely an individual will conform. Such attachment can and do vary over time.
- *Commitment.* This bond reflects Hirschi's understanding of the rational actor: the more an individual invests in

conformity (i.e. commits themselves to a particular lifestyle) the more they have to lose by deviating from it.

- *Involvement*. The more an individual spends their tine engaged in behaviour that is conventional or law abiding the less time they have for other things.
- *Belief*. If an individual has been brought up to be a law-abiding citizen then he or she will be less inclined to break the law.

It is possible to argue that these four dimensions of social bonds are interconnected and interdependent. In addition, it is also possible to see the links between these ideas and common sense ones, for example, 'the devil makes work for idle hands' is not far removed from the notion of involvement above. However, many people have seen the strengths in Hirschi's ideas not as being theoretical strengths but empirical ones. In other words, these ideas have been subjected to a good deal of testing that has resulted in some sound empirical support. (The reader might like to review Braithwaite's 'facts' at this point and identify those that fit with the importance of social bonds.) Empirical support notwithstanding, this version of social control theory cannot help us understand:

- Why the absence of social control leads some people into drug offences and other people into tax fraud.
- The role of changes in the law or levels of tolerance towards different law-abiding or law-breaking behaviours.
- How one individual's deviant or law-breaking behaviour is recognized and labelled as such and the same behaviour by others not.

These kinds of problems have led others, most notably Gottfredson and Hirschi (1990), to refine this original version of social control theory into what they called 'A General Theory of Crime'. This version of social control theory is intended to explain all crimes at all times and draws much more closely on rational choice theory as discussed earlier adding in the importance of understanding 'self-control' to the previous emphasis on social control. The combination of these two concepts led to much attention being paid to one central mechanism of control that arguably has an impact on both: the effectiveness or otherwise of parenting. Although this focus certainly won appeal in the policy arena, it still did not address all crimes at all times as the authors claimed. Again the reader might like to think about the validity or otherwise of ineffective parenting and its contribution to, for example, insider dealing! An absence from this conceptual debate that provides a neat example of the construction of the Criminological Other discussed in Chapter 1.

In an interesting development of social control theory, Charles Tittle, an American social scientist, introduced **control balance theory** in 1995. He made the observation that whilst too little control might lead to deviant behaviour, so might too much control. So if control is balanced (whether that be of individuals or organizations), then conformity followed; if control is unbalanced, then deviancy and/crime was the result. The kind of imbalance, too much or too little, equates with the kind of behaviour that might follow. However, for deviant or criminal behaviour to occur a number of elements needed to be present: a pre-disposition for deviant behaviour (motivation), a trigger mechanism that highlights the control imbalance, recognition of and opportunity for deviant/criminal behaviour and the ability to overcome any constraints on such behaviour (these could be situational, moral or simply the presence of others). From this brief overview, you can probably see the way in which Tittle's work tries to integrate some of the other ways of thinking about crime that we have discussed so far, and as he himself observes (Tittle 2006) it remains to be seen whether or not this intervention has any real promise in terms of practice.

The impact of social control theory, in the nature of the theory itself, has arguably been much more subtle and piece meal in the policy arena. As a social theory, focusing on the importance of the social, it does not lend itself so readily to easily measurable policies whose effectiveness might be demonstrated in a relatively short period of time. Even the effectiveness or otherwise of parenting interventions needs some time, and quite a complex process, to demonstrate their effectiveness. Therefore, despite some of the relevance of the empirical findings that lend support to social control theory, in a social context, both in the United Kingdom and elsewhere, that has increasingly demanded quick fixes for social problems, the impact of social control theory has inevitably been very subtle if it has been there at all. Our next theoretical framework had its origins in the United Kingdom rather than in the United States.

RELATIVE DEPRIVATION

Walklate (2007: 61) states that relative deprivation:

> refers to conditions in which people may not only be (or may not at all be) objectively deprived, but also may feel so deprived and perceive themselves to be so deprived in comparison either with others in the same social category or others in a different social category.

As a concept, relative deprivation has a long history of use primarily in social psychology. In the context of criminology, it has been used most recently as a key explanatory concept within what came to be called '**left realism**' (as distinct from 'right realism' discussed earlier; the differences and similarities between these two ways of thinking about crime will be discussed in detail later). Jock Young (1992), a UK criminologist whose work over recent years has largely been associated with left realism, argues that the concept of relative deprivation is very powerful for three reasons:

1. It can be applied to circumstances throughout the social structure.
2. It can be applied to all kinds of crime not just those deemed to be economically motivated.
3. It is a concept that is not dependent on identifying some absolute standard of deprivation or poverty.

The importance of this concept to left realism is best explained by putting it within a more detailed appreciation of the left realist framework.

Left realism emerged in the United Kingdom during the 1980s in part as a response to the way in which the early British Crime Surveys seemed to be downplaying the importance and impact of crime in people's everyday lives. So, in many ways the political purpose of left realism, in challenging what the received view of the crime problem then was, has never been in doubt. However, there has always been more to the left realist project than politics.

Left realism centralized the need to address crime 'as people experienced it' (Young 1986: 24) and 'necessitates an accurate victimology' that 'must also trace accurately the relationship between victim and offender' and must take account of the fact that 'crime is focused both geographically and socially on the most vulnerable sections of the community' (ibid: 23). To understand the complete picture of crime, its production as a social problem and its impact, it was argued that criminology needed to take account of the 'square of crime'; that is, the way in which the victim, the offender, the reaction of the formal agencies of the state and the reaction of the public, all interacted with each other to produce crime as a social problem. Within this square of crime, relative deprivation is the concept that helps to understand the way in which crime may be differently constituted in different circumstances. So, the motivation for criminal behaviour has to be understood as the product of what people see going on around them, how they see themselves in relation to that understanding and how their behaviour may or may not be reacted to within the particular set of social circumstances in which they find themselves. As Young (2001: 244) states:

> Discontent can be felt anywhere in the class structure where people perceive their rewards as unfair compared to those with similar attributes. Thus crime would be more widespread, although it would be conceded that discontent would be greatest amongst the socially excluded.

As Young himself is at pains to point out the cause of crime cannot be explained by material deprivation alone and yet, at the same time it must be seen related to the social order. For the left realist the concept of relative deprivation connects material circumstances with the social order since human beings can and do reflect on their material circumstances and of those around them. As he goes on to observe, the changing relationship between merit (working hard for what you get) and reward, which can be observed in contemporary society, from for example, English footballers who are paid £250,000 a week, to the bonuses paid to bankers despite their shortcomings displayed during the economic crisis of 2008–10, has an impact on rich and poor alike: 'Thus relative deprivation, and a crisis of identity affects both parts of society although the direction of the hostility conjured up and the poignancy of its impact are very different indeed' (Young, 2007: 46).

The policy agenda that flows from left realism emphasizes such strategies as multi-agency intervention that have become almost commonplace in the United Kingdom since the first development of these ideas. However, these ideas, such as those discussed elsewhere in this chapter, have not proceeded without criticism. For a detailed analysis of these see Walklate, 2007, chapter 4 and Hopkins-Burke, 2001, chapter 15. One key problem that remains is captured by the following question:

> Given that this theory assumes no absolute condition of deprivation, this means that we can all feel relatively deprived in relation to some other group with whom we are comparing ourselves. So what makes some people, as relatively deprived as their neighbours, whether this is in relation to how they each feel or what they each might have (i.e. both subjectively and objectively), turn to crime and their neighbours do not?

In real terms this question reflects one of the ultimate problems for theory and explanation within criminology; is it the individual 'at fault'; is it society 'at fault' or is it some mix of the two? Each of the theories we have discussed here offers us different solutions to this question. However, before taking this further perhaps this is the point where it will be useful to revisit the five questions about theory that we began with. So consider:

1. What kinds of crime can each of these theories tell us about?
2. How do they fit with the ideas of the time in which they were formulated?
3. When, where and by whom were they written?
4. What policies flow from them?
5. How do they relate to the evidence?

Hopefully in thinking about your answers to these questions, you have become particularly sensitized to the importance of understanding the political context in which theories become popular, gain support or recede in significance. This is captured in the discussion here by some of the terms that have been used to describe the theories themselves: like right realism and left realism, both of which claim to take crime and its impact seriously. Where they differ, of course, is where they locate the cause of crime, and then, as a consequence what there is to be done about it. However, of particular importance to the discussion here is how each of these theories performs in relation to question five. This we shall explore in a little more detail.

HOW DO THESE DIFFERENT THEORIES PERFORM IN RELATION TO THE EVIDENCE?

The evidence presented in this chapter by which to evaluate these theories were the 13 facts that Braithwaite said any theory of crime should be able to fit in. It has already been observed that his 'facts' do not necessarily allow for all kinds of crime and that much of Braithwaite's work could itself be situated within the social control model of crime. However, now being aware of those limitations, it is still a useful exercise to consider how each of the theoretical frameworks that have been discussed here perform in relation to his facts, and also to consider the extent to which that performance might connect or not connect with common sense knowledge about crime. So, stop for a minute and complete the following table.

Braithwaite's 'facts'	Rational choice	Social control	Relative deprivation	Common sense
	Yes/No/Maybe	Yes/No/Maybe	Yes/No/Maybe	Yes/No/Maybe
1				
2				
3				
4				
5				
6				
7				
8				
9				
10				
11				
12				
13				

Think about your evaluation in the table above. Which of these 'facts' do the three theories we have discussed so far explain? Which are left unexplained? What are the differences and similarities between what is included and excluded by these theories? Are all kinds of crime covered here? If not, which are included and excluded? Which key fact is highlighted by Braithwaite but left out by all these theories? Do any of them take account of gender?

LOOKING AT THE EVIDENCE: THE QUESTION OF GENDER

Chapter 1 introduced the different ways in which criminology and victimology, as areas of study, made some issues more visible than others. In that chapter, this was discussed in terms of the 'criminological other' and the 'victimological other'. Issues around gender featured strongly in these constructions and yet from the evidence of Braithwaite's 'facts' and that produced in Chapter 3, it is clear that crime is predominantly a problem to do with being male. However, from the evaluation of the theories discussed in this chapter so far, it can be seen that the extent to which gender, as a variable, is apparently accounted for within them is pretty minimal. It must be said that the proponents of these theories would argue that their theories are either gender neutral (that is, could apply to men or women; rational choice theorists and social control theorists might say this).

At this point, you might like to consider Frances Heidensohn's (1985) use of the concept of control to make sense of women's lives, understood as either being

- under control (by men);
- or out of control (being deviant);
- or possibly being increasingly 'in control' as some have entered the world of work in relatively powerful positions.

How does this use of the idea of control compare with Hirschi's or Tittle's use of the concept?

In addition, others might argue that the concepts they use are inclusive of gendered issues (those committed to the concept of relative deprivation might say this). Nevertheless, those committed to looking at the effect that gender has on both the propensity to commit crime and on the ways in which we might think about the victim of crime, would have a different view. Moreover, given that questions relating to gender and crime have been given a good deal of criminological press in its recent history, it is important to consider what the issues are about this that concern people.

First of all it is important to recognize the difference between gender and sex. Put simply, sex is a biological given, male or female (though in a small number of cases there can even be confusion here); gender refers to the socially ascribed attributes of being male or female (man or woman). Second, when the term gender is used, it does not only refer to women. It refers to men as well. Third, some would argue that there can be no such thing as a gender neutral concept; because the world is divided into men and women, concepts or theories reflect either a male view of the world or a female view. It is on this third point that many feminists initially, and latterly theorists interested in masculinity, had (and some still do have) problems with respect to criminological work. Their common concern is reflected in this statement made by Brown (1986: 35), a UK criminologist:

> the more one seeks to show that male criminologists take leave of their senses when the question Woman looms on the agenda, the more one implies that they are in their right minds when they talk about male crime.

By implication, the reason for raising the gender question is not just to ensure that women are included within criminological theorizing and explanation, but also to ensure that criminology is also thinking critically about how the *maleness* of crime (back to Braithwaite's facts) is theorized and explained. In recent years some criminologists have tried to do this by employing the concept of 'hegemonic masculinity'.

HEGEMONIC MASCULINITY AND CRIME

Jefferson (2006: 199), a UK sociologist, defines hegemonic masculinity in *The Sage Dictionary of Criminology* in the following way:

The set of ideas, values, representations and practices associated with 'being male' which is commonly accepted as the dominant position in gender relations in a society at a particular historical moment.

Given the maleness of the crime problem and the dominance of men within the criminal justice professions, some criminologists most notably Messerschmidt in North America and Jefferson in the United Kingdom have explored the extent to which an appreciation of the dominance of men in society as a whole is the starting point for understanding the dominance of men within criminal behaviour. Much of the focus of this work owes a good deal to the work of Connell (1987, 1995) an Australian social scientist.

According to Connell (1987), the ways in which men express their masculinity in contemporary society is connected to the powerful cultural position given to normative heterosexuality. In other words, it is expected and considered normal for men to see themselves as different from women and at the same time to desire women. This deep-rooted expectation of what it is to be a man is reflected in all kinds of social relations. So, for example, it is found in the idea of the man being the breadwinner, in the criminalization of homosexuality, and in making women the objects of pornography. Normative heterosexuality underpins all these examples and for Connell defines the structure and the form of manhood that any individual man is constrained to live up to. If the question of ethnicity is added to this framework, it suggests that the white heterosexual male is in the position of power and at the same time suggests that other forms of manhood are downgraded (such as the homosexual male or the ethnic minority male) as are forms of femininity. The powerful position of this version of masculinity is maintained and sustained by consent. As we are all gendered subjects, we all benefit to a greater or a lesser degree by the framework of hegemonic masculinity. So far, maybe so good; but how does this relate to crime?

Messerschmidt (1993, 1997) relates these ideas to crime in three key locations: the street, the workplace and the home. In each of these locations, he provides a detailed account of the variety of ways in which masculinity is given expression to: from the pimp on the street to the sharp business of the rising white collar executive and to expressions of male proprietary in the forms of various violences in the home. All these can be understood as different ways of doing manhood within the framework of dominance highlighted by Connell. They all demonstrate the ways in which men display their manliness to others and themselves. So, while the business executive might use his position and power to sexually harass his secretary in perhaps more subtle ways than the pimp who controls his women, the effects are the same. In this particular example, the women are 'put in their place' and the men are confirmed as men.

This way of thinking about crime and criminality certainly puts to the fore the maleness of crime and the criminal justice industry. It has even been used to facilitate an understanding of how men deal with victimization. An experience that men often struggle with as the demands of masculinity would suggest that being a victim is something highly contradictory for them. (This is discussed again in the next chapter.) However, as a way of thinking it has not proceeded without its critics and, whilst it is not necessary for such a critique to be explored in detail here, the following question from Hood-Williams (2001: 44) captures the essence of the problem:

> The question remains, however, why it is that only a minority of men need to produce masculinity through crime rather than through other, non-criminal means?

In many respects, the tensions that are inherent in the masculinity thesis in its search for an explanation of crime are the tensions inherent within criminology itself. The reader will recall from Chapter 1 that criminology has to be understood as a 'modern' discipline. This means that it is intimately implicated in the search for universal explanations that can better inform the policy-making process. As a consequence it does look for explanations that will fit all things. So, as Hood-Williams suggests, criminology is constantly left with the dilemma of identifying a concept or a theory that works for some of the time but not all of the time. Yet, some would argue that there is still much to be gained by exploring the extent to which hegemonic masculinity or indeed masculinities takes the criminological agenda forward. This is not the place to explore this debate but the reader might still like to reflect on its value, as an idea, in relation to Braithwaite's facts.

Summary and conclusion

This chapter has illustrated that:

1. There is a good deal of difference between common sense and criminological sense. So, what we know about crime as members of the public can sometimes connect with what criminologists know about crime but this is not always the case
2. Criminologists do not all agree on how to explain crime. One of the key tensions for criminologists is how much of their explanation to attribute to the individual and how much to attribute to the social. This tension is, of course, connected with the fact that criminology as a discipline is multi-disciplinary in character and so people from different backgrounds will emphasize different variables. Moreover, this tension should not be seen as a problem. It is after all what makes criminology interesting and the subject of much debate!
3. No one criminological theory connects that well to all the known facts about crime. This suggests that it is time for criminology to stop looking for grand explanations and that it might be more fruitful now to search for more middle range explanations perhaps focusing on particular crimes or particular contributory factors towards criminality
4. Different criminological theories lend themselves to different policy interventions and it will depend on the political climate how successful any theory or policy intervention may be. (Crime prevention policy is discussed in more detail in Chapter 8.)
5. Different theories make different crimes, criminals and victims visible and invisible. None of the theories discussed here makes 'crimes or victims of the powerful' highly visible. This does not mean that they could not just that they have not generally been applied in this way. This comment, of course, encourages us to think about the extent to which 'crimes of the suites' have achieved the same kind of criminological attention as 'crimes of the streets' or 'crimes behind closed doors' at all, and is clearly one arena in which common sense theory about crime and criminological theory share in similar assumptions about what kind of crime is harmful, and as a consequence is made visible, in how we think and talk about it as well as what kind of crime is considered to be not so harmful. This question is explored in detail in Chapter 6.

Much of what has been considered in this chapter has focused our attention on the kinds of ideas that criminologists work with that help us to understand why people commit crime and remember we have only considered here some recent sociological approaches to this question. In the next chapter, we are going to consider the kinds of ideas that criminologists work with to help us understand the nature and impact of crime. This is the area of work known as victimology and as its label implies it is intended to focus our attention on understanding the victim of crime.

EXERCISE

1. In your own words define the following terms:

   Bounded rationality
   Control balance
   Relative deprivation
   Hegemonic masculinity

   How do your definitions match with those found in Glossary?

2. Which of these concepts would you use to explain what kinds of crime, or do you think they can be applied to all crime?
3. Define right realism.
4. Define left realism.
5. What do you think are the key differences and similarities between these two ways of thinking about crime?

RECOMMENDATIONS FOR FURTHER READING

For those who want a further introduction into the contemporary nature of criminological theory and its relationship with criminal justice policy, take a look at Walklate, S. (2007) *Understanding Criminology* (third edition) (London: McGraw Hill–Open University Press). In addition, there is also the text by Hopkins-Burke (2001) *An Introduction to Criminological Theory* (second edition) (London: Routledge–Willan). This covers not only contemporary theory but also situates it within an appreciation of the historical emergence of contemporary theoretical concerns. Of course, anything by the authors referred to in this chapter will develop your understanding of the nature of criminological concerns in specific areas. See for example, M. Felson and R.L. Boba (2010) *Crime in Everyday Life* (fourth edition) (London: Sage), J. Braithwaite (1989) *Crime, Shame and Reintegration* (Cambridge: Cambridge University Press) and J. Young (1999) *The Exclusive Society* (London: Sage). Reading any of these will deepen your understanding of rational choice theory, social control theory and relative deprivation, respectively. The material dealing with *gender* tends to be a little more specialized as many university courses have units dedicated to just exploring the *gender*ed nature of crime, but for a deeper appreciation try Walklate (2004) *Gender, Crime and Criminal Justice* (second edition) (London: Routledge–Willan).

THINKING ABOUT THE VICTIM OF CRIME

This chapter is concerned with the impact of crime. You will recall that in Chapter 1 some introductory comments were made about the area of analysis within criminology called victimology. In that chapter, you were introduced to the ideas that have historically informed the way in which those criminologists who have been interested in the victim of crime have gone about their work. You were also made aware of the way in which the work of feminists challenged those ideas and the way in which these processes resulted in the assumption that men cannot be victims. In Chapter 1, this was called the 'victimological other'. In this chapter, the criminological concern with the victim of crime will be explored in detail building on what has been learned about the nature and extent of crime from Chapter 3.

INTRODUCTION

The central purpose of this chapter is to offer a more complete picture of the kinds of things that interest criminologists and victimologists about victims of crime. As was stated in Chapter 1, the study of criminal victimization has its origins in the work of lawyers who fled the Nazi regime prior to the Second World War, and they, alongside many others, were concerned to understand how such mass victimization could occur. However, the concepts that these early theorists employed focused very much on what it was about the victim that had resulted in the events that had happened to them. In other words, they were looking to establish what made victims different from non-victims, thus mirroring early criminological work. It was not until the 1960s and 1970s that the interest in the victim of crime took a different shape as a result of the emergence of the feminist movement, on the one hand, and the development of the criminal victimization survey, on the other. These developments in their different ways clearly pointed to a patterning of victimization and that such a patterning could not be explained by reference to the individual alone. There had to be some structural explanation. Awareness of this patterning has led criminologists interested in the victim of crime to be concerned with four main questions:

1. What does this patterning of criminal victimization look like and why does it look this way?
2. What impact does crime have on both individuals and their wider communities?
3. What role do victims have in the criminal justice process and what do they think of that role?
4. Why do some victims get more attention than others?

We shall discuss each of these questions in turn but first a word about the concept of victim.

WHAT DOES THE TERM 'VICTIM' MEAN?

For many people working with victims of crime either as practitioners or academics, the term 'victim' is highly problematic. It is particularly problematic for those working within the feminist movement. So, what do these problems look like?

When the word 'victim' is gendered, as in French, for example, being la victime, it is denoted as female. If the genealogy of the word 'victim' is examined, it is connected to processes of sacrifice in which again the victim was more often than not female. The links between this word and being female implies that the passivity and powerlessness associated with being a victim are also associated with being female. It is this link that is problematic for those working within the feminist movement who prefer to use the term 'survivor' to try to capture women's resistance to victimization. At the same time, the idea of being a victim or being a survivor is also problematic for others interested in criminal victimization because the either/or distinction fails to capture the processes of victimization. In other words, it is possible that an individual at different points in time in relation to different events could be an active victim, a passive victim, an active survivor, a passive survivor, and might have a whole range of experiences in between.

You might like to stop and think about this for a minute and try to identify people you know who might fall into any of these categories. Does the label 'victim' work for you? If so, how and under what circumstances? You might reach the conclusion that the label 'victim' really seems quite sterile.

There is, however, another problem associated with the word 'victim' that is derived from appreciating the process whereby an individual becomes a victim. This problem is connected with what Nils Christie, a Norwegian criminologist, has called the 'ideal victim'. In other words, there are certain assumptions attached to the label 'victim' that means not everyone actually acquires the label of victim. For Christie, the ideal victim is the *Little Red Riding Hood* fairy story victim; a young, innocent female out doing good deeds who is attacked by an unknown stranger. Indeed, this ideal victim fits all the common sense stereotypes of the 'legitimate' victim of rape, particularly someone who suffers an unprovoked attack from a stranger. In other words, some people who acquire the label of victim very readily and easily are deserving victims, and other people who may never acquire the label of victim at all are undeserving victims. This distinction between deserving and undeserving victims and how it impacts on people's experiences of the criminal justice process is one of the issues that has pre-occupied criminologists interested in the victim of crime and has led Carrabine and other UK sociologists (2004: 117) to talk of a 'hierarchy of victimization'.

This hierarchy captures a sense of the way in which different individuals and/groups are more readily identified as victims than other. For example, at the bottom of this hierarchy would be the homeless, the drug addict and the street prostitute: all those for whom it might be argued that their lifestyle renders them prone to victimization and nearer the top would be the elderly female victims of violent crime the least prone to crime but assumed to be vulnerable and readily assigned victim status. Hidden from view, but nonetheless illuminating the power of this hierarchy, would be young offenders who find themselves in prison but who might be there because of their experiences of victimization [see the work of Chesney-Lind and Pasko (2004), who suggest that such experiences are one pathway into crime for young women]. This hierarchy is most readily identifiable in the media construction of the elderly female as the victim of violent crime and the readiness with which such events are given full and graphic coverage by the media. This is despite the evidence that the group of people most likely to be the victims of violent crime are young males who go out drinking two or three times a week. Understanding this hierarchy draws attention to not only the way in which different victims acquire a legitimate status as victims or not but also the politics that lie behind this. We shall return to this at the end of this chapter. Despite the problems inherent in the term 'victim', some of which have been discussed here, it is nevertheless the word that is in common usage, and we shall use it for the rest of this chapter having acknowledged its problematic status.

UNDERSTANDING THE PATTERNING OF CRIMINAL VICTIMIZATION

Chapter 3 presented some recent findings on the nature and extent of crime and criminal victimization, and on the basis of that kind of data, criminologists are in agreement that there are four important social variables that frame experiences of criminal victimization; they are social class, age, gender and ethnicity. In summary, criminologists would say that the patterning of criminal victimization can be understood by reference to the following four variables:

1. The risk of having your house burgled is much higher for the poorer sections of the population.
2. The younger you are the more likely you are to be murdered or abused in some way, and the more hidden this is, the less likely this is to be reported or recorded as a crime.

(This is especially the case for children living in institutions and the elderly.) Even theft and street crime are more likely, the younger you are, with teenagers most likely to victimize each other rather than older people.

3. Men are most likely to be victimized violently by other men who are their acquaintances and women are most likely to be victimized violently and/or sexually by men that they know and in their own homes.

4. People belonging to ethnic minority groups are more likely to be criminally victimized than white people.

The relevance of these variables and their relationship with the likelihood of criminal victimization seems to be fairly consistent across different societies but especially the United Kingdom and the United States. However, recognizing that these variables pattern criminal victimization in important ways does not explain the pattern. To explain this pattern, victimologists and others concerned with criminal victimization have used a range of concepts and theoretical perspectives. Here we shall focus on the value of three of them. The concept of 'lifestyle' as associated with positivist victimology referred to in Chapter 1, the concept of patriarchy associated with the work of radical feminism and the relevance of hegemonic masculinity as discussed in Chapter 4.

LIFESTYLE AND CRIMINAL VICTIMIZATION

As was suggested in Chapter 1, the concept of lifestyle was important in underpinning the kinds of questions asked in the development of the criminal victimization survey first in the United States and then embraced in the United Kingdom and elsewhere and more recently in the efforts to measure criminal victimization on an international scale. So in this respect, at least the concept of lifestyle has been very influential. It was developed initially and related to criminal victimization by Hindelang *et al.* (1978) in their book *Victims of Personal Crime: An Empirical Foundation for a Theory of Personal Victimization*. In this book, they present a way of thinking about personal victimization in which lifestyle refers to 'routine daily activities, both vocational activities (work, school, keeping house etc.) and leisure activities' (ibid.: 241) and in which individuals are constrained by role expectations and structural characteristics that are reflections of their demographic positions (class, age, sex, ethnicity etc.). The way in which individuals adapt to these constraints is reflected in their daily routines, and in their lifestyles. They argue that there is a direct link between an individual's routine daily activity and their exposure to high-risk victimization situations from which personal victimization occurs. From this starting point, they go on to posit eight propositions. These are worth reiterating in detail to get a better feel for this way of thinking about the patterning of criminal victimization.

HINDELANG ET AL.'S EIGHT PROPOSITIONS

1. The probability of suffering a personal victimisation is directly related to the amount of time a person spends in public spaces particularly at night-time.
2. The probability of being in a public space at night varies as function of lifestyle.
3. Social contacts and interactions occur disproportionately among individuals who share similar lifestyles.
4. An individual's chances of personal victimisation are dependent upon the extent to which the individual shares demographic characteristics with offenders.
5. The proportion of time an individual spends with non-family members varies as a function of lifestyle.
6. The probability of personal victimisation, particularly personal theft, increases as a function of the proportion of time that an individual spends among non-family members.
7. Variations in lifestyle are associated with variations in the ability of individuals to isolate themselves from persons with offender characteristics.
8. Variations in lifestyle are associated with variations in the convenience, the desirability and the vincibility of a person as a target for personal victimisations.

(Ibid.: 250–66)

There are both strengths and weaknesses associated with these propositions; some of which have been recognized by the authors themselves, but before we go on to consider them, the reader might like to think about the following:

- Which, if any, of these propositions fit with what is known about the patterning of criminal victimization?
- What kinds of crimes these propositions fit best with and why?
- What might the policy implications of these propositions look like?
- What do you think the strengths and weaknesses of these propositions are?

There are at least three strengths that can be identified with this way of thinking about the patterning of criminal victimization:

1. It is grounded in the data.
2. It does relate to the patterns that are found rather than just focusing on the individual.
3. It does encourage a critical thinking about policy; for example, would encouraging the elderly to go out more expose them to more risks of criminal victimization and how could those risks be managed?

However, there are also at least three weaknesses as follows:

1. Is lifestyle the kind of objectively measurable entity proposed as the propositions suggest or is it something a little more vague and fuzzy and more about process?
2. How do we make sense of the criminal victimization that takes place in private rather than in public?
3. Do people adapt to their social demographic position or are they made to? Put another way, is it just as important to talk about racism, sexism, ageism and so on as it is to talk about race, sex and age? In other words, what about relationships of power?

So, this way of thinking about the patterning of criminal victimization works for some crimes and not for others (crimes of the streets but not crime behind closed doors or crimes of the suites) and has some value in the policy arena. However, this conceptual starting point is limited because of the way in which lifestyle is understood. The key limitation in this model lies in its lack of appreciation of power relationships. However, it is power relationships that are put to the fore for radical feminism and its application and understanding of patriarchy.

PATRIARCHY AND CRIMINAL VICTIMIZATION

Chapter 1 discussed the way in which work emanating from the feminist movement challenged much criminological and victimological thought. Moreover, while it is important to acknowledge that there are different kinds of feminism all of which pose different questions for both of those areas of concern, in this section, we are going to focus on the importance of just one strand of feminism: radical feminism. (If you are interested in a fuller discussion of the relationship of the different strands of feminism with criminology and victimology, then take a look at Walklate [2004], *Gender, Crime and Justice*, 2nd edition.) Our purpose is to understand how and to what extent radical feminism has contributed to an understanding of the patterning of criminal victimization, so first of all, it is important to offer a little more detail about radical feminism.

Radford, a UK feminist, defines radical feminism in *The Sage Dictionary of Criminology* in the following way:

> Radical feminism offers a systematic analysis of the nature of women's oppression; including the ways in which it is sustained through law and the criminal justice processes. Its aim is not only to understand male dominance and control of women and children but also to end it.
>
> (2006: 336)

So radical feminist analysis focuses on the ways in which men oppress women (and children) and how the structure of society helps to sustain that oppression. This structure and its impact are referred to as patriarchy. The key variable is, therefore, men's power over women. This power is reflected in all aspects of social life, and at its centre for the radical feminist lies the question of sexuality. Tong (1989), a North American feminist, puts the issues that concern radical feminism in this way: who rapes whom, who batters whom, for whom does pornography exist, for whom does prostitution exist and for whom female sexuality exist? The answer in each case is men.

In the context of making sense of the patterning of criminal victimization, it is relatively easy to see both the kinds of crime and victimization that radical feminism helps to make sense of. Put simply, radical feminism clearly focuses attention on all those criminal victimizations that go on in private between people who are for the most part known to each other. This means rape, sexual assault and domestic violence. In focusing attention on these kinds of criminal victimizations, radical feminism also emphasizes that the offenders are men. At this point, the reader might like to consider the following:

- What kinds of victimizations are excluded from this analysis and whether or not you think that this exclusion is appropriate?
- What might the policy implications be of adopting the radical feminist view of criminal victimization?
- What do you think the strengths and weaknesses of this way of thinking about the patterning of criminal victimization look like?

It is fair to say that despite the ideological tensions between radical feminism and victimology over the use of the term 'victim' as discussed earlier, the work of radical feminism has contributed enormously in widening both the understanding of this kind of crime and criminal victimization. Both criminology and victimology now take these issues much more seriously than they once did especially in understanding the impact of this kind of crime. This will be discussed in detail later. This work has also clearly placed men, the understanding of men's behaviour and how this is mediated by men's relationship with masculinity(ies) at the centre of such agendas. This is what constitutes a gendered analysis. However, some of you might have already realized that despite this impact, understanding crime and criminal victimization is not so straightforward. What about social class, age and ethnicity? In other words, how do we make sense of the impact of these other variables that are clearly evidenced in the data we have discussed in Chapter 3. This is a problem that criminology and victimology struggle with. There is also another problem here that was alluded to in Chapter 1.

Chapter 1 discussed how victimology along with the influence of feminism had served to construct a 'Victimological Other'. Put more simply, as a result of the kind of work done on criminal victimization, women (and children) are much more visible as victims than men are. In part some would argue that this is a result of their greater vulnerability. A concept that will be discussed in detail when the impact of crime is considered in detail. However, before we proceed to do that, it will be useful to think about the invisibility of men as victims by asking the question: can men be victims? To answer this question, we shall revisit the concept of hegemonic masculinity that was introduced in Chapter 4.

HEGEMONIC MASCULINITY AND CRIMINAL VICTIMIZATION

In Chapter 4, the concept of hegemonic masculinity was introduced as being an important one that criminologists work with as a way of understanding the maleness of offending behaviour. Here we shall consider its value in helping us to understand the relationship between being male and criminal victimization.

While much victimological work leaves us with the impression that victims are not likely to be male, this is clearly empirically not the case. Much male violence is committed against other men, and in recent years, there has been an increasing awareness that much of that male violence is sexual violence. So quite clearly men can be victims, but what is problematic is understanding how they experience that victimization and its impact. Increasingly, criminologist and victimologists have used the concept of hegemonic masculinity to understand this experience. In other words, how men see themselves as men. For example, Goodey (1997), a UK criminologist, in researching male reaction to violence, used the phrase 'big boys don't cry' to help to explain how it was that young men struggled with being victimized. Put simply, it contradicted their understanding of themselves as men. The following quote is taken from Etherington (2000), a UK social scientist, who has worked with men who were sexually abused as children. One of her respondents said about his experiences of being abused by his mother:

> Apart from being my mother, she was a woman. I'd been educated by my father that women were there for the cooking, cleaning and sex. They were put on earth for our benefit and every man should have several. They were not the abusers they were abused upon. So how could she abuse men when I was the man?

(24)

This quote captures some of the confusions existing for men when they experience violence or other forms of victimization especially at the hands of women. Perhaps made worse when they know that this is likely to be a minority experience. The concept of hegemonic masculinity helps us to understand some of the confusions that this generates for men. Of course, not all men will experience victimization in the same way, but the general unwillingness of men to identify themselves as a victim and the greater likelihood of men reporting anger at being criminally victimized is only just beginning to be understood by criminologists and victimologists. Both may go some way to help us to understand the relative invisibility of men in the patterning of reported criminal victimization. The reader might like to consider then the following:

- What does the concept of hegemonic masculinity help us to understand about the patterning of criminal victimization?
- What kinds of criminal victimizations are included and excluded by this concept?
- What might the policy implications look like that would follow from putting the concept of hegemonic masculinity at the centre of our understanding of criminal victimization?
- How might men who do report such criminal victimization experience the criminal justice process?

Arguably, one of the key areas that the concept of hegemonic masculinity puts to the fore of criminological and victimological understanding is the way in which men and women might differently experience the impact of crime. So that is the issue to which we shall now turn.

UNDERSTANDING THE IMPACT OF CRIME

Some would say that the now well-documented 'fear of crime' is one of the key areas in which crime, to a greater or lesser extent, has impacted on us all over the past 30 years. However, criminologists and victimologists work with four important distinctions in understanding the impact that crime may have on individuals. These are **primary victimization, secondary victimization, indirect victimization** and vulnerability. We shall discuss each of these in turn.

Primary victimization refers to the direct impact that a crime has on the victim. That impact may vary with the nature of the crime, of course, from physical injury, to financial loss, to loss of earnings as a result of the required involvement in the criminal justice process. However, for some people, this kind of impact is made worse by the stress, shock and sense of invasion of privacy that may go along with burglary, along with feelings of fear, difficulty in sleeping, to the post-traumatic stress syndrome reported by some victims of rape. This kind of impact can sometimes be made worse by the way in which the criminal justice system responds to such victims. This is what is referred to as secondary victimization. Research has indicated that individuals who are involved in the criminal justice process, as either victims or witnesses, frequently feel let down by that process. This can happen in different ways from not being kept informed of what was happening in their case, to being treated unsympathetically by the professionals working in the criminal justice process, to not being believed when they are giving their evidence. These kinds of experiences all, arguably, add to the feelings of victimization. In other kinds of cases, such as murder, the families of both the murderer and the murder victim can also feel victimized by their experiences both in relation to feelings of bereavement, to maybe being under suspicion themselves for what has happened as well as just not being able to make sense of what has happened. All of this is referred to as indirect victimization. However, the extent to which any individual may experience crime in any of these ways is frequently related to their personal or structural vulnerability. In other words, not all victims of crime will experience their victimization in the same way or with the same level of impact. The variations that can be found in people's experiences, criminologists refer to as their vulnerability.

Overall, those most affected by crime look very similar to those most likely to experience criminal victimization. Mawby and Walklate (1994: 54), two researchers from the United Kingdom, listed those most affected by crime in the following way:

1. Those on low incomes;
2. Those in rented accommodation;
3. Those from ethnic minorities;
4. The elderly and the very young;
5. Single person or one-parent households;
6. Women compared with men.

Table 5.1: Relationship between risk from crime and impact of crime according to victim survey data

	High risk	*High impact*
Class	Poor, living in private-rented housing	
Gender	Males	Females
Age	Young	Elderly
Ethnicity	Ethnic minority groups	
Marital/family status	Those living in households with no other adults	

Source: Updated from Mawby and Walklate (1994: 55).

If this is put together with those most at risk from crime, then the picture looks as shown in Table 5.1.

So from Table 5.1, it can be seen that those for whom crime seems to have the most impact are those least at risk, elderly females. Moreover, thinking about the relationship between risk and impact in this way seems to hold for both UK data (on which it is based) and US data. Indeed, it seems reasonable to suggest that vulnerability works in this way in other societies too. However, it is important to remember that Table 5.1 is derived from criminal victimization survey data, and that if we were to incorporate some of the work emanating from the feminist movement into this, then the impact of being criminally victimized by someone you know, an intimate, would need to be taken into account. In addition, if we were to incorporate some of the concerns addressed by those criminologists and victimologists interested in corporate crime, we might also want to consider the structural and global dimensions to the impact of crime. For example, globally the most casualized workers are the most at risk from workplace injury that results from offences against health and safety legislation, women have been most at risk from poor quality breast implants and 'product dumping' in general exploits poorer countries in the search for work. This is indeed an extensive agenda and one that we take up in detail in the next chapter.

So criminologists and victimologists work with a range of different concepts to help to understand the impact of crime. Some of that work has resulted in increasing attention being paid to the role that victims have in the criminal justice process, since more often than not victims who get involved in the criminal justice process feel victimized twice: once by the offence and once by the process. It is to that issue that we shall now turn.

VICTIMS AND THE CRIMINAL JUSTICE PROCESS

It goes without saying that victims play a crucial role in the criminal justice process in any jurisdiction. Without their role in reporting crime, and their subsequent presence as complainants at court, much more crime would remain invisible and not prosecuted. However, the change in terminology in the last sentence encapsulates the key change in status for the victims once they enter the court. At this point, they cease to be a victim but become a complainant in the same way that an offender ceases to be 'an offender' and becomes a defendant. This is because the purpose of the criminal justice system is to establish the 'truth' of a particular case and the associated guilt or innocence of the accused. The terms offender and victim prejudge the outcome of that process. However, because of the central importance of the victim to the criminal justice process in ensuring cases do proceed, increasingly efforts have been made to look for ways of both to better improve the experience that victims have of the criminal justice process and to ensure their continued involvement in it. A good deal of campaigning work has been focused on this both from within the feminist movement and from those who are involved in the range of victim support organizations that now exist in many different societies. Much feminist work has concerned itself with challenging and changing the laws to do with sexual offences, whereas much of the victim support work has focused on the question of campaigning for victims' rights. These campaigns take a different shape and form in different societies and have had a differential impact dependent on whether or not the criminal justice system is *adversarial* or *inquisitorial*. The difference between these systems is taken up in Chapter 7, but at this juncture, the reader might like to do the following:

- Make a list of all the different organizations that you are aware of who claim to represent the interests of the victim of crime. What are the similarities and differences in those claims?

- Make a list of what the strengths and limitations might look like of looking for ways of improving the involvement of victims in the criminal justice system.
- Make a list of the kinds of questions you think that a criminologist interested in the victim of crime might ask about policy initiatives that claim to give victims 'rights' in the criminal justice system (e.g. the Victim Impact Statement).

So far in this chapter, the kind of crime victim we have talked about has either been the victim of 'crimes of the streets' or 'crimes behind closed doors'. We have yet to consider the victim of 'crimes of the suites' in detail. At this point, then it is worth thinking about why some victims of some kinds of crime get more attention than others.

WHY DO SOME VICTIMS GET MORE ATTENTION THAN OTHERS?

Part of the answer to this question returns us to the issue of vulnerability. In one sense, it is obviously quite reasonable, at the level of understanding the harm done to an individual, for a highly vulnerable elderly female who has suffered from trauma of being attacked by an intruder in her own home, intent on burglary receives all the attention necessary from victim support workers and the criminal justice process. This kind of response to this kind of individual clearly returns us the image of the ideal victim with which this chapter began. So in some respects, the nearer an individual fits the 'ideal' stereotype, the more attention they are likely to receive. Indeed, the more sympathetic attention they are likely to receive. However, it is also clear that while there are differences in attention received at an individual level, there are differences in attention received by victims of crime at a structural level. Think back to the documentation of the nature and extent of crime discussed in Chapter 3. In that chapter, you were presented with a number of case studies in which law-breaking behaviour had occurred. Yet despite the dramatic nature of those case studies, they were neither necessarily nor readily identified as criminal. As a consequence, neither were the victims of those case studies readily identified as victims of crime. Nevertheless, there are criminologists who spend their time exploring these less visible crimes and victims despite the lesser attention that they receive. Described here as victims of 'crimes of the suites', the work that criminologists do in this area is discussed in detail in the next chapter. For the purposes of this chapter, it is sufficient to be aware that criminologists would argue that there are both individual reasons and structural reasons as to why some victims of crime receive more attention than others. It is also important to remember that recognizing the process of victimization, of who may become a victim of what kind of behaviour, is not a static one. New 'victimizations' can be recognized and responded to. In the light of this, we shall spend just a little time thinking about one 'newer' victimization: hate crime.

HATE CRIMES

In part a concern with 'hate crime' has emerged as a consequence of understanding how minority groups, in particular, experience crime. In the United Kingdom, there is no legislative status that delineates hate crime from other kinds of crime though there is a range of legislation that can be used to prosecute behaviours motivated in this way. This is in contrast to the United States. There, the Federal Bureau of Investigation (FBI) defines hate crime as offences that are 'motivated in part or singularly by personal prejudice against others because of a diversity – race, sexual orientation, religion, ethnicity/ national origin, or disability'. Despite these kinds of jurisdictional differences, the term 'hate crime' does have some currency especially in the media and its portrayals of particular crimes and their impact. Consider, for example, the nail bombing of a 'gay' pub in London in 1999 and the brutal murder of James Byrd in Texas in June 1998. Whether or not bigotry motivated the offender in either of these cases is not our concern here, but who the victims are likely to be is. The FBI report on hate statistics for 2008 states that racial bias accounted for nearly 51 per cent of incidents, religious bias 17.9 per cent, ethnic or national bias 12.2 per cent and sexual orientation bias 17.6 per cent. So although the actual behaviour perpetrated as a hate crime may be just the same as other kind of crime, that is, vandalizing property or violence against the person; recognition of who the victims are most likely to be offers additional appreciation to this kind of criminal behaviour and its impact.

Summary and conclusion

In this chapter, we have explored the kinds of questions that criminologists interested in the victim of crime might be concerned with. In doing so, we have considered some of the data that those questions have produced, some of the concepts that have been used to make sense of the data, how we might think about the impact of crime from the victim's point of view and what some of the policy developments might look like from the victim's point of view. Hopefully, what you have learned is that criminology shows that:

1. The chance of being criminally victimized is unevenly distributed across any population, with poor people from ethnic minorities, especially males, being most likely to be victimized by a stranger and women most likely to be victimized by someone they know, though criminologists differ on the primacy that they give to each of these variable. Some think that race is the most significant, others explore gender, others social class and others focus on age. It is likely that all these variables interact with one another and have a compounding effect when impact is considered.

2. The impact of crime is wide and varied and is most likely to take its greatest toll on those sections of society who can least afford to deal with it either in terms of material resources or personal resources, that is, the most vulnerable that frequently reflects how the variables listed under point one interact.

3. The closer someone fits with the idea of the ideal victim, the more likely they are to receive a response, help and support from the criminal justice system.

4. Victims are central to the working of the criminal justice system, and much effort has been made and continues to be made across different jurisdictions to make the criminal justice system more victim centred.

EXERCISE

The reader might like to critically assess each of the statements above, and in doing so think about the following:

- How the kinds of stories you might come across in the media match or fail to match with these statements and why?

- What are the problems in re-orienting the criminal justice system, so that its concerns match more closely with the victim of crime?

Thinking about these two questions will act as good preparation for the two chapters that follow.

RECOMMENDATIONS FOR FURTHER READING

There are a number of textbooks that are intended to introduce the reader to the sub-discipline of *victimology* that has been the focus of this chapter. One of the most popular ones is written by a North American, Andrew Karmen, and is simply called *Crime Victims: An Introduction to Victimology* (Pacific Grove, CA: Brooks Cole) first published in 1990 and now in its seventh edition. A more comparative approach that address the question of victims' rights is offered by Lorraine Wolhutter *et al.* (2009) *Victimology: Victimisation and Victims' Rights* (London: Routledge-Cavendish). A more advanced collection edited by Sandra Walklate (2007) *Handbook of Victims and Victimology* (London: Routledge-Willan) is a collection written by experts on various issues relating to victims of crime. However, this is for the ambitious only.

6

CRIMES OF THE SUITES

An introduction to critical criminology

This chapter will extend our thinking about crime and criminology by developing our understanding of the nature and impact of 'crimes of the suites'. Chapters 2 and 3 were concerned to explore some of the problems inherent in counting crime and assessing how much crime there might be. In both these chapters, some consideration was given to the kinds of crimes that were more easily countable and as a result featured more readily in pictures of the extent of crime. It was clear from these two chapters that the crime and criminals most visible both in the criminal justice system and in the various crime statistics are crimes of the streets. In addition, it was observed that the criminal activities that might loosely be termed the 'crimes of the suites' were much more difficult to count and as a consequence it was much more difficult to offer an assessment of their nature and extent. Partly as a result of this, such crimes are much less likely to be seen as criminal either by the general public or by the criminal justice system. The purpose of this chapter is to pay a little more attention to these 'crimes of the suites', to review the way in which criminology and criminologists have paid attention or failed to pay attention to them and to suggest why this may be the case. So, to get most benefit from this chapter, the reader is advised to revisit the relevant pages in Chapters 2 and 3 to refresh his or her memory on some of the issues related to measuring this kind of crime.

INTRODUCTION: THE RICH GET RICHER
AND THE POOR GET PRISON

This heading is borrowed from the title of a book published in 1979, now in its ninth edition, by Reiman, an American social scientist. In the first edition of this book, Reiman produced statistics designed to challenge conventional thinking about what counts as crime. For example, he stated that in 1974 the total number of people 'murdered' in the United States was 168,600: 114,000 deaths occurred as a result of occupational hazard; 20,000 from inadequate emergency medical care; 15,625 were a result of a knife or other cutting instrument, including a scalpel; 13,987 resulted from the use of firearms; 2,000 from hypodermics or prescriptions and the remainder included a range of different weapons. These figures clearly indicated quite a different understanding of the context in which, for example, murder might occur. More recently in the United Kingdom, for example, the Union of Construction, Allied Trade and Technicians (UCATT) reported that the death of five construction workers in the same week that the government announced a 35 per cent cut in the budget of the Health and Safety Executive (UCATT 5/11/10) and a visit to the website www.curethenhs.org will give a feel for some of the issues surrounding the deaths in a Staffordshire hospital from 2005 to 2008. In a similar vein, Box (1983), a UK social scientist, argued that (using the Health and Safety Executive's own statistics) between 1973 and 1979, there were 3,291 deaths recorded as homicide by the police and a total of 11,436 deaths resulting from occupational accident or disease. In a more up-to-date assessment of the figures for the United Kingdom, Whyte (2004a: 136) suggests that 'the total number of deaths at work, that result from health and safety *crimes* are likely to exceed 4,500 each year and this is before we factor in the largely unknown deaths caused by other occupational diseases'. Moreover, as Tombs and Whyte (2007: 37) state, 'In contemporary societies, work routinely kills workers and members of the public through acute injury and chronic illness'. The widely reported and celebrated rescue of the miners trapped underground in Chile in 2010 both serves to remind us of the particularly hazardous nature of some work environments as well as the global variations in experiences of those workplaces. In addition, Whyte (2004a) reports on findings in the United States that suggest corporate fraud costs up to 20 times more than the cost of 'traditional' crime. The question is, what are the common concerns for these authors in the context of criminology? There are at least four:

1. To draw our attention to a wider understanding of law-breaking behaviour.
2. To emphasize that law-breaking behaviour frequently has serious consequences.
3. To point to the extent to which such behaviour is at least connected with, although not a product of, economic imperatives.
4. To draw our attention to the fact that such behaviours are not necessarily subjected to the criminal justice process but other kinds of regulatory agencies, and as a consequence the perpetrators are not criminalized, that is, labelled as criminal.

This chapter will explore each of these concerns in more detail, but first what kind of crime is under consideration here?

CRIMES OF THE SUITES: PROBLEMS OF DEFINITION

Chapter 3 offered case studies of the kind of 'crime' under consideration here that were huge in their impact and widely covered in the media. However, what kinds of crime do these case studies, and the statistics presented above, represent? Different criminologists use different terms to try to capture the kind of criminal behaviour under discussion here. Terms such as white-collar crime, corporate crime, business crime, crimes of the powerful, commercial crime are just a few terms that are used to capture this kind of criminal behaviour. The problem is what do all of these terms mean? Or put another way, as it is by Nelken (2007: 738), a UK criminologist who works in Italy: 'What, if anything, is there in common between the marketing of unsafe pharmaceuticals, the practice of insider trading, the "long-firm" fraud, computer crime, bank embezzlement and fiddling at work?' Of course, one commonality in all of these activities is that they do not normally feature in common sense understandings of crime. This is partly because these behaviours invoke confusing images between what are considered to be respectable activities or occupations with that which is considered to be unrespectable, the criminal. However, in *The Sage Dictionary of Criminology,* Tombs and Whyte (2006: 462) offer the following definition of white-collar crime:

> A heterogeneous group of offences committed by people of relatively high status or enjoying relatively high levels of trust, and made possible by their legitimate employment. Such crimes typically include fraud, embezzlement, tax violations, and other accounting offences, and various forms of workplace theft and fiddling in which the organisation, its customers, and other organisations are the victims.

The same authors (2006: 74) offer the following definition of corporate crime:

> Illegal acts or omissions, punishable by the state under administrative, civil or criminal law, which are the result of deliberate decision-making or culpable negligence within a legitimate formal organisation. These acts or omissions are based in legitimate, formal, business organisations made in accordance with the normative goals, standard operating procedures and/or cultural norms of the organisation and are intended to benefit the corporation itself.

Before continuing, the reader might like to reflect on these two definitions and think about the following questions:

- What are the main points of similarity and difference between these two definitions?
- What kinds of behaviours do they draw attention to?
- What kinds of offenders are they drawing attention to?
- Who are the victims likely to be?
- From what you have read so far in this book, what kind of attention do you think the criminal justice system pays to these offences, offenders and victims?

These two definitions of 'crimes of the suites' draw into our understanding of crime and criminology a wide spectrum of activities that, as earlier chapters have shown, might reach the headlines of the newspapers from time to time but do not regularly feature in the kinds of crimes that people worry about on a routine, daily basis. Yet there is a strong tradition within criminology of exploring not only what people do worry about (crimes that they see) but also what does not concern them so much (crimes that they do not see). According to Nelken (2007), part of the explanation for why we see some crimes and not others lies within the ambiguity that is associated with crimes of the suites. Nelken (2007) uses the term white-collar crime in his discussion of this ambiguity, and in presenting his arguments his label will be used. However, the reader might like to note that he uses this term to cover all the kinds of crime that are of concern here in 'crimes of the suites'.

NELKEN'S AMBIGUITIES

WHITE-COLLAR CRIME AS A CONTESTED CONCEPT

The term white-collar crime was first coined by Sutherland, in 1949, who defined it as the kind of crime committed by 'a person of high status in the course of his occupation' (ibid.: 9). This kind of definition, by implication, focuses attention on the status and respectability of the offender as much as the illegality of the offence and, as a consequence, has generated much confusion as to what kind of behaviour is to be included and/or excluded by it. For example, following this definition has led some researchers, especially in the United States, to focus on what might be called the routine criminal behaviour of the middle classes (tax fraud, false claims and accounting) and has led others to argue that white-collar crime is a normal and well organized part of business life: rooted in the same principles as more conventionally understood organized crime 'permitted' as a product of collusion with those there to regulate such practices. In between these extremes, others have attempted to generate different categories of white-collar crime: crimes in the workplace, economic crime, environmental crime, with some extending these kind of categories to include such things as genocide and so on. Croall (2001), a UK researcher in this area, suggests that it makes sense to work with a distinction between crimes committed against organizations (by their employees and others) and crime committed by organizations (either on their employees and others or on each other).

As Nelken (2007) argues, problems of definition should not be ignored. These problems reveal that not all criminologists in this area are necessarily talking about the same kind of behaviour. By implication, this means that the problems of measurement and explanation will also look somewhat different. However, those of you who have already read Chapters 1 and 2 will now be fully aware of the contested nature of criminology and its concerns.

IS WHITE-COLLAR CRIME REALLY CRIME?

This ambiguity is quite clearly connected to the first because if we are not sure what white-collar crime is, how can it be considered criminal? This ambiguity reflects the tensions that exist between those who take the criminal law as the defining point for the study of criminology and those who might want to take a wider legal remit and include civil and administrative offences as being part of the criminological agenda. There are, of course, those who would take a much broader understanding of what might be included as criminal by considering not the law per se but the question of the harm done as being crucial to defining the criminal. While the recognition of this ambiguity is a useful reminder of the diverse nature of criminology, it should also be remembered that even taking the narrow definition of the criminal law as the defining point of criminological investigation poses particular problems with white-collar crime. For example, the diffusion of responsibility that exists within many organizations makes it difficult to identify who is both legally and criminally responsible for an event. In addition, the ever-changing nature of technology in the workplace makes it difficult for Health and Safety legislation, for example, to keep up with such changes.

WHAT CAUSES WHITE-COLLAR CRIME?

If there is ambiguity about what white-collar crime is, and whether it is really criminal in the ordinary sense of the term, then it follows that there will be ambiguity about explaining it. This ambiguity rests on the extent to which the normal explanations of criminology fit or do not fit with the white-collar criminal. (At this juncture, the reader might like to reflect on the extent to which the different explanations for crime discussed in Chapter 4 might be applied to the crime under discussion here.) Different criminologists within this area take different positions on this question. Some opt for explanations that focus on the individual (put simply, greed rather than need). Others adopt the view that it is capitalism itself that sets the framework, which generates criminal behaviour of this kind (put simply, the pursuit of profit will be maintained by whatever means, legal or illegal). An early Dutch criminologist, Willem Bonger (1876–1940), argued that capitalism itself produced the condition under which exploitation as a system and a practice became valued. This view is linked with the fourth ambiguity.

WHITE-COLLAR CRIME IN ITS EVERYDAY SETTING

Any search for explanation requires that we understand the meaning and the context in which the behaviour under investigation occurs. In the case of white-collar crime, some commentators argue that the same requirements also apply. So, if such behaviour is put in its social context, then it does not look so criminal. This social context involves recognizing that, on one hand as Croall (2001) points out, victimization is diffused, indeed people might not be aware that they have been victimized at all, and on the other hand, there is the question of intentionality, did the offenders intend to cause harm or was their behaviour not intended to deceive anyone but simply a product of what might be considered to be normal business practice? The American Bernard Madoff, serving 150 years for fraud, is reported as saying, 'People just kept throwing money at me. Some guy wanted to invest, and if I said no, the guy said, what am I not good enough? (*The Daily Telegraph* 21 June 2010). What do you think? Of course, there are some well-known cases in which neither of these conditions could be said to have applied. The way in which the P&O Ferry Company ignored safety advice for their roll-on/ roll-off ferries might be a case in point (see Slapper and Tombs, 1999). However, such cases notwithstanding, placing white-collar crime in its everyday setting not only adds to its ambiguous status but also makes it a bit easier to understand why detection is more difficult.

RESPONDING TO WHITE COLLAR CRIME

The main issue here is the use of a range of different regulatory agencies and enforcement methods to deal with white-collar infringements. Agencies that more often than not are not that well funded or well equipped to fulfil their task are required to complete a task that more often than not is rooted in the need for the compliance of the offender. These factors add to the problems of detection, prosecution and conviction. For example, Whyte (2004a: 138) reports that in the United Kingdom, the Health and Safety Executive employs a total of 1,651 inspectors (as compared with 133,336 police officers as of 1 March 2003) who are responsible for 736,000 registered premises and that on average a workplace will receive a Health and Safety inspection once every 20 years. These figures, while only a small part of a much wider picture, offer some insight into the problems of regulation and enforcement of white-collar crime. Indeed, in a recent study, Tombs and Whyte (2010) present evidence that suggests a collapse of regulatory practices in respect of health and safety legislation in the United Kingdom as the tightening economic climate has taken its toll on the resources of the Health and Safety Executive – the agency charged with the enforcement of the legislation. Add to this the need for the cooperation of the offender (compliance) in order to pursue any complaints at all, then the ambiguous message sent out with respect to white-collar crime becomes evident. Moreover, as Croall (2001) observes, even when prosecuted and found guilty, sentences are frequently seen to be lenient with the vast majority of such offenders given fines. Putting all of this together, it can be seen that the response to white-collar crime is very ambiguous indeed.

WHITE-COLLAR CRIME AS AN INDEX OF SOCIAL CHANGE

Nelken's sixth ambiguity has two dimensions to it. One dimension points to the view that there is less public concern about this kind of behaviour and therefore less support for more severe punishment. The other points to a slightly contradictory view that changing social attitudes results in the penalizing of behaviour that was previously considered acceptable. From a point of view, it is this kind of contradictory ambiguity that lends itself to what Walklate (1989) called the 'ideology of disaster'. Under these kinds of fluid circumstances, it is much easier to define events as disasters and/or accidents than frame them as criminal acts that connect with the last of Nelken's ambiguities (see also the case studies in Chapter 3).

THE COLLATERAL COSTS OF CONTROL

Here Nelken is pointing to the more general dilemma posed by the title of this chapter: the rich get richer and the poor get prison. What would be the costs of reorienting the law enforcement process to focus on white-collar crime (defined all inclusively) in terms of enforcement, prosecution and conviction? Whose interests would such a reorientation serve and what would the outcomes actually look like? As Nelken (2007: 761) states, 'Industry tends – with the collusion of the state – to balance the safety of workers against the increased costs of production'. What would the costs and benefits of behaving differently look like, especially in the contemporary global market?

Nelken's ambiguities have provided a useful insight into some of the problems associated with taking white-collar crime seriously. As a result, it is possible to add to the problems of measurement discussed in Chapter 2 a list of difficulties identified by Croall (2001) that white-collar crime suffers from:

- low visibility
- complexity
- diffusion of responsibility
- diffusion of victimization
- difficulty of detection
- difficulty of prosecution
- lenient punishment
- ambiguity in the law
- ambiguity in criminal status.

Moreover, the nature of these difficulties tends not to vary much from society to society. At this juncture, the reader might like to revisit the case studies presented in Chapter 3 and identify the extent to which they suffer from any or all of the difficulties in the above list.

By way of illustrating some of these problems, you might like to do the following:

- Choose two daily newspapers from the same day: a quality one and a 'popular' one.
- Count how many articles there are in each of them on crime and note the pages in the newspaper where they occur.
- What kind of crime is covered in each of the papers? Are they similar or different? What kind of language do the newspapers use in discussing the crime covered?

- Are there any reports that cover the kind of crime we are discussing here? How do those reports compare and contrast with reports on other kinds of crime?
- What kinds of ideas can you find that try to explain the different kinds of crimes covered? Are these ideas the same, or used in the same way, for different kinds of crime?
- How does this coverage, if at all, illustrate the ambiguities we have been discussing here?

If we put all these problems in relation to white-collar crime together, it is no wonder that it is the view of some criminologists that the rich get richer and the poor get prison. But a question remains: who is the victim of this kind of crime? As was discussed in Chapter 1, the victim of such crime is rarely seen or heard. However, concern about this victim of crime has been taken up, most notably, by Elias, a North American victimologist.

CRIMINAL VICTIMIZATION AND CRIME OF THE SUITES

A key condition for the perpetuation of white-collar crime, as the term has been used in this chapter, is as Geis (1973) observes 'victim **responsiveness**'. Or put another way by Box (1983: 17), 'the majority of those suffering from corporate crime remain unaware of their victimisation – either not knowing it has happened to them or viewing their "misfortune" as an accident or "no ones fault"'. The disaster scenario of some of the case studies presented in Chapter 3 constitute a good example of this victim responsiveness. But, of course, as we have observed in this chapter, it is not victim responsiveness alone that permits such crimes to happen. We also need to add to that the different and differential policing of such activities (by regulatory authorities rather than the criminal justice system), the imperative of the profit motive and, in relation to some aspects of white-collar crime, the presence of trust between the victim and the criminal. (At this juncture, the reader might like to think back to the discussion of the case of Harold Shipman in Chapter 1 in relation to trust and the crimes of this potentially powerful individual. Indeed, the exploitation of trust and trust relationships is also a key in understanding some aspects of fraud.) Taking these factors together, Box (1983: 67) concludes that:

> If employees, consumers, and other corporate victims had their awareness sharpened and supported by trade unionism, consumerism and environmentalism, and the state and legal institutions could be shamed into closing the gap between lofty principles and tawdry practices . . .

Thirty years on the question remains whether or not anything has changed. Elias (1986, 1993) argues that the growth and development of victims' movements, in particular that have emerged in the intervening years, have amounted to little more than political manipulation.

As an illustration of this, the reader might like to consider the policy response by the Home Office in England and Wales that produced a Victims' Code of Practice under legislation passed in 2004. This was introduced in April 2006, and if you want to read the charter in full then it is available from cjsonline.gov.uk. This is a substantial document covering all that a victim of crime might expect from the criminal justice process. For our purposes, here we shall just consider one aspect of it – the standards of service you can expect after the reporting of a crime. You can expect the following:

1. A crime you have reported to be investigated and to receive information about what happens.
2. The chance to explain how the crime has affected you and your interests to be taken into account.
3. To be treated with sensitivity if you have to go to court as a witness and be offered the support of the Witness Service at the Crown Court.
4. To be offered emotional and practical support.

All of these standards of service are discussed in much more detail in the code and space dictates that it is not possible to cover them all here, so just a few aspects of the first expectation will be considered.

In relation to the first standard of service, much is made of what a victim of crime might expect from the police, and from their response to them and to the crime, and how they will keep them informed. It goes on to say that victims of serious crime may receive extra help, if a member of their family has been killed as a result of a crime, in cases of rape or where a child is the victim of serious crime. There are a number of issues that you might like to think about in relation to these kinds of statements and the kind of crime victim highlighted (and especially if you do make the effort to read it in more detail).

- What kind of crime is presupposed as being the problem here?
- Who is considered to be the victim of such crime?
- Who is considered to be the appropriate agency to deal with such crime?
- What, and who, is included and excluded from these suppositions?
- Why do you think the various governments of England and Wales have sought to endorse such charters since the early 1990s?

You may have found answering some of these questions easier than others; however, one theme that you may have considered is the way in which *conventional* understandings of crime and the crime problem predominate. You may have also come to the conclusion that there is nothing here that actually gives the victim of crime anything more than a reassurance of good service but with no guarantees that such service can be or will be delivered. It is in the gaps between what actually happens and what could happen that the political manipulation of which Elias speaks occurs. Moreover, this code of practice is not intended to make failure to comply with it the basis for legal proceedings. However, failure to comply may be taken into account in considering the possibility of such proceedings. If you have read it further, you might find it interesting to think about what it says about what kinds of crime and what kinds of victims are included and excluded by it. So, for example, section 4.5 says that only individuals or businesses with fewer that nine employees are entitled to receive services under the code and the code itself does not apply to criminal conduct as a result of driving a motor vehicle or where criminal conduct is subject to investigation by the Health and Safety Executive. These provisions further endorse a very conventional understanding of what counts as crime and who counts as a victim of crime. This is rather different than the kind of crime and criminal victimization that has been under discussion in this chapter.

In a recent and wide-ranging study of fraud in the United Kingdom, Mike Levi, a UK criminologist, along with other colleagues adopted

Table 6.1: A typology of fraud by victim

Victim sector	Victim sub-sector	Examples of fraud
Private	Financial services	Cheque fraud, counterfeit goods and/or money, data compromise fraud, embezzlement, insider dealing/market abuse, insurance fraud, lending fraud, payment card fraud, procurement fraud
	Non-financial services	Cheque fraud, counterfeit goods and/or money, data compromise fraud, embezzlement, insider dealing/market abuse, insurance fraud, lending fraud, payment card fraud, procurement fraud
	Individuals	Charity fraud, consumer fraud, counterfeit goods/money, investment fraud, pension-type fraud
Public	National bodies	Benefit fraud, embezzlement, procurement fraud, tax fraud
	Local bodies	Embezzlement, frauds on council taxes, procurement fraud
	International (but affecting UK public)	Procurement fraud (by UK against non-UK companies to obtain foreign contracts) EU funds fraud

Source: Adapted from Levi, Burrows, Fleming, Hopkins, and with Matthews (2007: 12).

what they call a victim-centric approach to fraud from which they developed the following typology of fraud (see Table 6.1).

This typology illustrates the complexities of just one example of what we have chosen here to call white-collar crime. However, it would be useful for the reader to think about this typology, relate it to the case of Bernard Madoff and think about the following questions:

- Where does his behaviour fit in relation to this typology? (There may well be more than one category).
- Who were his victims and what were they victims of?
- He was one who got caught, why?
- What were the wider national and international consequences of his activities? Can these be quantified?

Summary

The discussion so far has tried to extend what it is that might count as crime and who as a consequence might count as a victim of crime. It can be seen that extending our understanding in this way is highly problematic both in terms of common sense understandings of these issues and in terms of legal understandings of these kinds of activities. There is a fine line between what might be considered sharp business practice and criminal fraud for example. However, extending our understanding of what might count as criminal has been an important aspect of criminology, so now it will be important to consider what kinds of ideas criminology has used to make sense of this kind of criminality.

HOW HAS CRIMINOLOGY ATTEMPTED TO EXPLAIN WHITE-COLLAR CRIME?

Much of the previous discussion in this chapter has drawn implicitly on an understanding of crime and the problem of crime that might be best understood as being the 'criminality of the state'. This view of crime and criminology relies, in different ways, on the work of Karl Marx.

Marx drew attention to the way in which the powerful in society use the range of resources available to them, including the law, to secure and maintain their dominant position in society. In this view of society, the law and the processes that underpin the law and its practice are at the centre of critical scrutiny. Such scrutiny puts to the fore the way in which some groups in society are targeted by the law and its practice and others are not. Put simply, the law and its enforcement become arenas in which the powers of the state are made legitimate. For a criminologist working within this kind of framework, these powers express themselves especially along class, race and gender lines. Hence, the rich get richer and the poor get prison. This way of thinking about the nature of crime and criminal victimization is an important dimension to criminology and, though it takes a variety of forms, we shall discuss three of them briefly here: Marxist criminology, radical criminology and critical criminology.

MARXIST CRIMINOLOGY

Marx himself had little to say about crime or the law, but the general tenor of his views can be translated into the context of criminology. Two important writers who have done this are both North American, Chambliss (1975) and Quinney (1977). Chambliss argued that capitalism creates the desire to consume, and as not all members of society are able to earn enough to match the levels of consumption generated by capitalism, this puts the haves and the have-nots in conflict with one another. This view does not presume therefore that only the have-nots (the poor) will engage in criminal behaviour but does presume that it is their behaviour that will be the focus of the criminal law. He says:

> Criminality is simply not something that people have or don't have; crime is not something some people do and other don't. Crime is a matter of who can pin the label on whom, and underlying this sociopolitical process is the structure of social relations determined by the political economy.
>
> (Chambliss, 1975 in Muncie *et al.* 1996: 228)

So, for Chambliss, the underlying cause of crime (remember criminology, as was outlined in Chapter 1, is still about the search for the causes) lies with the state and the political and economic interests that are necessarily served by the law and its implementation. As Chambliss argues, 'The state becomes an instrument of the ruling class enforcing laws here but not there, according to the realities of political power and economic conditions' (ibid.: 230). A similar emphasis can be found in the work of Quinney (1977).

Quinney used the term 'politicality of crime' to suggest that criminal behaviour was not the product of a deficient personality or poor socialization but a political expression. By that he meant that it was not an individual's behaviour itself that was criminal but the action that was taken against it that rendered it criminal. It was his view that the ways in which some behaviours were deemed problematic and other were not were embedded in social relationships. These relationships were structural, that is, rooted in power relationships, and should not be seen to be conspiratorial but part of the social relations of society. Taking this as a starting point, Quinney constructed a typology of crime. So, he talks of crimes of domination (police brutality, white-collar crime, governmental crimes), crimes of accommodations and resistance (theft and homicide produced by the conditions of capitalism) and terrorism (a response to the conditions of capitalism).

Both these versions of Marxist criminology clearly put all crimes of the powerful (including white-collar crime) on the agenda and see such crime as the product of either the authorities themselves or endemic to the conditions of capitalism that result in some behaviours being targeted more consistently and more effectively than others. Not many criminologists in the present decade take such a simplistic view of the cause of white-collar crime in particular or the cause of crime in general, but these ideas were influential in the development of the second two strands of Marxist-oriented criminology to be discussed here: radical criminology and critical criminology.

RADICAL CRIMINOLOGY

Radical criminology has its origins in the United Kingdom rather than the United States and is largely associated with the work of Taylor, Walton and Young (1973) in *The New Criminology*. Arguably, this work paved the way for the later work of Young and others that focused on relative deprivation that was discussed in Chapter 4. *The New Criminology* was written as a critique of the then dominance of criminology by psychological explanations of crime. It strived to create what they called a fully social theory of deviance: a concern to take account of (among other things) the nature of the criminal process as a whole and how its constituent parts produced the whole.

However, developments in Marxist theory, especially in relation to understanding the nature of the state, rather left this kind of criminology stranded. Arguably with the exception of the well-known work done in the United Kingdom by Hall and others called *Policing the Crisis*. This work attempted to make sense of how, during the mid 1970s in London, the crime of 'mugging' was constructed as not only a social problem but also as the archetypal 'black' crime. Their analysis of this process was controversial, but in terms of the development of a Marxist oriented criminology, it led people to think much more critically about the role of the law in relation to crime and the criminalization process. In other words, how some groups and/or sections of society were much more likely to receive the attention of the criminal justice process for their behaviour, moreover, behaviour that might not be too different from the behaviour of other groups in society. (The reader might like to think of some examples of this: raucous behaviour at the rugby club or a football match as compared with raucous behaviour elsewhere is a good place to start!) Arguably, understanding this process of criminalization is the starting point for critical criminology.

CRITICAL CRIMINOLOGY

The final strand of Marxist-oriented criminology to be discussed here is that known as critical criminology. This is a label that still has some resonance for contemporary criminology and criminologists though it is often difficult to ascertain its precise meaning. It is a term used here as a way of bringing together a range of different work that is concerned with the various ways in which the state uses its power to maintain and sustain itself. So, critical criminology is still concerned with the criminality of the state but recognizes that the way in which the state has vested interests in the way things are (rather than the way they might be) frequently work in very subtle and socially nuanced ways.

For some criminologists, understanding those subtleties has meant focusing on how classism, racism, sexism, heterosexism are an intrinsic part of the way in which institutions work, how policies are formulated, what becomes an agenda item or not and so on. In others words, they become part of the structural relationships in which people work, that require constant work and self-reflection on the part of individuals to change them. For other criminologists this being 'critical' means focusing on how some state practices marginalize and criminalize some groups and not others. For others it has meant focusing more critically on the victim of crime and endeavouring to establish a more subtly nuanced understanding of why some people are more likely to be seen as victims and others not. All of which are quite legitimate questions for understanding white-collar crime. Yet in many ways, criminology still struggles to put white-collar crime at the centre of its concerns. Why is this the case?

CRIMINOLOGY AND WHITE-COLLAR CRIME: HAPPY OR UNHAPPY BEDFELLOWS?

To formulate an answer to this question, read the following observations made by Whyte (2004a: 145), a critical criminologist in the

United Kingdom, think about what you have read in this book and write down your reasons for agreeing or disagreeing with him.

1. 'The criminal justice system remains pre-occupied with a relatively limited number of interpersonal crimes, and criminology by and large obediently falls into line behind the "official" version of the crime problem'.
2. 'The punitive gaze of criminal justice looks the other way when it comes to crimes of the powerful'.
3. 'The law's embedded bias therefore forces us to think about a much more profound question in relation to regulation: in capitalist social orders, can state regulation ever adequately guarantee our protection'?
4. '. . . we have to recognise that some of the most destructive and deadly harms committed by corporations are not crimes at all but are activities sanctioned and legitimated by states'.
5. 'A bigger question for criminology is therefore to think about how we change a system that encourages both corporate *crime* and corporate *harm*'.

In devising your response to these statements, hopefully you have considered a number of things, including the following:

- The nature of criminology as a discipline and its umbilical link with modern society and as a consequence, the policy-making process.
- The kind of data available to criminologists.
- The inherent difficulties of accessing data about white-collar crime.
- The kinds of crimes that people take seriously and expect the criminal justice system to 'do something about'.
- The role of the law in defining what is and what is not criminal.
- The role of the law in defining who can be and who cannot be an offender.
- The role of the victim in all of the above.

You may, of course, have thought about other things too and may have concluded by agreeing or disagreeing with all, some or none of Whyte's statements. However, what is important in relation to thinking about them and thinking about criminology is to recognize that what is understood by 'crime' can never be taken for granted and that if serious consideration were to be given to the victim of crime then the question of the harm done by a wide range of illegitimate activities (like not adhering to health and safety legislation) might be a more meaningful one to pursue.

Summary and conclusion

In this chapter, our understanding of crime, what crime is, who can be considered a criminal and who can be considered to be a victim of crime has been extended considerably. Hopefully, some of this has served to challenge further both your own common sense understandings of all of these issues and also what criminology is about. While small in number in relation to the criminology community as a whole, critical criminologists have a very important role to play in challenging not only what we might all take for granted about the crime problem but also what the discipline itself takes for granted about the nature of the crime problem. Given that much of the policy arena in relation to crime works with a very conventional understanding of crime, the impact of critical criminology and critical criminologists is likely to be rather limited. This fact, however, should not deter the reader from appreciating the value of asking questions about what this strand of work represents like, for example, whose crime and whose justice are we putting to the fore here? The answers that are given to such questions form the basis of understanding how criminologists think about the criminal justice system and crime prevention, the focus of our next two chapters.

EXERCISE

Given the concerns of critical criminology as outlined in this chapter and the financial crisis of 2007–2010, you might like to think about the following questions:

1. In what ways, if at all, is such a crisis a concern for criminology? Why?
2. How, if at all, does such a crisis impact on society and whom?
3. What might the relationship be between this impact and criminal behaviour, and what kind of criminal behaviour?

4. What role, contributory role, if any, did the regulatory agencies play in this crisis?
5. How, if at all, can such crises be prevented?

You might want to hold on to your answer to the last question and think about it again after you have read Chapter 8.

RECOMMENDATIONS FOR FURTHER READING

A thorough discussion of white-collar crime can be found in H. Croall (2001) *Understanding White-Collar Crime* (Buckingham: Open University Press), and G. Slapper and S. Tombs (1999) *Corporate Crime* (London: Longmans) offer a good case study analysis of particular white-collar crimes. More recently, Tombs and Whyte (2007) have taken a detailed look of infringements associated with health and safety legislation in Safety Crime (London: Routledge-Willan). Reiman, J and Leighton, P. (2009) *The Rich Get Richer and the Poor Get Prison* (Pearson Education), now in its ninth edition and first published in 1979, is a must if you want to read a very radical approach to the issues addressed in this chapter. R. Elias (1993) *Victims Still* (London: Sage) is a sound, if somewhat polemical, discussion of the way in which the victims' movement in the United States has been the object of political manipulation. For a more advanced appreciation of the problems that white-collar crime poses for criminology, take a look at Nelken's chapter on White Collar Crime in M. Maguire, R. Morgan and R. Reiner (2007) *The Oxford Handbook of Criminology* (fourth edition; Oxford: Oxford University Press).

7

A QUESTION OF JUSTICE

This chapter will pay particular attention to the nature of the criminal justice system in England and Wales. In Chapter 1, it was made clear that criminologists not only concern themselves with the problems of defining, measuring and explaining crime, they are also concerned with how the criminal justice system works, or fails to work, for the criminals, victims and the professionals who are involved with it. For many criminologists, their concern with the criminal justice system is around the question of whether or not it works in a fair and equal way for the people who come into contact with it. To do that, of course, it is necessary for a criminologist to have some kind of understanding of how the criminal justice system works before they can offer an understanding of what its strengths and weaknesses are. So this chapter will introduce the reader to some understanding of the nature of the criminal justice system and highlight the kinds of questions that criminologists might ask about it.

INTRODUCTION

Before it is possible to consider whether or not any particular criminal justice system does work fairly or not, it is important to be able to appreciate what the different parts of the system are supposed to do. Of course, being concerned about fairness or equality ultimately means that criminology and criminologists also have something to say about justice. However, justice is a difficult concept both to understand and to define.

Some would argue that justice, like beauty, is in the eye of the beholder. Such a view implies that justice is as variable as beauty itself and as a consequence, because it is so variable, cannot be achieved by any criminal justice system. However, it is clear that any criminal justice system in any society, as its title implies, is expected to deliver justice. So the purpose of this chapter is to explore some of the ideas on which different criminal justice systems are based and to examine the extent to which these ideas reflect different understandings of how justice might be achieved. First, we shall consider different definitions of justice. Second, we shall consider the nature of different criminal justice systems; namely, that of England and Wales (there are differences in Scotland and Northern Ireland), the United States and features of systems of continental Europe. In doing so, we shall reflect on the similarities and differences between them in what they consider to be part of the process of delivering justice. But first, how might justice be defined?

WHAT IS JUSTICE?

Ways of understanding what counts as justice have changed over the centuries. The ancient Greeks took the view that justice was rooted in the logic that gave the world its order. In this sense, justice (logic) was something opposite to chaos, and it could be applied everywhere and objectively measured. However, more modern understandings, to be found especially in the work of the philosopher Immanuel Kant, argued that justice was rooted in moral principles (i.e. ideas about right and wrong) that also could be applied everywhere. More recently, the twentieth-century philosopher Richard Rorty has argued that justice is not so much connected with moral principles (what might be referred to as ethics) as it is connected with consensus. In other words, justice is what people agree that it is. One extension of this view of justice is that expressed in the following quote from Alasdair McIntyre, a contemporary moral philosopher, who states:

> So rationality itself, whether theoretical or practical, is a concept with a history: indeed since there are a diversity of traditions of enquiry with histories, there are, so it will turn out, rationalities rather than rationality, just as it will also turn out that there are justices rather than justice.
>
> (1988: 9)

So, what 'justice' means has been, and still is, highly contested. Feminists argue, for example, that when you begin to unravel what rationality means within the criminal justice system, it refers to a particular kind of rationality: the rational man of law. Ngaire Naffine (1990), an Australian socio-legal scholar, suggests that this man of law is a middle-class, entrepreneurial man, a successful market individual. If he is the man of law whose rationality counts in the legal process, then such presumptions fail to speak to other kinds of men as well as women. So the law, and the courts in particular, cannot 'hear' the working-class man, the ethnic minority man or the woman who may come before it. Hence, criminal justice professionals may advise defendants to wear a suit or to look presentable if they are required to attend court. This is a fairly low key way, but nevertheless important one, in which the 'man of law' impacts on the processes of delivering justice.

Nevertheless, there is still the expectation that the purpose of a criminal justice system is to deliver justice, and in the context of the criminal justice system, this has been and is intertwined with the idea of punishment. The way in which justice and punishment are, or should be, connected is also an issue of considerable debate. For example, the United States still uses capital punishment for those convicted of first-degree murder, whereas most European countries no longer have this option on their statute books for this kind of offence (though in some instances it is still retained for offences of treason). However, each of these different practices would argue that the crime and the punishment for the crime are connected. This is usually referred to as the 'principle of **proportionality**', that is, the idea that punishment is not arbitrarily imposed but has been subjected to debate, agreed on and considered appropriate for the crime committed. Put more colloquially, there is some sense that the 'punishment fits the crime', though quite clearly this does not mean that the punishment will be the same everywhere for the same crime.

Recognizing that there is a connection between justice and punishment acknowledges that one focus of concern for the criminologist are the policies that any particular criminal justice system implements in relation to justice. These policies symbolize what is considered to be a reasonable way of connecting justice and punishment in any particular society. However, such connections are themselves neither simple nor straightforward. Indeed, there are theoretically a number of different ways in which this relationship might be articulated. Following is a list of concepts that arguably articulate different ways of considering the relationship between justice and punishment. The reader is encouraged to think about each of these terms and to reflect on the questions that follow.

- Revenge
- Retribution
- Restitution
- Reparation
- Restoration

1. What do each of these terms mean?
2. What do they each imply about punishment?
3. What do they each imply about justice?
4. How might they be represented in criminal justice policy?
5. What do each of them suggest about the relationship between the victim and the offender?

If you have thought about the terms listed above and tried to answer the questions that follow, you are probably now aware that no one criminal justice system's approach to punishment and justice comprises just one of these responses. More often than not criminal justice systems reflect a mixture of policies that have elements of each of these kinds of responses. In addition to being aware of this kind of complexity, it is also important to be aware that there are different principles on which any particular criminal justice system might operate in relation to its policies. These different principles are referred to as 'natural justice', 'due process', 'crime control' and 'social justice'. Barbara Hudson, a UK criminologist, writing in *The Sage Dictionary of Criminology* defines natural justice in the following way:

NATURAL JUSTICE

> A concept of natural justice emphasises basic principles necessary to ensure fairness in legal proceedings; principles of justice deriving from the nature of humanity; principles of justice which would obtain in a state of nature and which are independent of social relationships.
>
> (Hudson 2006: 258)

In practice, this means fair procedures: for example, that idea that no one should be a judge in their own case and that no one should be found guilty without having the choice of being represented.

DUE PROCESS

Lorraine Gelsthorpe, another UK criminologist, writing in the same dictionary defines 'due process' as follows:

> A due process model or perspective emphasises the need to administer justice according to legal rules and procedures which are publicly known, fair and seen to be just.
>
> (2006: 144)

In practice, this means, for example, arrested persons should know what they have been arrested for, why they are going to court, that there should be standards of proof in relation to evidence and that each side should have the opportunity to present their case. So the due process model implies more than just the establishment of fair procedures, it also implies that those procedures must be administered fairly and equitably and that there is impartiality about the judicial process.

CRIME CONTROL

Defining crime control she states,

> A crime control perspective or model stresses that the primary function of the criminal courts is to punish offenders and by doing so, control crime.
>
> (Ibid.: 81)

The crime control perspective on criminal justice therefore values the criminal justice system in general, but the courts in particular as being the means whereby the law is upheld regardless of question of impartiality. Put another way, the due process perspective values the importance of identifying the innocent and ensuring they are acquitted, even if this means that a guilty person goes free.

SOCIAL JUSTICE

And finally, Barbara Hudson defines social justice in the following way:

> Fair distribution of opportunities, rewards, and responsibilities in society. Principles and institutions for the distribution of meaningful social goods – income, shelter, food, health, education, freedom to pursue individual goals.
>
> (Hudson 2006: 404)

Defined in this way, it might be difficult to see how a concept of social justice relates to the criminal justice system, but if the criminal justice system is understood as a social good (such as the institutions for education and health, in other words something that we can all benefit from), then the question of fairness becomes one in which it is useful to consider how, if at all, the criminal justice system should take account of social inequality when it comes to the question of punishment. This is an important area of debate for those criminologists who would argue that it is through improving social policy that crime can be tackled, not by sending people to prison. Indeed, for some commentators, the relationship between criminal justice and social justice is paramount. Dee Cook, a UK social scientist, states:

> If a society cannot guarantee 'the equal worth of all its citizens', mutual and self-respect and the meeting of basic needs, it cannot expect that all citizens will feel they have an equal stake in abiding by the law, and it cannot dispense justice fairly and enhance confidence in the law.
>
> (2006: 21)

In this sense, criminal justice policy and social policy are intimately connected. So, it is important to think about how changes in one area might impact on the other, like for example, policy decisions made in 2010 by the coalition government in the United Kingdom as a part of the Comprehensive Spending Review, to limit people's access to state support for housing, might render some people homeless and expose them to criminal victimization.

These different understandings of justice become particularly pertinent when we add them to the notion of the rational man of law commented on earlier. The observations made some time ago by Kathy Kendall, a Canadian sociologist who now works in the United Kingdom, illustrate one dilemma that debates on justice raise for feminists. She asks:

> The question feminists face is whether justice for women is best achieved through legal recognition of sexual difference (special treatment) or by regarding sexual difference as largely irrelevant (equal treatment).
>
> (Kendall 1991: 80)

Given the rational man of law principle, then it is quite possible to ask the same question on behalf of the working-class man or the man from an ethnic minority, rendering the questions that might be raised for the working-class, ethnic minority woman problematic indeed. Moreover, the question of special treatment or equal treatment is overlaid by what we understand by justice, captured by the different definitions stated earlier and how justice might be achieved as a process. Is justice about making sure everyone experiences due process in the same way, or it is about outcome? That is ensuring that such cases receive the same punishment?

It is possible to see elements of each of these ideas on the practice of justice present in many contemporary criminal justice systems. For example, consider the amount of time and effort that is spent on high-profile cases, like that of the serial killer Harold Shipman discussed in Chapter 1. This time and effort reflects a commitment to due process since the last thing any barrister wants with this kind of case is for it to go to appeal on a 'technicality', that is, on an issue(s) relating to the defendant's rights not having been adhered to. In contrast, much of the work of the magistrate's court might fit with the crime control perspective in which there is little argument between the prosecution and the defence with more than 90 per cent of defendants pleading guilty. Issues pertaining to 'natural justice' are not so easily identifiable, but as more and more people appeal to the European Court of Human Rights, and the human rights legislation takes a deeper hold on the working of the criminal justice system, it is likely that this perspective will have greater importance. A social justice approach can be delineated in some of the policies that are intended to keep young offenders out of prison, for example, some of the inter-agency work in **restorative justice**. Increasingly too, the 'victim' has been given a greater voice in the justice process as more and more jurisdictions introduce variations on victim impact statements.

EXERCISE

Search any national newspaper archive on the Internet for victim impact statements or family impact statements for the past 12 months. (Many newspapers get permission to publish these once a case has reached a conclusion.) When you have found and read perhaps two of these, think about the following questions:

- What influence, if any, do you think these kinds of statements should have on the decision-making of the court?
- What other purpose might these statements serve?
- What do these kinds of policy developments have to say about justice?

What conclusions did you reach? One might be that justice can take many forms and can be practised in many different ways. It is highly contested, and part of the interest for the criminologist is how this contest plays itself out both in individual cases and in the case of social groups and their experience of the criminal justice system. (The reader is invited to remember the data from Chapter 3 here and reflect on how it relates to the workings of the criminal justice system.)

In democratic societies, the practice of justice is the responsibility of different agencies that comprise the criminal justice system. In England and Wales, these agencies are overseen by the Home Office, the Ministry of Justice and the Office of the Attorney General, which each has different responsibilities in relation to the delivery of the criminal justice system (Table 7.1).

In the rest of this chapter, we shall consider the role of the different parts of this system and the relationship that they have with each other. First of all in England and Wales and then we shall consider how this system compares with the system in the United States and continental Europe with respect to the relationship afforded to the

Table 7.1: England and Wales criminal justice system

Ministry of Justice	Home Office	Office of Attorney General
Criminal law	Security and counter-terrorism	Director of public
Criminal courts	Policing	Prosecution
Sentencing	Immigration and asylum	Crown prosecution service
Youth justice	Inspectorates	Serious fraud office
Judicial appointments	Crime reduction/community safety	Revenue and customs
Human rights	Identity and citizenship	Prosecutions
National Offender Management System (NOMS)		

Source: Taken from Newburn (2007: 545).

victim and the offender in these different jurisdictions. Lack of space means that it is impossible to offer a detailed appreciation of the workings of different criminal justice systems, but given the coverage given to the victim of crime in this book, a look at how those different jurisdictions handle the victim is justified and might even be interesting to the reader! Finally, we shall consider whether or not there is anything to be gained, and for whom, by changing the balance in the relationship between the victim and the offender; something that has preoccupied those interested in researching victims of crime and enhancing the rights of victims of crime in recent years in the United Kingdom especially. But first who comprises the criminal justice system?

THE CRIMINAL JUSTICE SYSTEM: ENGLAND AND WALES

The criminal justice system in England and Wales, like many other criminal justice systems worldwide, comprises six key components:

> The police
> The Crown Prosecution Service (CPS)
> The courts

The Probation Service
The Youth Justice System
The prison service

The purpose here is to consider the function of each of these component parts; however, key to understanding how each of them operates in relation to each other is the concept of **discretion**. We came across the importance of discretion in Chapter 2. Eugene McLaughlin writing in the *Sage Dictionary of Criminology* defines discretion in the following way:

> The power conferred on criminal justice professionals to use their judgement to decide what action to take in a given situation. This includes the decision to take no action. Discretion is officially delegated within the criminal justice system and it is not limited to one decision point. Because it extends to all points of decision-making and encompasses procedures and working methods, flows back and forth through all parts of the criminal justice system.
>
> (2006: 134)

As we shall see, understanding discretion is crucial to understanding the criminal justice process.

THE POLICE

The role and function of the police in England and Wales and elsewhere has been subjected to much debate over the past two decades. However, it is clear that the essential role of what will be called here 'blue uniform policing' has hardly changed at all despite this debate. Brogden *et al.* (1988) defined the role of the police in the following way:

> The police is an occupation defined by its specific mandate (given in the oath which all must take), its specific powers and its specific form of accountability. The mandate entails upholding 'law and order'. The powers to fulfil this include a range of extra powers over and above those of citizens. And the form of accountability is accountability to the law, not to politicians or more generally to the 'democratic' polity. All of these are unique-specific to police officers of the state.

The importance of this unique role of the police is self-evident when the number and range of organizations that now 'police' behaviour are considered. These organizations range from school teachers, to youth justice workers, to security guards operating in a shopping mall, traffic wardens to police community safety officers and special constables. All these groups of people are concerned with policing behaviour, that is, trying to ensure that social control/social order is maintained. However, it is only the blue uniform police officer who has the mandate to uphold law and order and who is accountable to the law in the way in which they do this. This makes the work of the police both more subject to public scrutiny and more likely to have an impact on those subjected to police action all at the same time. (Those of you unsure as to the validity of this last statement might like to consider whom they would complain to, and the likely effectiveness of their complaint, if a security guard in a shopping mall behaved inappropriately.) The central feature of the combined effect of the police mandate and their accountability to the law is to be found in the concept of discretion.

The mandate of upholding law and order requires police officers to make judgements as to whether or not the behaviour that is the object of their attention is criminal, or disorderly or in some instance both. This process of making a judgment implies discretion: making a decision in the light of the circumstances presented to them and in the light of their understanding of the law. All that a police officer needs to do is to ensure that any decision that they make can be defended in law. Clearly, the presence of discretion means that the police do not (nor indeed could they) enforce all of the law all of the time in all kinds of circumstances. A police force that did this would truly be a police state. The question arises, however, whether or not their use of discretion is applied fairly, that is, in line with some sense of justice. In recent years in England and Wales, this question has been raised most frequently in relation to their use of stop and search as a method of apprehending suspected criminals especially in relation to people from ethnic minorities.

Focusing on the police use of discretion directs attention much more to their law enforcement role than their maintenance of order role. Yet it is clear that the police are expected to work with both functions: enforce the law and maintain order even though on occasion these two functions might contradict one another. For example, enforcing the law in the context of policing a public demonstration might incite the crowd to greater disorderly behaviour, whereas the use of discretion done with authority might diffuse crowd behaviour. In other words, there is always a balance to be struck between these two functions. Nevertheless, it is the case that historically the police have implicitly taken on board the view that the maintenance of order equates with dealing with unruly behaviour on the streets: drunks, young people hanging about, prostitution and so on. Although clearly in recent times, the police function in relation to the maintenance of order has concerned itself with such issues as domestic violence, its historical focus of order maintenance from the 1830s to the present day is also part of the backcloth against which to understand the stop and search statistics presented earlier. All of that notwithstanding it is evident that some groups of people are much more likely to find themselves arrested, charged and taken to court (see Table 7.1). It is at this juncture that the CPS takes over.

THE CROWN PROSECUTION SERVICE

Having been arrested and charged the decision as to whether or not to proceed with a prosecution is taken by the CPS. This organization was established in 1985 and began its work in 1986. At the head of this organization is the Director of Public Prosecutions, and its role is to conduct criminal prosecutions on behalf of the state. In other words, the role of the CPS is to make decisions, either to prosecute or not to prosecute according to what it considers to be in the public interest.

The notion of the public interest points to another important area in which discretion can play its part in the decision-making process. The CPS decides whether or not proceedings are in the public interest and in so doing will take account of a number of factors focusing on the costs of proceedings: economic, social and whether or not justice will be served as a result. This can be quite a contentious issue, but one of the key concerns is to avoid frivolous or unnecessary proceedings.

Prior to the establishment of the CPS, prosecutions had been conducted by the police; however, the introduction of this system was intended to transfer the process of prosecution to lawyers with no previous involvement in the case as a way of trying to ensure a more impartial approach to prosecution. However, the extent to which this has been achieved has been subject to some debate with some evidence suggesting that the CPS remains on balance guided by the police in its decision-making. Moreover, there have been a number of other accusations lodged against the CPS since its inception. These have been summarized by Joyce (2001: 195), a UK political scientist, in the following way:

The Economic Politics of Prosecution

- The CPS is understaffed resulting in people with too many cases and poor preparation.
- The decision not to prosecute is high. About 1 in 7 cases is not pursued reflecting the extent to which the CPS test of success at court may also be guided by cost factors. (Cheaper to drop the case earlier than later.)
- Downgrading offences so that they are heard at magistrate's court rather than crown court. This is quicker and cheaper.

The reader might like to think about what kind of perspective on justice are reflected in these accusations of the CPS: natural justice, due process, crime control or social justice?

THE COURTS

Once the decision has been made to prosecute for an offence, the next stage in the proceedings is for the defendant to appear in court. The court system has undergone some change in the United Kingdom recently introducing an American style 'Supreme Court'. Figure 7.1 offers an illustration for the structure of the court system.

Technically, at the top of this structure sits the House of Lords but that is a final place for appeals that are considered to be in the wider public interest. For criminal offences, there are two key levels in this system: the Magistrates' Court and the Crown Court. It is important to remember that there are two important features of this system:

1. The purpose of the prosecution process is to prove 'beyond reasonable doubt' that the accused committed the offence of which they are charged.
2. To achieve this outcome the British courts use the **adversarial system**. In this system, the defence and the prosecution seek to prove the validity of their case by the strength of their argument in interpreting the evidence. This does not necessarily equate with a search for evidence about what actually happened or the 'truth'.

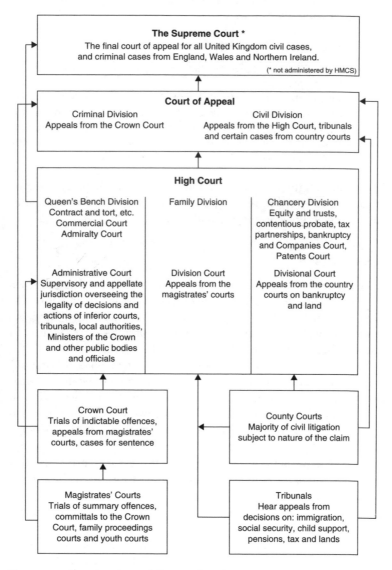

Figure 7.1: The structure of the court system

Source: Her Majesty's Courts Service www.hmcourts-service.gov.

These two principles would also apply to the court system in Canada and the United States, and they are the principles that often leave complainants and witnesses somewhat confused especially by how they have been treated in the witness box. However, it is the function of the court proceedings to cast doubt on all evidence brought before it for the argument to be won or lost. This is the essence of the adversarial system: winning (or losing) cases. A process in which it is essential to cast 'reasonable doubt' on any testimony or evidence brought before the court. (Again the reader might like to think about what concept of justice is reflected in this process.)

In addition, these two courts deal with different kinds of offences. Magistrates' Courts deal with less serious criminal offences referred to as summary offences. Here, most defendants plead guilty to the offence they have been charged with and the magistrates (usually three of them more often than not an ordinary member of the public) guided by the clerk to the court will impose the appropriate penalty for the offence. (There are quite detailed guidelines given to magistrates as to what kind of penalty is appropriate for what kind of offence, though they do have discretion with these guidelines.) Life becomes a little more complicated at Crown Court. Here, more serious offences referred to as indictable offences are heard before a jury (although again here in the region of two-thirds of cases are guilty pleas and heard by a judge only), and it is here that the adversarial system comes into its own with both sides trying to convince the jury on the merits of its case. In between there are 'triable either way', offences in which either the magistrate or the defendant can choose to have heard at Crown Court.

Whatever the offence or the court where the defendant appears, the majority of people plead guilty. Indeed, much of the work of the professionals involved in the pre-trial process is arguably geared towards obtaining a confession or securing a guilty plea to a lesser offence (plea bargaining), which means that much of the work of the court is concerned with sentencing, thus illustrating perhaps the crime control aspects of the criminal justice system. In making decisions on sentencing the courts are guided by three things:

1. sentencing guidelines;
2. information about the offence;
3. information about the offender.

Latterly, a fourth factor has come into play:

4. Information about and from the victim

The level of involvement of the victim (complainant) in the criminal justice system is one of the key areas of difference between the criminal justice systems under discussion here (see later). In England and Wales, there has been some movement over the past 15 years to give the victim of crime a bigger voice in criminal justice proceedings. This has taken a number of forms from the court having the option at its disposal to order the offender to pay compensation directly to the victim, to the introduction of the Victim Personal Statement Scheme (an opportunity for the victim's statement on what happened to them and the impact it has had to be presented to the court) and the increasing popularity and development of restorative justice as an option of disposal for the court. (There are many and varied interpretations of restorative justice, but for the purposes here, it is simply important to note that they provide an opportunity for the offender to make amends to the victim; see also Chapter 8.) The extent to which any of these developments with respect to the victim amount to anything more than a symbolic reference to the victim is a moot point but they do point to the increasing importance being given to the role of the victim in the criminal justice process in England and Wales.

In making recommendations for sentence, the courts have an increasingly diverse range of options most of which will either involve the probation service, the youth justice service or the prison service. A little will be said about the role of each of these in turn. Though it should be noted that, following the North American model, the probation service and the prison system in England and Wales in June 2004 have been combined into a kind of correctional services system called the National Offender Management System (NOMS).

THE PROBATION SERVICE

The role of the probation service has undergone considerable change over the past 20 years. Traditionally concerned with the task of befriending offenders, it is now much more likely to be preoccupied with dealing with the victims of crime and cognitive behavioural programmes designed to reduce offending behaviour as befriending people. This change in emphasis in the kind of work that probation officers might do and who with has been matched by a change in organizational structure. In 2001, a National Probation Service was formed and organized to match the 42 police areas, with each of these areas being headed by a probation panel. (Readers might like to visit the National Probation Service website to get a detailed feel of what this new organization looks like and what its central purpose is considered to be.) However, for the most part, the work of the probation service is focused on the delivery of an effective and standardized service.

THE YOUTH JUSTICE SYSTEM

The 1998 Crime and Disorder Act introduced widespread reform to the youth justice system in England and Wales. These reforms, stemming from a White Paper produced by the labour party in 1997 called 'No More Excuses', which itself took on board major criticisms of the youth justice system contained in an Audit Commission Report of 1996 called 'Misspent Youth', aimed to put in place three principles in relation to youth justice: restoration (the idea that young people should make amends for their offending behaviour), re-integration (that this process of making amends should ensure their inclusion in society) and responsibility (that young people and their parents take responsibility for the prevention of their offending behaviour). In putting these principles into practice under the 1998 legislation, the youth justice system in England and Wales is now overseen by the Youth Justice Board. This board is responsible for the effective delivery of the youth justice service through inter-agency Youth Offending Teams. These teams are supposed to work within a common framework of practice to ensure consistency across all local authority areas with the range of options for dealing with young people now available from the court. A visit to the Youth Justice Board's own website will give the reader a good feel for the range of work being done and how successful the Board believes its work to be.

THE PRISON SERVICE

The role of the prison service is in many ways self-explanatory. Their statement of purpose for 2010 is given below.

Statement of Purpose

Her Majesty's Prison Service serves the public by keeping in custody those committed by the courts. Our duty is to look after them with humanity and help them lead law-abiding and useful lives in custody and after release.

Our Vision

To provide the very best prison services so that we are the provider of choice.
To work towards this vision by securing the following key objectives.

Objectives

To protect the public and provide what commissioners want to purchase by

Holding prisoners securely
Reducing the risk of prisoners re-offending
Providing safe and well-ordered establishments in which we treat prisoners humanely, decently and lawfully.
In securing these objectives, we adhere to the following principles:

Our Principles

In carrying out our work we

Work in close partnership with our commissioners and others in the criminal justice system to achieve common objectives.
Obtain best value from the resources available using research to ensure effective correctional practice.

Promote diversity, equality of opportunity and combat unlawful discrimination.

Ensure our staff have the right leadership, organization, support and preparation to carry out their work effectively.

Source: www.hmprisonservice.gov.uk.

Think carefully about the words used in this statement and think about the following questions:

- Do you find anything problematic in this statement?
- Are there any tensions or contradictions here?
- Whose interests do you think are prioritized in this statement?

Of course, one persistent and inherent tension in the use of prison as a form of punishment is whether the prison is for punishment or for rehabilitation. Those who opt for the 'prison works' view reflect a crime control perspective of justice, and those who are persuaded by the rehabilitation argument are more inclined to the social justice stance. Whichever view is adopted, it is clear that prison is the principle form of punishment used in all societies for what they consider to be serious crimes. Yet, not all societies use prison as a punishment at the same rate or for the same kinds of crime. Table 7.2 illustrates some of these differences.

Table 7.2: Rates of imprisonment per 100,000 of national population for 2000–2002

England and Wales	139
France	99
Sweden	64
Iceland	37
Russian Federation	607
Poland	260
Turkey	89
Slovenia	56
United States	730
Canada	116
Panama	359
Mexico	156
Brazil	137
Venezuela	62
New Zealand	155
Australia	112

Source: Adapted from Christie (2004: 52–3).

Consider Table 7.2 and think about the following questions.

- What, if anything, do these figures reveal about penal policy in each of these countries?
- How would you explain the differences between, for example, England and Wales, Sweden and the United States?
- Is there anything that you find surprising in these figures? Why?

It must be remembered that in the absence of the death penalty, prison (as the most serious form of punishment for an offender) may account for some of the differences in Table 7.2 but probably not very much. The differences shown in the table are probably mostly explained by different policies on punishment and different levels of public tolerance of the use of imprisonment. The reader might also speculate that the differences in the figures reflect different levels of offending behaviour but that argument would be a difficult one to sustain. (Just think about the problem of attrition discussed in Chapter 2 as a starting point.) However, the figures do make interesting reading and clearly make the point that the use of prison, as an option for offending behaviour is highly variable. Of course, there are a range of ways in which an offender can be dealt with by the criminal justice system depending on the kind of offence they have committed.

Range of dispositions from the court

- Caution
- Final warning
- Absolute discharge
- Conditional discharge
- Fine
- Compensation order
- Community service
- Combination
- Probation order
- Prison sentence (with wide variety of length and variety in level of security).

In addition to this list, there are a range of possibilities for young offenders that might involve all kinds of conditions from parenting orders to re-education projects to community-based supervision orders.

This list indicates a number of things:

1. The complexity of the criminal justice system relating to the way in which it might dispose of offenders.
2. The potential difficulty of matching a particular disposition from the court with what might work for a particular offender.
3. The importance of recognizing that for each of these dispositions carries a criminal record, which for some offences stays with the offender for ever (e.g. in the case of sex offences and in others can be considered 'spent' after 5 years).

So not only is this a highly complex process but it is also quite a difficult one in which to monitor and track effectiveness, that is, to identify with confidence what will work with what kind of offender. This is a question that preoccupies many criminologists. It is also important to recognize that many of the decisions made in this process from the decision to arrest, to the decision that proceed with a case, to the decision of what kind of sentence to give are made with the discretion of the professionals involved being central to that process.

Discretion runs throughout the criminal justice system. This discretion is not unfettered. In other words, it is subjected to the law, rules, guidelines and ultimately public scrutiny; yet, it is still an important part of the process. So, while for particular offences there are clear guidelines indicating maximum and minimum levels of punishment, it still remains in the hands of the court what particular sentence is imposed. Also, as was seen with the CPS, not all cases are always proceeded with. The CPS may choose not to take a case further because they decide that it is not in the public interest to do so. The role that discretion plays within the criminal justice system is important in keeping some flexibility in response to the circumstances of a particular case and, in a liberal democracy, keeping the criminal justice system cognisant of its role in delivering justice. However, criminologists are particularly interested in how, through the cracks and crevices of discretion, justice is dispensed and what kinds of patterns of decision-making can be identified.

Summary

So far, we have discussed the key features of the criminal justice system in England and Wales and highlighted some of the areas that particularly attract criminological attention. What is of interest is the extent to which those features repeat themselves or do not repeat themselves in other jurisdictions. Obviously, in an introductory book of this kind, it is impossible to deal with other criminal justice systems in detail. What are presented here are at best pen portraits. However, the reader interested in other jurisdictions would do well to pursue the recommendations in the Further Reading. It should be remembered that in each of these jurisdictions, the conditions under which the criminal justice system operates and the kind of relationship that is presumed by the people party to that system are framed by the presence or the absence of constitutional rights, the relationship between federal governments and central government and the respective powers that each of these have, along with the different political traditions that may exist in different countries. All of which means that, while each jurisdiction will have similar components (the police, the courts, a prosecution service etc.), the powers that these components have and how they relate to each other can be very variable. However, given the policy emphasis on England and Wales on looking for ways to better integrate the victim of crime within the criminal justice system, that emphasis will provide the lens through which we shall look at the criminal justice system in the United States and some features of the systems in continental Europe.

THE UNITED STATES

From Table 7.1, it can be seen that the United States sends more people to prison per 100,000 of population than any other country for which there are reasonably reliable statistics available. Taking this kind of statistic on its own might lead to the conclusion that in that jurisdiction there had been an unequivocal acceptance of the view that prison works! However, while the United States has a written constitution that guarantees all of its citizens certain rights (e.g. the right to arms) that does make it quite different from the United Kingdom, each of the states within the United States can make its own laws with their own associated recommendations. This is exampled in the case of capital punishment with not all states having this on the statute book, and those that do, not necessarily using the same kind of capital punishment.

The role of the victim in the criminal justice system can also vary from state to state. However, subsequent to the 68 recommendations made by the President's Task Force on Victims of Crime in 1982, much has been put in place for the victim of crime, with all 50 states of the United States having passed victims' rights laws. What these rights translate into in practice, however, does vary from state to state. One area of common practice is in allowing the victim to give evidence on the impact of a crime either as part of a pre-sentence report or at the point of sentencing, with most states allowing for both opportunities though with some leaving it to the discretion of the judge. However, the majority require that the court take account of the impact of a crime on the victim in setting the sentence with some states specifying the kind of information that should be included in such a statement. Other rights included at state level cover such issues as the right to information, the right to restitution and the right to protection from the offender. While such rights may be on the statute books, there is still recognition that ensuring compliance with those rights can be problematic. As a result, some states have introduced the equivalent of a Crime Victims Ombudsman to investigate complaints when these rights are not adhered to.

The United States and the United Kingdom share in what is referred to as the Anglo-Saxon model of law, which, despite some of the complexities in variation referred to above, encourages policy comparison, policy transfer from one jurisdiction to the other and other like initiatives. (The question of policy transfer is discussed again in the Conclusion section.) However, European countries are rooted in a different legal tradition.

LOOKING TO EUROPE

Many of the countries in Europe also have a federal system of government, like that in the United States, which makes it important to understand the relationship between the region or the locality and central government before it is possible to appreciate how the criminal justice system works. This is the case, for example, in France where in the context of policing it is important to understand the different roles accorded to the local gendarmerie as compared with the Police Nationale. There are similar differences in Germany and Italy. However, one of the important differences to understand is the underlying structure of the legal system.

In countries where the legal system is based on Roman law as opposed to Anglo-Saxon law, there exists what is referred to as the 'partie civile' system. This system exists in France, Belgium, Italy and Spain and is called the 'adhesion' procedure in Germany, the Netherlands and Czechoslovakia. The importance of these systems lies within the potentially different role it offers to the victim (or complainant) within criminal proceedings as it permits the victim to present a civil claim against their offender as part of the criminal proceedings. The extent to which victims make use of this is, of course, a moot point. However, it does lay down the potential for a different structural relationship between the victim and the offender that is connected with the different principles on which such criminal justice systems proceed. Rather than being adversarial systems like the United Kingdom and the United States, many criminal justice systems in Europe are *inquisitorial*. This means that the purpose of the proceedings is not so much about winning or losing a particular case but in finding out what actually happened and on the basis of that information, a magistrate may frequently take the decision on the question of who is to be proceeded against for what kind of offence. This can result in quite a different experience of the criminal justice system especially for the victim of crime. For example, they can, if they choose, be more involved in all the proceedings, but perhaps more importantly they have a tendency to feel less under scrutiny since the central purpose of the **inquisitorial system** is to find out what happened in which the role of the victim has a different purpose.

COMPLEX JUSTICE?

Hopefully, this chapter has demonstrated the importance of understanding some key features of how any particular criminal justice system operates. It is important to consider the following:

1. What the key function of any particular criminal justice system might be: crime control, due process, natural justice or social justice.
2. The central importance of discretion; where that is located, how it is used and who benefits or does not benefit from it.
3. That while all criminal justice systems might have similar component parts, those parts are not necessarily connected in the same way and do not necessarily attribute the same importance to the same parties in the process. This is especially the case in relation to the victim of crime.
4. Given these kinds of differences, it makes it very difficult for criminal justice policy to travel from one jurisdiction to another. However, those difficulties are not only technical ones of understanding how different legal systems work but they are also cultural ones to do with what people expect the criminal justice system to deliver.

The reader might like to consider the extent to which these issues are reflected in the following report.

In the international news section, *Guardian* newspaper on 8 March 2004, there was an article headlined 'Buried Alive Under California's Law of "Three Strikes and You're Out"'. This article was reporting on a protest demonstration that had taken place at a vigil held at Leimert Park in south Los Angeles in which mock gravestones had been constructed with photos of people who were considered to be 'victims' of California's three strikes law, marking the tenth anniversary of its implementation. Under this law, any third offence results automatically with a 25-year prison sentence with no chance of parole, and in California, this is not confined to crimes of violence. The article reports that 65 per cent of those imprisoned were for non-violent crimes with 354 of them receiving 25 years to life imprisonment for petty theft of less than US$ 250. It goes on to comment that counties in the north of California who have not used this legislation have seen crime drop 22 per cent more than in those parts of California where this law has been applied rigidly.

On the basis of this summary, what do you think this kind of report conveys about:

- justice
- discretion
- punishment
- cultural tolerance in relation to criminal justice policy.

These are some of the questions that a criminologist might be asking about policies such as those outlined in the report above; can you think of any other?

In conclusion, then it is possible to see that justice is complex, and understanding how criminal justice systems work is not easy or straightforward either.

Summary

The purpose of this chapter so far has been to introduce the reader to the nature of the criminal justice system in different jurisdictions and to offer an insight into its complexity. It is important to appreciate this since criminologists spend a good deal of their time trying to understand who it is who comes to the attention of the criminal justice system, what happens to them when they do and why what happens to them does so in the way that it does. All of which connects with the question of what kind of a society do we think we live in or want to live in. In others words, it connects with our understanding of justice and who is it for. As the findings in Chapter 3 illustrated, some people are much more likely to be subjected to the processes of the criminal justice system than others, and as that chapter and Chapter 5 suggested, there are a whole range of crimes that are never criminalized and never subjected to the criminal justice process but may be subjected to other 'regulatory' agencies. However, the discretion that is an inherent and important part of the way in which all criminal justice systems operate has led to a considerable concern, in the United Kingdom in particular, that the criminal justice system is 'institutionally racist'. As a way of encouraging the need for critical thinking highlighted in Chapter 1, it will be useful to consider what this actually means in the light of what we have learned about the nature and extent of crime and the criminal justice system from this chapter and Chapter 3.

IS THE CRIMINAL JUSTICE SYSTEM 'INSTITUTIONALLY RACIST'?

The charge of 'institutional racism' was made against the criminal justice system in the United Kingdom by the Macpherson Report. This was produced in the wake of the murder of Stephen Lawrence in London in 1993. The inquiry that followed the failure to secure a conviction for the murder of this young, black man resulted in the Macpherson Report. That report concluded that a catalogue of compounding factors had contributed to not only the death of Stephen Lawrence but also the failure to secure a conviction for his murder. This end product the report attributed to 'institutional racism' that it defined as:

> The collective failure of an organisation to provide an appropriate and professional service to people because of their colour, culture, or ethnic origin. It can be detected in processes, attitudes and behaviour which amount to discrimination through unwitting prejudice, ignorance, thoughtlessness, and racist stereotyping which disadvantage minority ethnic groups.
>
> (Macpherson Report 1999: 321)

The publication of this report and its conclusions led many police forces in England and Wales in particular to 'declare' their institutional racism and to put in place procedures and practices to combat it. Whether these practices have proved to be successful or not is not of concern here. Our concern is to understand how and why such a conclusion was reached, given what we have learned so far about the nature of crime, offenders, victims (Chapter 3) and the complexity of the criminal justice system (this chapter). At this juncture, it will be useful to review some of those findings.

In Chapter 3, we relied on the conclusion drawn by Maguire (2002). Put simply, when we look at what we know about known offenders it is possible to see that they include a higher proportion of males, young males, black males, people from poor background and people with disturbed childhoods, than might be predicted from their presence in the general population as a whole. In other words, these kinds of people are over-represented in the criminal justice system. In this chapter, we have concluded that the working of the criminal justice process is neither simple nor straightforward. So it might be fair to add that, who eventually ends up being a known offender, is also neither simple nor straightforward. Indeed, if we wanted a criminological answer to this question, we would need to trace quite a large sample of people from all kinds of backgrounds (including class, ethnicity, sex, culture etc.) from the moment that they are stopped by the police, through to the point at which they are dealt with at Crown Court, and all the points in between, and compare what happened to them. Such a study would be very difficult to mount and would require the co-operation of a large number of people. A study similar to this was conducted in the late 1980s by Tony Jefferson and Monica Walker, two UK criminologists, who were then based at the University of Sheffield. This study compared and contrasted the experiences of the criminal justice system of young white youths, young Asian youths and young Afro-Caribbean youths. One of its findings was that in areas that were predominantly inhabited by white people, the young males from ethnic minority groups were considered problematic and often targeted by the police, and in areas that were predominantly inhabited by people from ethnic minorities, the white youth were considered to be problematic and often targeted by the police.

The reader might have their own hypotheses as to why this was their finding; however, the study is mentioned here just to point up how complex an issue like this can be. I have used it here to endorse the need for serious empirical investigation of experiences of the whole criminal justice process and its complexities. One conclusion might be that that one example (in this case the murder of Stephen Lawrence) neither proves nor disproves a general rule. From what we know so far, the criminal justice system in England and Wales could equally be charged with the 'offence' of 'institutional sexism' or 'institutional classism'! The important issue being that all of these 'charges' return us to the question of justice with which this chapter began but more importantly the question of whose justice?

CONCLUSION

This chapter has been concerned to unpick the complexity of the criminal justice system within the framework of trying to develop what it is that interests criminologists about the criminal justice system. Hopefully, this has drawn attention to a number of issues of criminological concern from how the criminal justice system works, whether or not that works in a fair way, what the patterns of decision-making within the criminal justice system look like and whether or not anything can be learned from other jurisdictions with respect to those practices. Moreover, some criminologists also concern themselves with the professionals involved in the criminal justice system and how they do their work. This has been especially the case with policing and prisons, for example, though less so with the judiciary. In this last respect, there is still much interesting work to be done. However, one of the over-riding questions of criminological concern is: what works? What kind of policy works for whom under what circumstances? Whether that is within the context of a greater use of prison or an increased involvement of the victim of crime within criminal justice decision-making. This preoccupation with what works also runs through the next chapter. This is concerned with crime prevention.

EXERCISE

The figures below are taken from a report compiled by the Fawcett Society, a UK organization whose main focus is to campaign for the equality of women, including within the criminal justice system as offenders, victims and professionals. The data below is about women working in the criminal justice system.

Facts on female staff in the criminal justice system

- In 2008, only 24% of police officers in England and Wales were female, compared with 64% of all police staff.
- In 2008, only 12% of officers at the rank of Chief Inspector and above were female, compared with 27% of women at constable rank.
- In March 2008, there were 29 female members of the Association of Chief Police Officers, out of a total of 209.
- A 1993 police survey, with a response rate of 65%, found that nearly all the policewomen participating in the survey had experienced some form of sexual harassment from policemen. In addition, 3 out of 10 policewomen had been subjected to offensive insults or unwanted touching and 1 in 5 were pestered for unwanted dates.
- 66% of Crown Prosecution Service staff are female, but they are concentrated in more junior positions.

- There are 13 female Chief Crown Prosecutors out of a total of 42.
- 44.3% of practicing solicitors are female.
- 66.5% of practising barristers are men and 33.5% are women. 91% of Queen's Counsels (QCs) are men, and only 9% are women.
- Males solicitors earn on average £19,000 more than females.
- There is only one woman judge out of 12 in the House of Lords and three women out of 37 in the Court of Appeal. Women represent 14.02% of High Court Judges, 13.98% of Circuit Judges and around half of all magistrates.
- Overall, in 2008, 19% of the judiciary were female. This has increased from 16.9% in 2005, 15.8% in 2004, 14.9% in 2003, 14.5% in 2002 and 14.1% in 2001.
- 41% of the new judges appointed from 2005 to 2006 were female.
- Within the National Offender Management Service, five of the ten Regional Offender Managers are women, as is the Chief Executive.
- 35.9% of Prison Service staff are female.
- 25% of Prison Service staff at Operational Senior Manager grades are female, but 77% of administrative staff are female.
- The leaving rate is 9% per year for female Prison Service staff, as compared with the overall leaving rate of 6%.
- 23% of prison governors are female, while only one of the eleven Prison Service Area Managers is female.
- At the end of 2006, women made up 67.53% of the probation workforce.
- Women account for 68.34% of Probation Officers and 89.53% of Administrative Support Staff but only 33.58% of board members. 47.5% of Chief Officers in the Probation Service are female.

(The Fawcett Society 2010)

In the light of these data, think about the following questions:

- In what ways, if at all, do you think this ratio of women to men in the workforce within the criminal justice system might impact on how justice is delivered?
- Will that impact look the same at all points in the criminal justice system?
- Given what we know about offending behaviour from Chapter 3, if this pattern is put alongside the figures here, does that mean that crime is men's work?

RECOMMENDATIONS FOR FURTHER READING

A good general introduction to the criminal justice system is to be found in P. Joyce (2006) *Crime and the Criminal Justice System* (second edition) (Cullompton, Devon: Willan). A very user-friendly edited collection by Anthea Hucklesby and Azrini Wahidin (eds) (2009) is *Criminal Justice* (Oxford: Oxford University Press). This has an online resource centre associated with it. Indeed using the Internet for access to information and up-to-date statistics about the various agencies discussed here would be a fruitful exercise. For those of you interested in the more general concept of justice, B. Hudson (2003) *Justice in the Risk Society* (London: Sage) provides an excellent review and critique of the debates, though it is fairly advanced reading so be warned!

8

CRIME PREVENTION

This chapter will consider some issues relating to crime prevention. The reader will recall that Chapter 1 placed a good deal of emphasis on understanding and appreciating the nature of criminology as a 'modern' discipline. This emphasis stresses the link between the things that concern criminology and criminologists and the desire to influence the way in which society responds to social problems, in this case the social problem being crime. Put more simply, criminologists do not just want to know about crime, many of them also want to be involved in developing policies that will help prevent crime. However, the link between knowing something about crime and devising policies that will help prevent it is not always simple or straightforward. In this chapter, we shall be exploring some of the difficulties associated with policy formation. We shall also be looking to understand some of the developments in crime prevention policy over the last 30 years and the links between them and criminology. In so doing we shall be re-visiting the distinction that was made in earlier chapters between crimes of the streets, crime behind closed doors and crimes of the suites.

INTRODUCTION

In this chapter, we shall consider the key trends in crime prevention that have occurred over the last 30 years and we shall explore their links with different strands of criminological thought. More importantly, however, this chapter will be just as concerned to demonstrate what has been made visible and invisible within these trends. In other words, the reader will be asked to think about what kinds of crimes policy trends have paid attention to and why. Thus, reinforcing another theme from Chapter 1: the importance to criminology of thinking critically about policy and the evidence used to support it. But first, it is important to say something about what is assumed by the idea of crime prevention.

WHAT DO WE MEAN BY PREVENTION?

In general terms, 'prevention' is taken to be a 'good thing'. Whether with respect to health, poverty or crime, prevention is assumed to be a good thing because social problems are seen to be bad things. However, in any context understanding prevention involves two connected processes: being able to predict the outcome of a chain of events and then being able to devise a way of intervening with or altering that predicted outcome. Within criminology crime prevention implies that we can identify the cause(s) of crime and on the basis of this devise policy that can stop crime from happening. (For those of you who have managed to make it this far through this book, you should already be aware of what a tall order this is!) The ever changing nature of crime, and the ways in which it is committed, indicate how complicated a relationship of this may be. Nevertheless, policy makers and politicians, sometimes informed by criminologists and sometimes not, spend a good deal of time being pre-occupied with crime prevention. In recent years, though it has become more popular to talk of crime reduction that has latterly been translated into community safety. This change in terminology sends out the message that the possibility of preventing crime; that is eradicating it as a social problem looks increasingly less likely, but we may be able to reduce it, that is manage it better as a social problem or make people feel better about it. The reader will undoubtedly make up his or her own mind on whether or not this is likely to be the case!

As this chapter unfolds it will become clear that there are different ways in which crime prevention is understood and subsequently acted upon. Ken Pease (2002), an internationally recognized criminologist who has frequently worked within the crime prevention area, argues that there are three broad approaches to the cause of crime. We have used his terms earlier in this book but to reiterate them here they are psyche, opportunity and structure and they all articulate different ways of thinking about crime prevention (reduction).

- Those who think that crime is caused by the criminal mind (psyche) might opt for solutions that emphasize the importance of deterrence or incapacitation.
- Those who adopt the view that circumstances lead to criminal behaviour (opportunity) look for solutions in changing the social and/or physical setting in which crime occurs.
- The structural approach tends to adopt the position that crime prevention can only be achieved if efforts are made to alleviate social and economic inequalities.

So, even from this brief review, it can be seen that the relationship between understanding the causes of crime and the kinds of policies that might flow from that understanding can be very varied. Despite this variety, different ways of thinking about this relationship have been popular at different points in time, so before it is possible to discuss the viability or otherwise of different policies, it will be useful to develop an overall picture of the trends in crime prevention over the last 30 years and what has been learned from them. Much of what follows is implicitly informed by the criminological and policy question: what works?

TRENDS IN CRIME PREVENTION

Over recent times, there have been five identifiable strategies deployed to tackle crime each with a different focus on where the cause of crime lies. These are not mutually exclusive strategies and frequently exist side by side, but they have varied in their political popularity. These are:

- offender-centred strategies;
- victim-centred strategies;
- environment-centred strategies;

- community-centred strategies;
- integration strategies.

In this section, we shall discuss some of the key themes within each of these.

OFFENDER-CENTRED STRATEGIES

As the label implies, crime prevention work under this heading focuses on the individual offender as both the cause and the cure for crime. Under this heading it is possible to situate all those initiatives that can be loosely grouped together under the 'prison works' heading. The view that prison works embraces the idea that prison acts as either a deterrent to crime or as a means of incapacitating the offender. As Ken Pease says prison 'acts as a quarantine for the criminally contagious'. This view of the preventive role of prison is most frequently associated with those who adopt a tough political stance on law and order that appeals to a wide range of people, including some feminists who favour a tough stance on domestic violence, for example. There is, of course, another view of the preventive role of the prison, not focused on its deterrent role but its rehabilitative role. In this view, prison can provide rehabilitation for the offender through learning or behavioural work with individual offenders. (The focus on the psyche as indicated by Pease above.) Such offender-centred strategies might also include the popularly labelled '**zero tolerance**' campaigns.

ZERO TOLERANCE

Zero tolerance has its origins in North America and it is possible to trace two sources of its origin: one rooted in feminist campaigns on violence against women and one rooted in the 'broken windows' thesis of two North American criminologists Wilson and Kelling (1982).

Feminist campaigns carrying the zero tolerance label have their origins in Canada in the aftermath of the murder of 14 female engineering students in Montreal in 1989. Subsequently imported to Edinburgh in 1992 and latterly other places, this version of zero tolerance has a number of policy characteristics but is focused on violence against women and children and has a strong punitive stance.

No violence against women and children is to be tolerated regardless of age, class, ethnicity or ability. However, it is a view that equally argues that policies addressing women's and children's needs across and between different agencies should be co-ordinated alongside a willingness for such policies to be backed by resources. Arguably, these campaigns have been quite successful in raising public awareness of the problem of violence against women and children.

The 'broken windows' variant of zero tolerance addresses somewhat different concerns and it is this version that has become particularly popular with both local and national politicians in the United Kingdom. Wilson and Kelling (1982: 32) argued:

> A piece of property is abandoned, weeds grow up, a window is smashed. Adults stop scolding rowdy children; the children, emboldened become more rowdy. Families move out; unmarried adults move in. Teenagers gather in front of the corner store. The merchant asks them to move, they refuse. Fights occur. Litter accumulates.

This view of crime suggests that such behaviours make an area vulnerable to crime, and if left unchecked, lead inevitably to urban and neighbourhood decline. However, the empirical evidence in support of their thesis was ambivalent. There does appear to be some relationship between what Wilson and Kelling call 'incivilities' and the fear of crime, but it is quite difficult to map causal connections between what would now be called anti-social behaviour, crime proper and urban decline because a range of other factors are also likely to come in to play such as the housing market, demographic changes, the job market, local road building policies and so on. All these kinds of changes have their different and differential impact on the rise and fall of particular localities.

These issues notwithstanding, Wilson and Kelling made the case that the police had a key role to play in warding off further decline by policing disorder, the rowdy, the prostitutes and those causing 'trouble'. Though again there is little acknowledgement of what happens when the disorderly are moved on; where, for example, are disorderly people moved to? Whilst Young (1997) argued quite cogently that this reflected a view of the 'social as simple' offering a 'quick fix' to quite complex problems, policing disorder through zero tolerance has proved to be very popular.

There are a number of lessons for the budding criminologists to think about here.

1. Not all criminological ideas are 'soft' on the offender. Think about the implications of the punitive stance of feminism and the disorder focus for policing from Wilson and Kelling.
2. Support for policies is often based on a partial reading of the evidence, and neither a criminologist nor anyone else has any power to influence that reading.
3. Reasoned critiques of policies can be frequently ignored.
4. The political will to move policies in one direction rather than another can sometimes override what might be considered reasonable.
5. Policies sometimes take on a life of their own regardless of the evidence that may or may not support their implementation.
6. There is very little criminology, per se, in support of zero tolerance policies yet they have consistently secured popular support.
7. None of the above necessarily means that zero tolerance policies will not work anywhere but no one really knows where, when and how they might work because of 1–6 above

In addition, there is another view of crime prevention that focuses on the offender that is sociological in orientation rather than psychological. This kind of offender-centred approach is found in the work of the youth justice system and social work that can be very focused on getting young offenders especially to make amends for their offence as a way of getting them to understand the impact that their offence has on their victim and/or the community. Here we shall discuss this version of offender-centred strategies under 'Integration strategies' as this focus derives from the important impact that restorative justice has had in more recent years on criminal justice systems in different jurisdictions.

So, offender focused work can take different forms, however, given the rate at which some countries send offenders to prison (see Chapter 7), it seems to be the case that some societies embrace the prison works view much more readily than others. Our next heading takes the victim as the focus of policy intervention.

VICTIM-CENTRED STRATEGIES

It might seem a little odd to talk of victim-centred crime prevention strategies, but the heading is intended to capture the increasing attention that has been paid to the victim of crime over the last 30 years, not only in terms of the impact of crime but also in terms of how the support of the victim might be harnessed in relation to crime prevention. Under this heading it is possible to situate all of that victim avoidance advice with which we have all become very familiar. For example, next time you pass your local police station or public library take the time to look at the range of crime prevention leaflets available and ask yourself the following questions:

- Who do they suggest in responsible for crime?
- Who do they suggest might help prevent crime?
- What kind of crime are they concerned with?
- What kind of prevention strategies do they suggest?

Chances are you will come across leaflets ranging from mobile phone theft, to burglary to keeping safe at night. Many of these leaflets are directed at the ordinary member of the public and what they can do to prevent crime happening to them. It is in this sense that they are victim centred, directing our attention to victimization avoidance. The increasing attention that has been paid to the way in which everyday behaviour affords opportunities for criminal behaviour is part of what David Garland (2001), a criminological theorist from the United Kingdom, has called the '**responsibilization** thesis'; that is the ever widening web of individuals and organizations involved in sharing the responsibility for crime prevention.

The focus on what it is that members of the public do to make crime easier or harder to commit and trying to encourage the public to reduce the opportunities available for such criminal behaviour has links with our third crime prevention strategy: environment centred.

ENVIRONMENT-CENTRED STRATEGIES

This approach to crime prevention focuses on the offence rather than the offender. It has two strands to it: those policies concerned with target hardening and those concerned with what is referred to as 'designing out crime'. Again target hardening is something with which we are now all familiar: fitting steering wheel locks to cars, window locks on properties, introducing chip and pin credit cards and security measures at airports are all good examples of target hardening. Designing out crime looks for ways in which housing estates or individual buildings can be better designed to either increase means of surveillance and/or reduce areas for which no one feels responsible. In some respects closed-circuit television (CCTV) systems straddle both ideas offering a technical fix in terms of increased surveillance to target both crime and disorderly behaviour. Indeed, it would be rare to find a shopping centre or a car park now that did not have a CCTV system in place. Yet, despite the popularity of CCTV, what it actually achieves is still subject to some considerable debate.

Think back to where we started with this chapter and in particular the idea that in order to prevent something you needed to have a fairly clear idea of what caused it in the first place. And, while the presence of CCTV might have an impact on the particular location where it is installed, there is no reason to think that this means that crime or disorderly behaviour has been reduced or eliminated because the crimes or behaviours might be committed somewhere else. Criminologists refer to this as the problem of displacement.

There are four different kinds of potential displacement as a result of increased surveillance such as CCTV.

Temporal – crime is committed at a different time
Spatial – crime is committed in a different place
Tactical – crime is committed in a different way
Target – different kinds of crime are committed

So although CCTV offers an increasingly attractive and popular technical fix for crime, and we are all increasingly tolerant of the ever-present cameras, it does not necessarily impact on crime itself other than possibly in the much localized area in which it is situated. Given the problem of displacement presented earlier, the reader might like to think about what kinds of crimes are targeted by CCTV and what kinds of crimes are not. You might also like to reflect on the extent to which the problem of displacement also applies to zero tolerance policies. Our next crime prevention trend focuses on a different kind of surveillance not that of technology but that of the community.

COMMUNITY-CENTRED STRATEGIES

There are four ways in which the community can be harnessed in the interests of crime prevention:

1. the introduction of neighbourhood watch schemes;
2. multi-agency co-operation;
3. a policy focus on community safety;
4. a wider concern with partnerships.

Much of what we have discussed under headings two and three above constitute what is often termed situational crime prevention; that is, they look to manipulate the specific dynamics of particular situations to render them less crime friendly. Community-centred strategies can be generally understood as **social crime prevention** strategies. As such they are looking to manipulate the underlying structural dynamics that make some areas or communities more crime friendly. However, as with situation crime prevention strategies, social ones reflect a range of problematic assumptions. However, before these are considered it will be useful to develop an appreciation of the four types of community-oriented policy listed earlier.

NEIGHBOURHOOD WATCH SCHEMES

Neighbourhood Watch Schemes are now popular both in the United Kingdom and the United States and aim to harness members of the community as the eyes and ears of the police with two objectives in mind. The first objective is to increase the kind of surveillance that routinely takes place within communities. In other words, the idea is to heighten the kind of watching and noticing that frequently occurs within localities but with a view to encourage people to report any suspicious behaviour that such activities generate to the police. The second objective lies in the hope that increased surveillance of the kind just described will also result in an increase of social cohesion in communities so that people will themselves feel able to challenge behaviour that is problematic for them.

MULTI-AGENCY CO-OPERATION

Multi-agency co-operation, as the title implies, starts from the premise that crime prevention is not the sole responsibility of the police but should be shared by all the agencies whose task is to work within any particular community. So attention is focused on how the police, social services, youth justice and education might work together within a particular locality to tackle the crime problems that an area has. Contemporarily, such multi-agency co-operation is probably taken as routine practice in most jurisdictions with respect to questions of child abuse and increasingly in relation to domestic violence, whether it works or not is another issue.

COMMUNITY SAFETY

A policy focus on community safety shares some of the same rationale as multi-agency co-operation but is more likely to start by finding out what people who live in a particular locality think the problems are in their area and develop policies accordingly. This is sometimes referred to as a 'bottom-up' approach as distinct from the 'top-down' approach of multi-agency co-operation. As the label itself implies in using the term 'safety' there is the potential for community safety strategies to operate with a much broader agenda than that of criminal behaviour as defined by the law and are just as concerned to get members of the community involved in working in the interests of their community as they are to involve the 'professionals'. Put very simply, community safety could be viewed as a mixture of the ideas of neighbourhood watch with multi-agency co-operation.

PARTNERSHIPS

The idea of partnership takes the notion of harnessing the community one stage further by both broadening and deepening the range of groups encouraged to take responsibility for crime prevention in a particular locality. In the United Kingdom, the special inclusion of local authorities in taking responsibility for crime prevention affords an opportunity for the clear and more direct involvement of those who are locally and democratically elected to have a say in how to tackle local problems as does the inclusion of the business community.

So, in a sense the idea of partnership working builds incrementally on the other three ideas discussed earlier.

Each of these policy themes can be found to have had a different kind of influence in different countries. Most countries seem to have embraced some form of multi-agency co-operation, for example, with neighbourhood watch being favoured in the United Kingdom and the United States and partnership working now a legal requirement in the United Kingdom. Where countries differ in their deployment of these kinds of policy strategies lies within their respective different understandings of community, and the relationship between the citizen and the state in their respective responsibilities for social problems. Given that criminologists are interested in what works in relation to crime prevention policy they are, as a consequence, also interested in what might work in different communities and what the respective role is of the citizen and the state so we shall consider the importance of each of these questions in turn. First of all, what do we understand by community?

Think about the following questions, make a note of your answers and then compare what you have said with the issues discussed below.

1. What do you understand by community?
2. Do you live in a community?
3. Write down what makes you think that either you live in a community or that you do not.
4. What other groups of people do you think live in your community?
5. Who is included and excluded from this list?
6. If you were to make a list of the things that people think are a problem in your community what would that list look like, what would you do about those problems and whose help would you ask for to solve those problems?

If you have tried the exercise above you may have got a sense of how difficult it is to define what a community is and then go on to design a policy that might work in a community. Quite some time ago, Peter Wilmott (1987), a British sociologist, commented that community was a 'seductive' word. Rather like prevention that was discussed at the beginning of this chapter, community carries with it all kinds of positive connotations, but what it actually means is a little more problematic. Wilmott offers three ways in which people use the term community: to refer to an area (territorial meaning), to refer to things that people have in common (an interest group meaning) and to refer to a sense of belonging (an attachment meaning). (In your own notes you may find traces of all of these meanings.) In criminology it is possible to find other ways of thinking about community: as disorganized (see the discussion of sociological positivism in Chapter 1), as disadvantaged (as localities in which the means to achieve the goals of society are not available) and as frightened (as localities in which the fear of crime is greater than the problem of crime itself).

So it can be seen that whilst the notion of community conjures all kinds of 'feel good' factors associated with sense of place, identity, family ties or neighbourliness, when it comes to translating these 'feel good' factors into policy not only is it difficult, it is a process that involves differentiating those 'communities' needing intervention and those that do not (hence the criminological use of terms such as disorganized, disadvantaged or frightened). Moreover, some would argue that in contemporary times that communities are characterized by quite different factors than the ones listed earlier. Jock Young (2001), for example, suggests that communities are now so 'de-territorialized' and no longer rooted in face-to-face interaction that they are increasingly characterized by fragmentation, separation and short-term relationships rather than a sense of place or neighbourliness. Indeed, communities may exist in quite different forms with different senses of belonging such as Internet chat rooms.

This brief discussion highlights how complicated the idea of community can be and therefore how difficult it might be to formulate policies that might work within any particular community. It also highlights a further range of questions that are worth thinking about:

- If the policy concern is with social crime prevention, for what kind of community and in what way?
- If the concern is to intervene in some communities, are some of them pathologized (made different and problematic); if so why are they, and are they blamed or not for the problems they have?
- Are all communities comprised of the citizens who all have the same personal and economic resources, free of intimidation, to put policies into effect? (Think about the kinds of

localities where being the 'eyes and ears' of the police might be problematic and where it might not be.)

- What is the relationship between local authorities and national authorities in providing for communities with problems and how might this be managed?

The third and fourth questions listed above encourage us to think about at least two other questions. The first encourages us to think about the more general question of how different societies present a different relationship between the citizen and the state. For example, fairly recent research from France, Germany and Italy suggests that not only does community carry with it different meanings in those societies, they also operate with different assumptions about who is responsible for what at the local level, at a regional level and at the level of the state, with some evidence suggesting that the state has retained more responsibility for social problems in those societies than has been the case in the United Kingdom. Understanding these differences might interest a criminologist in trying to understand what might work or not work in the United Kingdom. The second question encourages us to think about whether or not all members of a community have the same economic, social and personal resources to participate in community life and as a consequence participate in crime prevention initiatives. This re-introduces the importance of understanding power relationships in our thinking about crime prevention that we shall return to shortly. Our final trend in crime prevention I have labelled integration strategies.

INTEGRATION STRATEGIES

Integration strategies largely derive from the work of John Braithwaite (whose facts about crime we discussed in Chapter 4) and take the form of seeking ways to re-integrate the offender back into the community usually with the involvement of the victim in some way. These strategies are popularly termed 'restorative justice'. What is actually meant by restorative justice, however, is not very clear. It seems to be quite an elastic idea with one central feature: it looks to ways of bringing the victim and offender together so that the victim might better understand what has happened to them and have a say in what happens to the offender, and also so that the offender can appreciate the impact that their behaviour has had, be encouraged to make amends and hopefully behave differently in the future. The criminological legacy of this policy is found in the work of John Braithwaite and others in Australia who were concerned to develop ways of 'shaming' the offender, and through working with them, and the people that their behaviour had had an impact on (whether that be an individual or the wider community), find ways to reintegrate them into the community. However, all kinds of initiatives that endeavour to bring the victim and the offender together now carry the label 'restorative' and its popularity is echoed in developments in the United States, Australia and New Zealand. Why this has become so popular is worth reflecting on.

At the academic level it would be difficult to deny the powerful influence that the ideas of Braithwaite (1989, 2002) have had on capturing the policy imagination around the notion of the 're-integration' of the offender. It is difficult to identify a contemporary debate on these issues that does not start without referring to his work. However, despite the international recognition given to this work, we are only just beginning to develop some awareness of what Daly (2002) has called the 'real story' of restorative justice. Daly offers a detailed discussion of the myths of restorative justice. One of these myths is that restorative justice is not punitive but a soft option (see also Dignan 2002). However, the power of the myths of concern here is perhaps most tellingly revealed in this comment:

> Far from wilting in the face of controversy and resistance as so many other justice innovations of recent vintage have, restorative justice appears to be trading the temerity of cautious reform for a kind of *swagger*. Whether such self-confidence is justified, time will tell. It will however be very difficult to ignore.
>
> (McEvoy *et al.* 2002: 475. My emphasis)

So, while there may be quite detailed questions of evidence to be sought out on what works, for whom, under what conditions in relation to this particular way of dealing with victims and offenders (some of the myths that are sympathetically unpacked by Daly, see also inter alia Morris 2002), it is the question of RJ's *swagger* that is problematic. So where does this come from, what does it look like and how might this impact on the question of criminological research and vice versa? Arguably, to understand this, it is necessary to appreciate two further questions: the question of how criminal justice policies travel and the question of what the policy implementation process looks like. Each of these question are important for criminology and anyone aspiring to become a criminologist and we shall address each of them in the conclusion to this book, so it will be useful for the reader to refer back to this discussion then. For the purposes of this chapter, it will now be of value to return to an appreciation of what is hidden by these trends in crime prevention that we have discussed so far.

STRUCTURAL DIMENSIONS TO CRIME PREVENTION: CRIME OF THE STREETS, CRIME OF THE SUITES AND CRIME BEHIND CLOSED DOORS

The above heading is a fairly simplistic way of trying to capture the full range and diversity of the contexts in which criminal behaviour and consequently criminal victimization are likely to occur. However, hidden within it is a strong message about not only the diverse nature of crime but also about the relative visibility of underlying power relationships within those contexts especially in relation to crime prevention. Traditionally, much activity in relation to crime prevention has been focused on the crimes that people see and know about (crimes of the streets). In more recent years, increasing attention has been focused on that crime that people see less of and often know less about: crime behind closed doors (think particularly about child abuse, domestic violence or abuse of the elderly). Even less attention, in crime prevention terms especially, is paid to the kind of criminal activity multi-national business corporations might engage in (crimes of the suites).

In this chapter, we have so far paid attention to the different developments in thinking about crime and crime prevention that have fuelled different policy initiatives in different countries without paying too much attention to the question of what kind of crime these policies have assumed to be the problem. For the most part it is perhaps fair to say that those policies have frequently worked with the idea that street crime, burglary and car crime are problematic to people and have focused their attention in this way. Indeed, it is fair to say that for the victim of such crimes, they are certainly problematic. However, within that activity, especially in the development of multi-agency and partnership working (where it has to be said that there has always been a concern with child abuse), different foci of activity have developed. These developments have tried to address issues relating to the less obvious types of criminal activity such as domestic violence and/or racially motivated crimes. These we might loosely think of as 'crimes behind closed doors' so it will be useful to think about the kinds of issues that thinking about these kinds of crimes raises for crime prevention policy.

CRIMES BEHIND CLOSED DOORS: COMMUNITY, GENDER, ETHNICITY AND CRIME PREVENTION

In our discussion on community earlier, the question was raised as to whether all members of any particular community share the same economic power or have the same personal resources to participate in community life including crime prevention. In your own thinking about community, you may also have concluded that communities are made up of different groups whose socio-structural position means that they participate differently in their locality. For example, think about the position of young unemployed people in your community as compared with those who have worked all their life and are now retired. These differences, in relation to age and employability, put them in different positions in relation to their community. The same argument can also be made along the lines of gender and ethnicity. In this section then we shall consider what kind of crime prevention activity has tried to take these kinds of structural positions into account.

GENDER AND CRIME PREVENTION

Thinking about the gendered potential of crime prevention can lead to thinking about a number of different kinds of crimes. Rape especially comes to mind where much advice is directed towards the different ways in which women can keep themselves safe from rape. For example, not walking home alone, taking a registered taxi service or preferably a female only taxi service, not accepting drinks from people you do not know very well and so on. All of which can sound either rather patronizing or common sense or, if you think a little more deeply, rather miss the point because the majority of rapes occur between people who know each other. Nevertheless, much crime prevention advice with respect to rape takes this form. The questions that this raises in terms of crime prevention are returned to below, however another crime in which there has been some crime prevention-related activity in recent years has directed attention towards the issues of domestic violence. Women working both within and outside of the feminist movement have made strenuous efforts since the 1960s to make people more aware of the kinds of violence perpetrated for the most part by men on their female partners. However, it has only been over the last 20 years or so that that campaigning work has been taken on board and recognized as an issue requiring more than the intervention of feminist-informed volunteers.

The nature and extent of domestic violence was discussed a little in Chapter 3. Needless to say that far from being an abnormal crime it is for some people the normal and routine experience of their everyday lives. What follows is a fairly long quote from a British researcher, Hazel Genn (1988), who was involved in the research that informed the establishment of the British Crime Survey and she has this to say about some people's experience of crime:

> Becoming interested in what appeared to be examples of "victim-proneness" in one geographical area, I visited one particular block on a council estate over a number of months, tape-recorded interviews with several families, their neighbours and friends, and eventually moved in for a short period with the woman who had suffered the greatest number of victimisations in our survey. The views which I formed after this period of intensive observation have a substantial bearing not simply on the experiences of multiple victims but on the limitations of victim surveys that are currently designed . . . What also became apparent was the fact that the events reported to us in the survey were not regarded as particularly remarkable. They were just part of life.
>
> (92–3)

The idea that criminal victimization is 'just part of life' is a very powerful one in coming to terms with understanding some peoples' experiences of crime in general and women's experiences of domestic violence in particular. The same observation might also be made of racially motivated crime. (Indeed this is an issue that we shall return to at the end of this section.) However, policy responses in this area have been largely informed by developments in North America, where based on research by two American criminologists, Berk and Sherman published in 1984, much was made of the case for arresting the offender. Moreover, despite follow-up findings published by Sherman *et al.* in 1991 indicating that the case for arrest was not proven, crime prevention policy in the United Kingdom embraced what came to be called the 'pro-arrest stance'.

A Home Office circular published in 1990 and reinforced in 2000 and 2003, clearly stated that domestic violence was to be treated as seriously as violence between strangers and advised all those involved in the criminal justice system to adopt a pro-active stance towards arresting the offender and to look to improve ways in which the victim might be supported. These circulars have been very influential in informing policy and practices across the criminal justice system in the United Kingdom and have more recently been backed up with stronger legislation in civil law. (See for example, the Domestic Violence Act 2004.) Responses to domestic violence, and its priority as a crime, have recently been endorsed through the establishment of Multi-Agency Risk Assessment Conferences (resonant with the multi-agency working commented on earlier) and the establishment of Independent Domestic Violence Advisors. Both initiatives work with the 'at risk' victim to try and devise ways of keeping her safe. The question is do these kinds of initiatives constitute an effective crime prevention response?

It is important to remember that this chapter started by pointing out that to prevent crime it was necessary both to know its cause and to know what might impact on that cause. At this point, the reader might like to re-read this chapter and think about the following questions:

- How would you classify the emphasis in the policy response to domestic violence as outlined earlier: offender centred, victim centred, community centred, environment centred or integration centred? (Remember any particular policy might contain elements of all or none of these.)
- Having classified this policy response, what do you think are the strengths and weaknesses of its approach?

- Again, having classified this policy response, what policy elements are missing from it? Might they be important?
- Do you think that this kind of approach is likely to impact on the nature and extent of domestic violence? (You might like to think about the implications of the quote taken from Genn and cited earlier to develop an answer to this question.) Make a list of the reasons why you think it might and, why you think it might not work.

Hopefully, what the questions above have led you to think about are a number of issues relating to the crime of domestic violence and how to tackle it. Indeed, you may have thought about a number of issues including, who is the object of these policies and whether or not their behaviour is likely to change as a result of interventions of this kind, such as being arrested. Put simply, the evidence suggests that in cases of domestic violence (and rape with which this discussion began) the perpetrators are male and the victims are female. So, one of the questions to be tackled, if we are serious about addressing these kinds of crimes in a preventive way, is male behaviour. In other words, a truly *gender*ed crime prevention policy would tackle both male and female behaviour.

Margaret Shaw, a Canadian sociologist working for the United Nations, devised this list of recommendations published in 2002 as a way of ensuring that gender is fully incorporated into crime prevention policy.

1. The establishment and routine use of disaggregated data and indicators for crime prevention planning and evaluation.
2. Investigating masculinities and gender relationships.
3. Undertaking education and awareness training with men in professional roles, associations and leadership positions on gendered attitudes as well as the links with violence.
4. Recognizing gender-based violence to include male violence against men as well as male violence against women.
5. Greater representation and inclusion of women at all decision-making levels.
6. Integrating gender into strategic safety planning and urban design.
7. Taking account of gender at all stages of local crime-prevention partnership planning.

8. The development of tools for analysis, implementation and evaluation that are sensitive to gender.
9. Incorporating exploratory walk approaches used in safety audits in city-wide community safety audits, and school, institution or work-place settings.
10. Incorporating gender actively into school, youth, recreation and other youth prevention programmes.
11. Actively engaging the media to change stereotypical gender models.

You might like to think about this list and compare it with your earlier one on why current policies on domestic violence may or may not work. However, before we continue to explore some of the underlying problems that this discussion may have led you to think about, a few words about ethnicity and crime prevention.

ETHNICITY AND CRIME PREVENTION

The general complaint frequently made by members of ethnic minority communities whether in the United Kingdom, United States or other countries in Europe is that they are over-policed and under-policed all at the same time. Put simply, this means that in their view they suffer disproportionately from too much attention from the criminal justice authorities when it comes to the question of crime, but when they are the victims of crime they suffer disproportionately from too little attention from the same authorities. Chapter 7 covered some of the issues in relation to this complaint, but for the purposes of the discussion here, it is important to consider, as with the case of gender, whether or not the experience of people from ethnic minorities is similar to other sections of society who might make the same complaint (such as those communities of predominantly poor, unemployed, white people) or whether or not some of their experiences are qualitatively different. It is possible to draw different conclusions to this question but it is important to consider at least two areas in which the experiences of people from ethnic minorities might be qualitatively different and therefore carry different implications for crime prevention policy.

To appreciate the possible significance of the first of these differences, it is useful to think about the 'lived reality' of people from ethnic minorities in similar ways as the Genn quotes about the lived reality of living with violence. It is important to remember that for many ethnic minority people their routine daily life is constituted by racial harassment to such an extent that it becomes their normal experience. Basia Spalek (2006) working in the United Kingdom refers to this as 'spirit injury'. Despite efforts made from different criminal justice agencies and the law to recognize such 'racial' incidents, the question remains how to tackle/prevent what has become normal for people?

The second of the possible differences for ethnic minority people lies with their experiences of the criminal justice system itself as an institution. Since the murder of Stephen Lawrence in the United Kingdom in 1993, much has been made of the issue of 'institutional racism' within that jurisdiction: the question of the 'collective failure' of an organization to provide an appropriate service to all members of a community. This issue has provoked much debate within the United Kingdom as it is clearly the case that such embedded racism must permeate all institutions not just the criminal justice ones, the crime prevention question that might flow from this kind of awareness is neither simple nor straightforward. However, it does ask us to think very carefully about whether or not crime prevention looks the same for all sections of a community, and whether or not policies have appropriately considered other perspectives, as with the case of gender.

Summary

So thinking about 'crime behind closed doors' or perhaps more generally, that kind of crime that tends to be the less visible kind of crime, raises all sorts of questions about crime prevention policy, what kinds of crimes it is intended to effect and how it might work as well as by implication, all kinds of questions about what is meant by community and community safety and whether or not the idea of community safety means the same thing to all sections of a community. As a result, the reader might like to think about the following questions:

- When people talk about community safety, whose community and whose version of safety is being invoked?
- Do those terms mean the same for all members of a community?

- What other dimensions to a community (in addition to gender and ethnicity) might make a difference to the kind of crime prevention policy that is prioritized?
- Finally, in thinking about 'difference' that the previous discussion has encouraged, are we in danger of exaggerating the differences between people and ignoring the similarities in what people expect from their routine daily lives? What might those similarities look like?

However, there is one further structural dimension to thinking about community, crime and crime prevention that the previous discussion does not make very obvious. That structural dimension raises again the question of 'crime of the suites'.

STRUCTURAL DIMENSIONS TO COMMUNITY CRIME PREVENTION: CRIME OF THE SUITES

As has been indicated elsewhere in the book, crimes of the suites, all that kind of crime that might be associated with the world of business, whether that be the local builder taking a cash in hand payment to ensure the early completion of a job or 'insider dealing' of the stock market, receive much less attention from criminologists, politicians and policy makers. Nevertheless, this is an area of crime and criminal activity that carries 'costs' even if those costs are frequently hidden from view. What such costs look like is not of concern here, but what is of concern is the hidden nature of this kind of crime, and given its hidden nature whether or not crime prevention policy could impinge upon it.

In an interesting and novel consideration of the development of *crime reduction* programmes emanating from the 1998 Crime and Disorder Act in England and Wales, Whyte, a British criminologist, conducted a survey of the nature and content of those crime reduction strategies in the North West of England. His study revealed the top target issues for the 26 crime and the disorder partnerships in that region, which are provided in Table 8.1.

As Whyte notes this list replicates almost exactly the Home Office's list of priorities in a part of the country where there is a

Table 8.1: Targets of crime reduction strategies in the North West of England

Vehicle crime	26
Burglary	24
Drug-related crime	15
Violent crime	15
Anti-social behaviour	12
Youth offender causing a nuisance	12
Road safety/speeding	11
Domestic violence	8
Robbery	8
Fear of crime	7

Source: From Whyte (2004b).

recognized problem with other kinds of transgressions. For example, Whyte reports that in that same area

- The Environment Agency instituted 98 prosecutions in 2001–02: one for flood defence offences, one for industrial process offences, two for radioactive substance offences, 62 for waste offences and 32 for water quality offences.
- In that same region there is one of the most heavily concentrated sites of chemical production in western Europe, where just two plants release about 40 per cent of all the factory produced cancer causing chemical in the United Kingdom into the air every year.

Whyte's argument is that there is no logical reason why activities such as these should not be incorporated into local crime and disorder partnership agendas, and yet, despite their actual and potential impact on local communities, they are not. Given what you have read in this chapter and the previous chapter about this kind of crime you might like to think about why this is the case. In particular think about:

- What is and is not recognized as crime?
- Who is and who is not recognized as a criminal offender?

- What is the role of the victim here?
- Why do locally constructed agendas take the form that they do?
- Who and what is included and excluded from those agendas?
- What messages do those agendas convey about concepts of partnership, community and safety?
- What role, if any, might the media play in all of this?

CONCLUSION

This chapter has been concerned to offer an understanding of the ways in which different thinking about crime links with different policy agendas and to encourage some critical thinking about those links and the kinds of agendas that are constructed. It is important to remember that the chapter started with a fairly simple framework for making sense of the links that we have been concerned with. Using the labels offered by Pease (2002), if you think the psyche is the cause of crime then you will think of some way of dealing with the offender, if you think that circumstance results in crime you will try to reduce those opportunities; if you think that structure is the cause of the problem then you might focus on a deeper understanding of the nature of social structure and longer-term strategies designed to impact on that. Throughout the concern is with the question: what works? How might the nature and extent of crime be reduced? Despite the difficulties associated with putting together an answer to this question, whether that is offered in relation to psyche, circumstance or structure, it is nevertheless one that still drives the crime prevention/reduction agenda and still drives much criminology.

EXERCISE

The reader might like to take a few minutes to read the following passage taken from a UK government sponsored crime reduction panel that was put together as a part of the government's forward planning process called 'Foresight'. That panel produced a report in 2001 called 'Just Around the Corner' and in its appendices it offers two scenarios for the future of social life in the twenty-first century.

Below is a brief summary of one of them for you to think about. If you want to access the report in full then you can get it from www. foresight.gov.uk.

'Meg wakes to the sound of an alarm. It is the Brightlands perimeter siren. A few minutes later she is reassured to hear to "all clear". She doesn't stop to think that both sounds are perhaps a little too familiar these days. Joe doesn't stir. He drank too much again last night and is out cold. They seem to argue more since they moved in together but that was the only way they could afford to move to Brightlands – "the walled estate where people care". They were lucky to get in given the demanding approval criteria of the other neighbours. If Joe's tag (for a disorder offence 10 years ago) had not been removed some months earlier they wouldn't have been allowed to buy there but with one in two men now having a criminal conviction by their 30s, even Brightlands residents cannot be too picky. Both work from home but this is a necessity not a luxury. Neither wants to use the poor public transport with its high levels of violence to get to work. While the roads are safer they are not really safe. Drivers don't relax until they re-enter a "walled" areas – either another estate or the business parks (for those who can't work from home). Road users are therefore often tense and aggressive. All public space is potentially more hostile than before. People prefer the isolation offered by their personal technology systems and increasingly resent being disturbed, or even spoken to in public. Personal radar systems and security devices are relied upon for protection. All this means people in the walled estates don't venture out much. . .'

(26)

- What do you think of this scenario?
- Can you identify any elements in it that are already present in our response to crime? Make a list of them and think about the advantages and disadvantages associated with them that are implied in this scenario.
- Do you think that this scenario applies everywhere? (E.g. think about urban and rural differences.)

- Do you think this scenario applies in all countries? What elements of it might and what elements might not? Why might there be the differences that you identify?
- What is implied in this scenario about social relationships as a result of increasing preoccupation with security?
- What does it say about community? Do you think this is a trend in your community?
- Whose security and whose protection are presumed to be important by this scenario?

Of course you might think that the scene painted above is a rather pessimistic view of the future and the kind of society that might exist then. However, what it clearly points to is the importance of thinking through the consequences not only in the short-term but also in the long-term of the kinds of policies and practices that are being routinely put into place as a way of combating crime. The routine acceptance of CCTV in the United Kingdom and the United States, for example, is not so prevalent in continental Europe though that does vary. So it is important to be aware that there are other decisions that politicians, policy makers and criminologists could be making in exploring the nature and impact of crime and what there is to be done about it. Part of the role of academic criminology is to explore the alternatives and in doing so raise questions about what might or might not work, where and when.

RECOMMENDATIONS FOR FURTHER READING

The literature on crime prevention is now quite vast but a sound analysis of recent developments in crime prevention is provided by G. Hughes (1998) *Understanding Crime Prevention*. Karen Evans (2010) offers a useful and critical introduction in *Crime Prevention* (London: Sage). Some of the dimensions to crime prevention touched upon in this chapter are more fully developed in G. Hughes, E. McLaughlin and J. Muncie (2002) *Crime Prevention and Community Safety*. This offers a much more advanced theoretical and political analysis of developments in crime prevention and is really for the more committed reader, but this book does offer some useful comparative material. A sound overview of community safety and crime prevention is offered by Adam Crawford in M. Maguire, R. Morgan and R. Reiner (2007 fourth edition) *The Oxford Handbook of Criminology* (Oxford: Oxford University Press), though this again might be for the more serious reader. Much can be learned by accessing the kinds of documents that are publicly available to you in your local area; for example, your area's Crime Reduction Strategy Document as required by the 1998 Crime and Disorder Act (in some areas now entitled Crime and Disorder Reduction Strategy). Reading this in the light of the questions raised in this chapter and thinking critically about any crime prevention leaflets and other material you come across is a good exercise for any potential criminologists to engage in.

9

DEVELOPING YOUR CRIMINOLOGICAL IMAGINATION

INTRODUCTION

Hopefully, what you have read so far in this book has made you sensitive to the diversity and range of criminological interests. It should have also made you aware of the differences between media and common sense images of crime, the criminal and the victim, as compared with criminological understandings of these issues. As was said in Chapter 1, criminology as a discipline is peopled by a wide variety of individuals from a wide variety of academic backgrounds tied together by their common interest in crime. However, this interest in crime is not only an academic one. That interest is also an interest in crime as a social problem. In other words (again as you will remember from Chapter 1), it is an interest that is also concerned to look for ways of not only understanding the nature and impact of this social problem but also for ways of alleviating it. Hence, the links between what it is that criminologists study and do, and the question of criminal justice policy. By way of conclusion, this chapter will explore the changing nature of those links in the light of the increasing political nature of criminal justice policy and the changing nature of global relations. To understand some of this, it will be useful to offer a few comments on the growth and development of criminology itself over the last 30 years.

GROWTH IN CRIME? GROWTH IN CRIMINOLOGY?

Those of you reading this book as a way of finding out whether you wish to study criminology further may be surprised to discover that 30 years ago in the United Kingdom there were no undergraduate courses in criminology, though post-graduate training was available. Moreover, at that time the biggest employer of criminologists in the United Kingdom was the Home Office. A brief look at undergraduate university courses now would reveal a very different picture. The first undergraduate course in criminology-related subjects was launched at the University of Northumbria in the late 1980s and since that time such courses teamed with subjects like law, sociology, psychology and cultural studies have blossomed. In addition, of course, during that time in England and Wales, there has been a considerable growth in the kinds of jobs for which a criminology-related qualification might be deemed appropriate. This is particularly the case in the areas of youth justice and community safety. Indeed, the job title of 'Community Safety Officer' did not exist 30 years ago! All of these developments may or may not be related to the changing nature of the crime problem. Indeed, some of them have become especially acute at a time when the officially recorded rate of crime appears to be in decline. (Hopefully, by now the reader knows how problematic statements of the previous kind can prove to be!) Nevertheless, crime as a subject of study, as a subject for media viewing and as an opportunity for many different kinds of employment seems to be a significant feature in contemporary life. In this conclusion, we shall be considering some aspects of these developments. We shall consider three issues in particular.

- First, given the changing nature of society that is just as influenced by global trends as national ones, how has this been reflected within criminology and criminal justice policy?
- Second, given the cultural significance that crime seems to have now, what efforts has criminology made to make sense of this?
- Third, given the events of the twenty-first century that have been global in their impact (in particular, 9/11 New York, 3/11 Madrid, 7/7 London and Mumbai in November 2008), what has criminology got to say (if anything) about these kinds of events?

CRIMINOLOGY, CRIMINAL JUSTICE POLICY AND GLOBAL TRENDS

As was suggested in Chapter 1, criminology traditionally has had, if not a close, at least an informative relationship with criminal justice policy. Much of the early research work conducted by Lombroso and others, for example, were specific in the impact that they had in changing attitudes and practices towards offenders. However, in more recent years, and arguably over the last 30 years in particular, that relationship has become rather more complex. This, in part, is connected to the way in which issues around 'law and order' have become far more central to the political process and have featured in a far more important way in securing the election of governments especially in the United Kingdom. It is also in part the result of governments seeking policy solutions to crime problems from outside of the national domain. This is a feature of the processes of globalization. Newburn (2007: 868–9) reminds us what the key features of globalization are:

- instantaneous communication (crucial here is the role of the Internet), including the ability to communicate in 'real' time;
- the speed of technological development;
- the growth and extensive influence of multinational corporations;
- the move towards a global free market;
- increased movement of people.

Against this backcloth, national governments have looked to other jurisdictions for ways of managing all kinds of social problems (including crime), and in the context of the United Kingdom this has meant more often than not looking to the United States for appropriate policy interventions.

The economic conditions of the early 1980s marked the beginning of what Feeley and Simon (1994) were to call 'actuarial justice'. In the United Kingdom, these economic conditions dictated that the agencies of the criminal justice system were to be subjected to, for the first time, the demands of efficiency, effectiveness and value for money. As a result, not only was the world of business, as its associated management practices, introduced to the criminal justice system (hence actuarial justice) but also agencies were encouraged to look to the management practices of other criminal justice systems in other countries to improve local practices. As Garland (2001) has documented, much of that looking elsewhere has involved, for England and Wales especially, looking west across the Atlantic rather than looking to Europe. This Westward looking barometer has taken its toll on the criminal justice system as a whole in the United Kingdom but particularly from the early 1990s, as all political parties embraced penal populism as one way of securing election to government. The continued rise in the prison population, the use of electronic tagging, zero-tolerance policing, private prisons, are a few examples of this Westward looking agenda. This agenda is particularly evidenced in the United Kingdom in relation to the victim of crime by the in principle embrace of the victim impact statement, popular in the United States and elsewhere, that is discussed in Chapter 7. A significant part of this rising victim policy agenda has been the ever more refined use and development of the criminal victimization survey methodology (referred to in Chapters 2 and 3). However, policies with a global reach, following on from the work of John Braithwaite, have also emanated from Australia and New Zealand in the form of restorative justice. The influence of the restorative justice agenda, in particular, is remarkable. So much so that researchers have commented that, despite the fact that no one seems to have a clear idea of what counts as restorative justice, these are policy initiatives that have a good deal of 'swagger' (McEvoy et al. 2002; see also Chapter 8). Why and how policies that have originated in other parts of the world take route and flourish in particular countries is one aspect of the processes of globalization that is of interest to criminologists.

In 2002, a Special Issue of the journal Criminal Justice was dedicated to exploring the question of how crime policies travel. Reference has already been made to the powerful influence that the work of John Braithwaite has had on foregrounding the value of looking for ways to 'reintegrate' the offender into the community through restorative means. His hypothesis is that in societies where there is a strong commitment to place collective interests over individual interests, there are stronger incentives for people to conform and lower crime rates. His prime example of such a society is Japan. The practical implication of Braithwaite's hypothesis suggests it is necessary to establish mechanisms whereby offenders could be subjected to such collective processes, shamed by them, and subsequently re-integrated into the community with a resultant stronger commitment to those community norms and values (that is, unlikely to reoffend). To date, many examples of such practices have emanated from Australia and New Zealand in the form of 'community conferences' or 'family conferences'. The relative success or failure of such practices is not of concern here; what is of concern is how did such policies travel to England and Wales?

Prior to the election of New Labour in 1997, the youth justice system in England and Wales was subjected to the following criticism:

> The current system for dealing with youth crime is inefficient and expensive, while little is done to deal effectively with juvenile nuisance. The present arrangements are failing young people – who are not being guided away from offending to constructive activities. They are also failing victims . . .
>
> (Audit Commission, 1996: 96)

In the light of this kind of critique and the determination of the new government to be 'tough on crime' and 'tough on the causes of crime', much was made of a reparation scheme for young offenders run by the Thames Valley Police, following the Australian and New Zealand model. As Chief Superintendent, Perry is quoted as saying the following about the scheme: 'While young offenders feel ashamed of what they have done, this allows them to make good and to go back into their community' (Crime Prevention News, 1998: 12).

In the search for models of 'best practice' that has embraced criminal justice practice since the late 1990s, it is of no great surprise that the idea of restoration, celebrated as it was in Thames Valley, was seized with both hands in a political climate bent on success. However, Thames Valley success notwithstanding, no one stopped to ask, in the political and/or the policy arena, whether such ideas travelled and if they did in what form, how and with what degree of effectiveness. The absence of such questions has fed the restorative justice swagger. The continued absence of any real rigour around such questions has provided additional nourishment for the elasticity and lack of clarity associated with restorative justice commented on above. Indeed, this lack of clarity and elasticity is articulated, and thereby endorsed, in the government's own strategy documents. However, this is a process not just about the efficacy or otherwise, of travelling criminal justice policies. The questions raised here also relate to what happens to such policies after they have travelled. What does the implementation process look like?

In considering the question of how criminal justice policies travel, Jones and Newburn (2002) offer an interesting critical analysis of the extent to which there may or may not be criminal justice policy convergence between the United States and the United Kingdom. Using a conceptual framework on policy designed to distinguish between policy process and policy levels, they present a convincing argument of the need for more detailed studies of how criminal justice policy takes its shape. Using the example of zero-tolerance policing, they conclude that the policy process is not a linear one. It is also necessary to understand the complex interplay between content, substance, style and rhetoric. Using this kind of analysis, they conclude that 'zero tolerance policing has barely been copied at all in the U.K.' (ibid.: 195). To this conceptual framework, I would also add the importance of understanding the policy network (see inter alia Ryan, Savage and Wall, 2001). Arguably, in the context of RJ, understanding the influence of such a network facilitates our understanding of the content and substance of the Crime and Disorder Act 1998 and the style and rhetoric of the Youth Justice Board. Here, of course, it would be easy to point to the role of the Audit Commission, the Chief Constable of Thames Valley and his involvement with the Youth Justice Board and the subsequent influence of Thames Valley in RJ training. All of which have clearly played a role in the current fashion for restorative justice style initiatives. This kind of analysis takes us beyond considering the power of specific individuals in policy development to understand the way in which shared interests have resulted in this particular policy turn.

Looking to a critical understanding of the policy process as outlined above not only offers a more detailed picture of RJ's swagger but also opens the lens to a deeper understanding of the macropolitical context in which RJ and its associated research operates contemporarily. A range of questions might follow from such a framework for analysis. At what level does this policy operate (its substance as compared with its rhetoric); what was the policy process like and how did RJ become transformed from a 'dead duck' as Paul Rock observed in 2004 to a popularly accepted way of doing business in 2010. In addition, we need a detailed appreciation of its network: who are its protagonists, are they in positions to make a difference and what shape does this network have?

Little time or work has been spent on thinking about how, if at all, these policies, conceived in different socio-economic contexts, may or may not travel to the United Kingdom and what that process really looks like. Hence the importance of comparative work to criminology for what can or cannot be learned from responses to crime in different cultural contexts. As a consequence, there is a series of further questions both for the reader and for criminologists:

1. How, if at all, do criminal justice policies travel?
2. Can criminologists apply the same kinds of understandings from one place to another to policies that have travelled?
3. Can criminologists use the same ways of researching problems and policies in different places?
4. What importance, if any, should be given to national and/or international politics in these processes?
5. What importance, if any, should be given to questions of culture in these processes?

The last issue, the question of understanding culture, has provided some criminologists one way of thinking about the current state of the discipline. This has led to the emergence of what has been termed 'cultural criminology'. So, we shall spend a little time considering this development next.

A WORD ON CULTURAL CRIMINOLOGY

Jeff Ferrell writing in the *Sage Dictionary of Criminology* defines cultural criminology in the following way:

> An emergent theoretical orientation that investigates the convergence and contestation of cultural, criminal and crime control processes. Cultural criminology emphasises the role of image, style, representation and meaning both within illicit subcultures, and in the mediated construction of crime and crime control.
>
> (Ferrell, 2006: 104)

If we add to this the following statement from Jock Young:

> Cultural criminology is of importance because it captures the phenomenology of crime – its adrenaline, its pleasure and panic, its excitement, and its anger, rage, and humiliation, its desperation and its edgework.
>
> (Young, 2004: 1)

we get a sense of what it is that is the focus of attention for cultural criminology and the historical legacy from which it has emerged. Arguably, emanating from work of the 1970s that focused attention on the role played by the media in constructing and reconstructing the crime problem (a role that has certainly not diminished as any glance at newspaper and television coverage amply demonstrates), cultural criminology is concerned to understand how 'culture, crime and crime control converge' (Ferrell 2006: 105). This focus brings to the criminological table not only the role of the more traditional media in the crime process but also photographs, art, film and other kinds of expressive practices, and also the way in which these arenas feed back into everyday life of not only those defined as criminal but also criminal justice professionals. How might this focus be translated into a specific criminological agenda?

First, this way of thinking about crime and the problem of crime is situated squarely within the way in which the media (film, TV, newspapers, etc.) interplay with people's experiences on one hand or provide a vehicle for experiences on the other. Some would argue that in contemporary society, all experience is mediated in this way. You might like to think about how many people you know who use what has happened in their favourite TV series as a source of either information or experience, or in understanding their own world or that of others. Moreover, the media now frequently provides us all with 'instantaneous' experience, minute by minute reporting, of real events like wars or as in the US live reportage of criminal trials. The line between this kind of experience and real experience is for many people increasingly fuzzy, but whatever the line is, it is part of people's subjective experience that needs to be taken account of when thinking about crime. There is a similar fuzziness to the difference between belonging to a 'real' community and what might be called a 'virtual' community, and as a consequence, who people are using as his/her reference point moral or otherwise. A good example here is Internet chat rooms and the potential they offer for criminal activity for paedophiles, where the move from the virtual to the real may not be necessary at all in terms of what such people might be seeking. It is the way in which crime is constantly constructed and reconstructed against this kind of backcloth that is of interest to the cultural criminologist. So, their focus of attention becomes:

1. The motive for crime as being about thrill, pleasure seeking and risk-taking rather than it being rational (see Chapter 4).
2. The context of crime being the spaces left available to people in an increasingly bureaucratized society, the spaces in which they can be creative.
3. The recognition of crime as being a response to a rule bound society – so breaking the rules and doing something different becomes a part of living itself, of actually feeling alive.
4. Such behaviours can only be studied by being immersed in them and being reflective on that immersion. (In other words, quite different from basing your study on official data of any kind: see Chapter 2.)
5. As a result of all of the above, criminology cannot be a science in the positivistic sense (and some would say, in any sense). So, in cultural criminology, there are no rigid lines drawn between the expert and the criminal or between crime and normality.

The consequence of this focus is that cultural criminology itself is likely to produce quite challenging and alternative forms of knowledge, which according to Hayward and Young (2004) makes it dangerous. In particular, cultural criminology would challenge much of the material discussed in this book. It would challenge even the possibility of doing comparative work and would certainly challenge the possibility of their being a universal definition of crime. More importantly, it works with quite a different sense of motivation for the criminal, not as being rational but as being a risk taker, a thrill seeker – someone desiring sensation. In this sense, cultural criminology endeavours to capture the way in which the post-modern world (as opposed to the modern world in which criminology has its origins) results in individuals seeking out their own ways of making sense of the world. Here the emphasis on difference and diversity are put to the fore in the contemporary global world but also an appreciation of the ways in which that defined as 'criminal' needs to be contextualized within people's normal everyday lives. For example, in a seminal study by Winlow and Hall (2006), two UK sociologists, they explore the testimonies of young people in how they experience their everyday lives. These stories suggest no resistance to, let alone opposition to, the current state of advanced capitalism. These young people are both captured by, and captivated by, egoism, competition and consumerism, whether that is in relation to their own personal lives and relationships or in relation to what they wear and how they choose to spend their time. As Winlow and Hall observe, they occupy a 'perilous social terrain' (2006: 31) in which their social precariousness, to borrow a phrase from Young (1999), is punctuated by Saturday nights and having a 'good night out'. There seem to be a number of ingredients to a good night but two are key: alcohol and violence. Indeed, for some of the young people in this study (mostly the young males), there is the sense of some vicarious pleasure to be gained from witnessing violence on a 'good night out' in which the relationship between violence and leisure is almost normalized. These young men have a sophisticated understanding of what gives rise to violence and their relationship with it, both as victims and perpetrators, in which the boundaries between these two categories are very blurred indeed with many incidents never being reported to anyone. It is the cultural embeddedness of what might be viewed as criminal and the processes that surround it that fascinates the cultural criminologist.

In the study by Winlow and Hall, we can see the manifestation of some of the features of globalization, through style, fashion and music, which were listed at the beginning of this chapter. However, the contemporary global world challenges criminology in other ways too and that challenge is manifested in the threat of (global) terrorism.

A NEW AGE OF ANXIETY? TERRORISM AND CRIMINOLOGY

The events of 9/11 in New York, 11/3 in Madrid, 7/7 in London, and Mumbai in November 2008, among many others, transgress borders and certainly transgress conventional understanding of crime. As a result, they pose a number of interesting questions for criminologists, for example:

- What is terrorism? Is it crime, or is it something else?
- Why should criminologists be interested in terrorism?
- What kinds of concepts might help us understand this particular aspect of the contemporary global condition, including what has become increasingly referred to as 'new terrorism'?

WHAT IS TERRORISM?

First of all, it is important to recognize that terrorism itself is not a singular, coherent concept. Some writers trace its origins to the 'reign of terror' that took place during the French Revolution. Other might take a gendered approach and talk of stalking as 'terrorism'. And others still would use this term to refer to the terrorist activities of the state as opposed to those activities aimed at undermining the state. So, as a concept, it is contested. As a result, one way of making sense of the kind of terrorism governments are preoccupied with is to think of a continuum of terrorism.

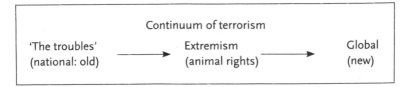

As you can see, this continuum (as it applies to the United Kingdom) situates 'new' terrorism against the backcloth of 'the troubles' in Northern Ireland and the mechanisms put in place to respond to those activities. It also accommodates other kinds of extremist activities. This then allows us to compare and contrast old and new terrorism along a number of dimensions – its organization, identity, focus and use of weapons.

Old terrorism	New terrorism
Vertical	Horizontal
Group	Cells
National	Global
Has infrastructure	Could be anyone
'Conventional' weaponry	Suicide bomber
Forewarning	No advance warning

Even this kind of analysis is rather crude, but it does give a feel for the complexity of identifying what is being discussed. For example, it does not readily lead us to think about 'state' crime as terrorist activity. Yet some critical criminologists would be very keen to ensure that the activities of states against their own people and other states are a central feature of understanding terrorist activities. (At this juncture, you might want to think again about the case study of Abu Ghraib we discussed in Chapter 3.) Indeed, given the long debated question around the legality of the war in Iraq from 2003 onwards, some commentators would want to include all the activities that have followed on from this, as terrorist. So, here we have some clues as to why criminology might be interested in terrorism.

WHY MIGHT CRIMINOLOGY BE INTERESTED IN TERRORISM?

Put simply, criminologists are interested in terrorism since it encourages us to think critically about the following:

- What is crime? (Does it include international law-breaking behaviour as well as more conventionally understood criminal law-breaking behaviour?)
- Who can be a criminal? (Individuals or governments?)
- By what processes are they identified as criminal? (Are the powerful always exempt?)
- Who is the victim of crime? (Individuals or states?)
- What does the 'fear of crime' mean? What are people afraid of and when?

In some respects, these questions are similar to those asked by cultural criminology, but rather than wanting to situate answers to these questions within specific cultural contexts, criminologists who are interested in questions relating to terrorism are just as preoccupied with the politics that underpin the questions listed above. Let us just pursue the issues that are raised for the 'fear of crime' for a moment as this was discussed in some detail in Chapter 2.

Furedi (2002), an English sociologist, has developed a provocative commentary on what he calls the 'culture of fear' that is present in the United Kingdom and possibly elsewhere, since the advent of the global terrorist activities of 2001. This culture of fear he argues is encouraged by sound bite politics and an uncritical mass media which transforms every human experience into a safety situation.

Everything from the food we eat, to the nature of our workplace, to the utensils we might use in our homes are classified as potential sites of danger. The paralysis that results from this is what he calls the 'culture of fear'. In addition, new fears emerge all the time: from terrorism to computer hacking. Add to this the local extension of the use of stop and search powers by the police under anti-terrorism legislation in which suspect people do not actually have to commit a crime to be identified as criminal. Indeed, we have now moved into a situation in which such pre-emptive activities are central to tackling terrorism. Indeed, the logic of anticipating the risk from terrorism requires that our response is driven by the question: what if? This question permits not dealing with crime but with the spectre of pre-crime.

The term 'pre-crime' is the name given to a specialized police unit in Phillip K. Dick's (1956) science fiction short story *Minority Report*. It is the primary duty of pre-crime officers to track down and arrest perpetrators *before* crime happens. Interventions are made on the basis of information about future crimes given by three 'precogs' – beings who are able to visualize impending criminal incidents. This short story, that was made into a relatively successful film, raises many of the dilemmas being faced in the contemporary context. The reliability of horizon scanning, the perils of preemptive intervention, the capture and utilization of personal data, the evidential standard of proof and the difficulty of establishing innocence in a changing environment are key themes in this story. Such concerns resonate very aptly with responses to terrorism. Indeed, the same could be said about the ever-increasing focus on young people as being problematic. It should be remembered, for example, that the current popularity of Anti-Social Behaviour Orders are not necessarily being invoked to challenge criminal behaviour but just that kind of behaviour that many young people engage in; hanging about and being a bit of a nuisance. Moreover on a wider scale, with the construction of the morally decent 'us' as against 'them' epitomized by the pronouncement by George Bush that 'you are either with us and against the terrorists or you are on the side of the terrorists', it is easy to see how not only new fears are being constructed but also new categories of offenders and victims are being created. The problem for criminology is how to make sense of these emergent processes. So here again there is a range of interesting questions for the discipline:

1. Is everyone experiencing this state of anxiety in the same way?
2. If not, then why not?
3. What is the role of culture in mediating the impact of global events such as terrorism?
4. What do such events tell us, if anything, about fear, risk or crime?
5. Who is most likely to have been the subject of government responses to terrorism and why?
6. What do those responses have to say about justice?
7. What has criminology got to offer in answering all of these questions?

For the most part, criminology has turned to the concept of risk to make sense of terrorism and other policy responses to crime, so to end, we will say a little about criminology's relationship with the concept of risk.

CRIMINOLOGY AND RISK

Criminologists have mostly drawn on the concept of risk to try and answer some of the questions that terrorism has posed for the discipline. 'Risk-oriented thinking' has become central to the criminal justice system, in areas such as crime prevention, offender behaviour, victim protection, policing and debates on imprisonment. Pat O'Malley (2010), an Australian social scientist, charts the influence of risk on criminology as both a macroform of structural regulation and a microform of self-management, in how people are categorized, ordered and regulated. You only need to reflect on how debates around immigration, asylum, policing, detention, sentencing, probation and human rights are shaped by understandings of risk. Think, for example, about the perceived risks associated with global terrorism that now affect all of us who want to, or need to, travel by plane, now in very real ways. This is a very good example of how structural regulation impacts on self-management and on the inter-relationship between the two.

Risk, of course, is a widely expansive concept and is differently interpreted by different social theorists for the purposes of this conclusion, we need not be too concerned about the similarities and differences between them. However, it is important to recognize that risk and risk assessment – informed either by asking questions about what was in order to make decisions about the future (a feature of parole decisions for prisoners for example) or by asking the question 'what if' based on information about what might happen in the future – are powerful influences within the discipline of criminology and for criminal justice practitioners. Both questions carry important implications for policy and justice.

CONCLUSION

As can be seen, many of the contemporary problems that are emergent within criminology in some ways transcend the problem of crime itself but their existence serves to illustrate the vibrancy and debate within the discipline as well as its variety of approach both in theory and in subject matter. So, the discipline continues to grow and develop despite what some might see to be its inherent weakness of being a 'rendezvous' subject. It is within that meeting place that there is challenge and diversity that exists not only at an academic level but also at the level of politics and policy. If this book has given you a taster for the challenge, diversity and difficulties associated with the discipline, it has succeeded in one of its aims. If it has encouraged you to think more critically and carefully about common sense and media presentations of crime, it has succeeded in another of its aims. If it has also broadened your understanding of not only the discipline of criminology but also what counts and does not count as crime, it has succeeded in another of its aims. What you now do with all of this is up to you!

EXERCISE

Either read Dick Francis's short story *Minority Report* or watch the film of the same title and think about the following questions:

- What practices does the story allude to that are already in place?
- How effective do you think these practices are?

- Who is most likely to be targeted by these practices, or are we all vulnerable?
- What questions do they raise about justice?
- What is the role for criminology in all of this?

RECOMMENDATIONS FOR FURTHER READING

On the contemporary nature of cultural criminology that is written in a very user-friendly and accessible style, see Jeff Ferrell, Keith Hayward and Jock Young (2009) *Cultural Criminology* (London: Sage). A short and very useful book on *Crime and Risk* is written by Pat O'Malley and was published in 2010 in the Sage Compact Criminology Series (London: Sage). If you want to take your understanding of criminology further, then it will be useful to have *The Sage Dictionary of Criminology* (2006, second edition) as a companion. It has useful definitions and key terms along with evaluations by experts in the field that will be invaluable if you decide to study the discipline further. The range of introductory textbooks designed for the first year student of criminology is vast with many of them offering a very similar diet of material to consider. Your pocket might help you decide which if any of these you purchase. Good luck!

GLOSSARY

There is a clear danger in offering a glossary of terms in a book of this kind that one fails to do service to the terms themselves or simply replicate what is available elsewhere. The reader is advised to use *The Sage Dictionary of Criminology* as the first reference point in any of their investigations of the terms and ideas used in this book and thereafter to use the recommended Further Reading at the end of each of the chapters here and the recommended Further Reading in *The Sage Dictionary of Criminology* to help further their ideas and understanding.

The terms that appear here are the ones that have not been fully defined in the text.

Adversarial system A way of describing the process whereby cases are won or lost in the criminal justice system of England and Wales.

Atavism A throwback to an earlier stage of biological development.

Attrition rate The process whereby offenders and victims are 'lost' as cases go through the criminal justice process.

Biological positivism A search for the cause of criminal behaviour that can be measured in biological differences.

Bounded rationality A recognition that criminal rationality is limited by the information they have available to them and therefore is not perfect.

Classical criminology A way of thinking about crime that gives the individual free will and the ability to make rational decisions.

Concentric zone theory A way of thinking about cities in terms of ever larger circles radiating outwards from the city centre.

Control balance theory Associated with the work of title; it is a view that recognizes both too much and too little control may result in criminal behaviour.

Crime reduction Policies intended to make the crime problem more manageable.

Crime science A commitment to seeking technical, design and opportunity reduction solutions to the problem of crime.

Criminal Other This depicts who is normally included and excluded from criminological attention.

Criminal victimization survey Data gathering from a general sample of the population designed to measure their experiences of crime.

Dark figure of crime The amount of crime that does not come to the attention of anyone.

Determinism Those variables that impact on behaviour but are beyond our control.

Differentiation The things that mark the differences between individuals or groups.

Discretion The gap between what the law says can and cannot be done and what is actually done.

Evolutionary psychology An approach to understanding human behaviour that connects psychological development with evolutionary (biological) development.

Gender The differences between men and women that are socially constructed.

Indirect victimization The impact that crime has on those not directly involved in the particular event concerned.

Inquisitorial system A way of describing a criminal justice process that is concerned to establish what happened and whether or not there is a case to answer.

Left realism A way of thinking about the problem of crime that emerged in the United Kingdom during the 1980s to reclaim the law and order debate from right-wing politics.

Pathology Abnormality.

Patriarchy A concept employed by (radical) feminists to emphasize the structure of male power over women.

Primary victimization The impact of crime on the victim.

Proportionality A principle of sentencing concerned to ensure that the punishment fits the crime.

Responsibilization The wide spread way in which ordinary citizens have been made to take increasing responsibility for crime and the response to crime.

Restorative justice A view of justice rooted in the belief of the need to reintegrate the offender into society through involvement of the victim.

Right realism Largely emanating from the United States during the 1980s, this label refers to a collection of theoretical and policy concerns that centre the cause of crime within the individual.

Secondary victimization The way in which contact with the criminal justice system may exacerbate already existing feelings of victimization.

Situational crime prevention Used in relation to crime prevention policy that emphasizes the opportunity basis of crime.

Social crime prevention Used in relation to crime prevention policy that emphasizes the social cause of crime.

Social disorganization Associated with the Chicago School of sociology during the 1920s and 1930s, this concept was used to describe the kinds of adaptations people made to their environment at a time of rapid social change.

Sociological positivism Locating the cause of individual behaviour within the measurable pattern of differences that could be observed across social groups.

Survivor A term used by feminists to capture the way in which women resist and overcome their oppression by men.

Victim culpability The extent to which the victim can be held to be responsible for what has happened to them.

Victim precipitation A focus on what it was that the victim did that resulted in their victimization.

Victim proneness The idea that some people or groups of people are more likely to be victims than others.

Victim responsiveness The willingness, conscious or otherwise, to be victimized.

Victimological Other The way in which victimology makes some groups of people more likely to be included as victims rather than others.

Victimology The study of victimization.

Vulnerability A way of emphasizing that the impact of crime is likely to be greater on some people than others.

Zero tolerance A proactive strategy designed to eliminate targeted crime.

Zone of transition That part of the city contemporarily referred to as the inner city.

APPENDIX

Throughout this text reference has been made to, and use has been made of, the Internet as a useful tool for gathering information about crime. Some of you maybe quite familiar, for example, with using Google as a source of information. You should always remember, however, that Internet sites vary enormously in the quality of the information they offer. Here are just a few suggestions as to how you might make best use of this kind of resource.

On crime and criminal justice policy in the United Kingdom: www. homeoffice.gov.uk has to be your first starting point along with www.justice.gov.uk. These websites allow you to search by putting in keywords and connect you with a whole range of research reports and statistical findings on crime, many of which can be downloaded free of charge. The British Society of Criminology (www.bsc.org.uk) offers information and links to other recognized websites. You can access similar material in the United States from the Federal Bureau of Investigation (www.fbi.gov) and the Justice Department (www. ojp.usdoj.gov), both of which will connect you with other sources of information. The Council of Europe website also offers some, if limited, information on crime as do the United Nations. The United Nations Office on Drugs and Crime (unodc.org) affords access to a wide range of resources on crime internationally.

There are more focused sources of information on victims of crime. For example, in the United Kingdom, www.victimsupport.org.uk provides useful practical information for and about criminal victimization with Criminal Justice System online offering an interactive virtual of the criminal justice system from the victim's perspective (www.cjsonline.org.uk). In addition, searching for international criminal victimization surveys, hate crimes or child and woman abuse will give you access to quite a disparate range of data, but you should remember that many of these are campaigning organizations and their websites will reflect that campaigning interest.

All of the different component parts of the criminal justice system also have their own web-based information, many of which you can access via the governmental sponsored links mentioned earlier. In addition, you might like to look at groups such as the Prison Reform Trust (www.prisonreformtrust.org.uk), the Police Complaints Authority (www.pca.gov.uk) and the UK Police Service Portal (www.police.uk) that links you to all the police services in England and Wales.

Newspapers also offer their own archive of material on the web, and these too can provide you with useful links to other sources of data. However, all of this is just a start. If you use whatever search engine you have access to sensibly and critically, the Internet can be a valuable sources of both information and research material, but do remember the quality does vary!

BIBLIOGRAPHY

Amir, M. (1971) *Patterns of Forcible Rape*, Chicago: Chicago University Press.

Audit Commission (1996) 'Misspent Youth', London: The Audit Commission.

Berk, R.A. and Sherman, L.W. (1984) 'The specific deterrent effects of arrest policy on domestic assaults', *American Sociological Review*, 49: 261–72.

Box, S. (1983) *Crime, Power and Mystification*, London: Tavistock.

Braithwaite, J. (1989) *Crime, Shame and Reintegration*, Cambridge: Cambridge University Press.

Braithwaite, J. (2002, Summer) 'Setting standards for restorative justice', *British Journal of Criminology*, 42(3): 563–77.

Brogden, M., Jefferson, T., and Walklate, S. (1988) *Introducing Policework*, London: Unwin Hyman.

Brown, B. (1986) 'Women and crime: the dark figures of criminology', *Economy and Society*, 15(3): 355–402.

Cameron, D. and Fraser, E. (1987) *The Lust to Kill*, Oxford: Polity.

Carrabine, E., Iganski, P., Lee, M., Plummer, K., and South, N. (2004) *Criminology: A Sociological Introduction*, London: Routledge.

Chambliss, W.J. (1975) 'Towards a political economy of crime', *Theory & Society*, 2: 149–70.

Chesney-Lind, M. and Pasko, L. (2004) *The Female Offender*, London: Sage.

Christie, N. (1986) 'The ideal victim', in E.A. Fattah (ed.) *From Crime Policy to Victim Policy*, London: Macmillan.

Christie, N. (2004) *A Suitable Amount of Crime*, London: Routledge.

Cohen, L. and Felson, M. (1979) 'Social change and crime rate trends: a routine activity approach', *American Sociological Review*, 44(4): 588–608.

Coleman, C. and Norris, C. (2000) *Introducing Criminology*, Devon: Willan.

Connell, G.W. (1987) *Gender and Power*, Oxford: Polity.

Connell, G.W. (1995) *Masculinities*, Oxford: Polity.

Cook, D. (2006) *Criminal Justice and Social Justice*, London: Sage.

Cornish, D. and Clarke, R.V. (1986) *The Reasoning Criminal: Rational Choice Perspectives on Offending*, New York: Springer.

Cornish, D. and Clarke, R.V. (2006) 'The rational choice perspective', in S. Henry and M. Lanier (eds) *The Essential Criminology Reader*, Boulder, CO: Westview.

Croall, H. (1992) *White-Collar Crime*, Buckingham: Open University Press.

Daly, K. (2002) 'Restorative Justice: The Real Story', *Punishment & Society*, 4(1): 55–80.

Dignan, J. (2002) 'Restorative Justice and the Law: the case for an integrated, systemic approach', in L. Waldgrave (ed.) *Restorative Justice and the Law*, Devon: Willan.

Etherington, K. (2000) 'When the victim is male', in H. Kemshall and J. Pritchard (eds) *Good Practice on Working with Victims of Violence*, London: Jessica Kingsley.

Fawcett Society. (2010) *Women and the Criminal Justice System: the Facts*, London: The Fawcett Society.

Feeley, M. and Simon, J. (1994) 'Actuarial justice: the emerging new criminal law', in D. Nelken (ed.) *The Futures of Criminology*, London: Sage.

Felson, M. and Boba, R.L. (2010) *Crime in Everyday Life* (fourth edition), Thousand Oaks, CA: Pine Forge Press.

Ferrell, J. (2006) 'Cultural criminology', in E. McLaughlin and J. Muncie (eds) *The Sage Dictionary of Criminology* (second edition), London: Sage.

Furedi, F. (2002) *The Culture of Fear* (second edition), London: Cassell.

Garland, D. (2001) *The Culture of Control*, Oxford: Oxford University Press.

Geis, G. (1973) 'Victimisation patterns in white-collar crime', in I. Drapkin and E. Viano (eds) *Victimology: A New Focus*, vol. 5. Lexington, MA: D.C. Heath and Co.

Gelsthorpe, L. (2006) 'Due process and crime control', in E. McLaughlin and J. Muncie (eds) *The Sage Dictionary of Criminology* (second edition), London: Sage.

Genn, H. (1988) 'Multiple victimisation', in M. Maguire and M. Ponting (eds) *Victims of Crime: A New Deal?* Buckingham: Open University Press.

Goodey, J. (1997) 'Boys don't cry: masculinities, fear of crime and fearlessness', *British Journal of Criminology*, 37(3): 401–18.

Gottfredson, M. and Hirschi, T. (1990) *A General Theory of Crime*, Stanford, CA: Stanford University Press.

Hall, R. (1985) *Ask Any Woman*, London: Falling Wall Press.

Hayward, K. and Young, J. (2004) 'Cultural criminology: some notes on the script', *Theoretical Criminology*, 8(3): 259–74.

Heidensohn, F. (1985) *Women and Crime*, London: Macmillan.

Henry, S. (2006) 'Crime', in E. McLaughlin and J. Muncie (eds) *The Sage Dictionary of Criminology* (second edition), London: Sage.

Hindelang, M., Gottfredson, M., and Garofalo, J. (1978) *Victims of Personal Crime: An Empirical Foundation for a Theory of Personal Victimisation*, Cambridge, MA: Ballinger.

Hirschi, T. (1969) *Causes of Delinquency*, Berkeley, CA: University of California Press.

Hobbes, T. (1968 originally 1651) *Leviathon*, Harmondsworth: Penguin.

Holmes, R. and Holmes, S. (1998) *Serial Murder* (second edition), Thousand Oaks, CA: Sage.

Hood-Williams, J. (2001) 'Gender, masculinities, and crime', *Theoretical Criminology*, 5(1): 37–60.

Hopkins-Burke, R. (2001) *An Introduction to Criminological Theory*, Devon: Willan.

Hudson, B. (2003) *Justice in the Risk Society*, London: Sage.

Hudson, B. (2006) 'Natural justice and social justice', in E. McLaughlin and J. Muncie (eds) *The Sage Dictionary of Criminology*, London: Sage.

Jefferson, T. (2006) 'Hegemonic masculinity', in E. McLaughlin and J. Muncie (eds) *The Sage Dictionary of Criminology* (second edition), London: Sage.

Jones, T. and Newburn, T. (2002, May) 'Policy convergence and crime control in the USA and the UK: streams of influence and levels of impact', *Criminal Justice*, 2(2): 173–203.

Joyce, P. (2005) *Crime and the Criminal Justice System*, Devon: Willan.

Jupp, V., Davies, P., and Francis, P. (1999) 'The features of invisible crimes', in V. Jupp, P. Davies, and P. Francis (eds) *Invisible Crimes: Their Victims and Their Regulation*, London: Macmillan.

Kendall, K. (1991, Spring) 'The politics of premenstrual syndrome: implications for feminist justice', *Journal of Human Justice*, 2(2): 77–98.

Laycock, G. (2006) 'Crime Science', in E. McLaughlin and J. Muncie (eds) *The Sage Dictionary of Criminology* (second edition), London: Sage.

Levi, M., Burrows, J., Fleming, M.H., Hopkins, M., and with Matthews, K. (2007) *The Nature, Extent, and Economic Impact of Fraud in the UK*, London: ACPO.

Lilly, J.R., Cullen, F., and Ball, R. (1995) *Criminological Theory: Context and Consequences*, Thousand Oaks, CA: Sage.

McEvoy, K., Mika, H., and Hudson, B. (2002, Summer) 'Introduction: practice, performance and prospects for restorative justice', *British Journal of Criminology*, 42(3): 469–75.

McIntyre, A. (1988) *Whose Justice? Which Rationality?* London: Duckworth.

McLaughlin, E. (2006) 'Discretion', in E. McLaughlin and J. Muncie (eds) *The Sage Dictionary of Criminology*, London: Sage.

McMullen, R. (1990) *Male Rape*, London: Gay Men's Press.

MacPherson, L. (1999) *The Stephen Lawrence Inquiry*, London: HMSO.

Maguire, M. (2002) 'Crime statistics: the "data explosion" and its implications', in M. Maguire, R. Morgan, and. R. Reiner (eds) *The Oxford Handbook of Criminology*, Oxford: Oxford University Press.

Mawby, R. and Walklate, S. (1994) *Critical Victimology*, London: Sage.

Messerschmidt, J. (1993) *Masculinities and Crime*, Lanham, MD: Rowman & Littlefield.

Messerschmidt, J. (1997) *Crime as Structured Action*, London: Sage.

Miers, D. (1978) *Responses to Victimisation*, Abingdon: Professional Books.

Miers, D. (1989) 'Positivist victimology: a critique', *International Review of Victimology*, 1: 3–22.

Mooney, J. (2000) *Gender, Violence and the Social Order*, London: Macmillan.

Morris, A. (2002, Summer) 'Critiquing the critics: A brief response to critics of restorative justice', *British Journal of Criminology*, 42(3): 596–615.

Muncie, J. (2006) 'Positivism', in E. McLaughlin and J. Muncie (eds) *The Sage Dictionary of Criminology* (second edition), London: Sage.

Myhill, A. and Allen, J. (2002) 'Rape and Sexual Assault: The Nature and Extent of the Problem', Home Office Research Study 237, London: HMSO.

Naffine, N. (1990) *Law and the Sexes*, London: Macmillan.

Nelken, D. (1994) 'Whom can you trust? The future of comparative criminology', in D. Nelken (ed.) *The Futures of Criminology*, London: Sage.

Nelken, D. (2007) 'White-collar crime', in M. Maguire, R. Morgan and R. Reiner (eds) *The Oxford Handbook of Criminology* (fourth edition), Oxford: Oxford University Press.

Newburn, T. (2007) *Criminology*, Cullompton, Devon: Willan.

O'Malley, P. (2010) *Crime and Risk*, London: Sage.

Pease, K. (2002) 'Crime reduction', in M. Maguire, R. Morgan and R. Reiner (eds) *The Oxford Handbook of Criminology*, Oxford: Oxford University Press.

Pease, K. (2006) 'Rational choice theory', in E. McLaughlin and J. Muncie (eds) *The Sage Dictionary of Criminology* (second edition), London: Sage.

Quinney, R. (1972, November) 'Who is the victim?', *Criminology*, 10(3): 309–29.

Quinney, R. (1977) *Class, State and Crime: On the Theory and Practice of Criminal Justice*, New York: McKay.

Radford, J. (2006) 'Radical feminism', in E. McLaughlin and J. Muncie (eds) *The Sage Dictionary of Criminology* (second edition), London: Sage.

Reiman, J. (1979) *The Rich Get Richer and the Poor Get Prison*, New York: John Wiley.

Rock, P. (1986) *A View from the Shadows*, Oxford: Clarendon.

Rock, P. (1990) *Helping Victims of Crime*, Oxford: Oxford University Press.

Rock, P. (2004) *Constructing Victims' Rights*, Oxford: Oxford University Press.

Ryan, N., Savage, S., and Wall, D. (2001) *Policy Networks in Criminal Justice*, London: Palgrave.

Shaw, M. (2002) *Gender and Crime Prevention*, Vienna: ICPC.

Sherman, L.W., Schmidt, J.D., Rogan, D.P., Gartin, P.R., Cohn, E.G., Collins, D.J., and Bacich, A.R. (1991) 'From initial deterrence to long-term escalation: short custody arrest for ghetto poverty violence', *Criminology*, 29(4): 821–49.

Slapper, G. and Tombs, S. (1999) *Corporate Crime*, London: Longmans.

Soothill, K., Peelo, M., and Taylor, C. (2002) *Making Sense of Criminology*, Oxford: Polity.

Spalek, B. (2006) *Crime Victims*, London: Palgrave.

Sutherland, E. (1949) *White-Collar Crime*, New York: Holt, Reinhart and Winston.

Taylor, I., Walton, P., and Young, J. (1973) *The New Criminology*, London: Routledge & Kegan Paul.

Tittle, C. (1995) *Control Balance Theory*, Boulder, CO: Westview.

Tittle, C. (2006) 'Control balance theory', in F.T. Cullen and R. Agnew (eds) *Criminological Theory Past to Present: Essential Readings*, Los Angeles, CA: Roxbury.

Tombs, S. and Whyte, D. (2006) 'White-collar crime and corporate crime', in E. McGlaughlin and J. Muncie (eds) *The Sage Dictionary of Criminology*, London: Sage.

Tombs, S. and Whyte, D. (2007) *Safety Crimes*, London: Routledge–Willan.

Tombs, S. and Whyte, D. (2010) 'A deadly consensus', *British Journal of Criminology*, 50(1): 46–65.

Tong, R. (1989) *Feminist Thought: A Comprehensive Introduction*, London: Unwin Hyman.

Walklate, S. (1989) *Victimology: The Victim and the Criminal Justice Process*, London: Unwin Hyman.

Walklate, S. (2004) *Gender, Crime and Criminal Justice* (second edition), Cullompton, Devon: Willan Publishing.

Walklate, S. (2007) *Understanding Criminology* (third edition), Buckingham: Open University Press.

Whyte, D. (2004a) 'Regulation and corporate crime', in J. Muncie and D. Wilson (eds) *Student Handbook of Criminal Justice and Criminology*, London: Cavendish.

Whyte, D. (2004b) 'All that glitters isn't gold: environmental crimes and the production of local criminological knowledge', *Crime Prevention and Community Safety: An International Journal*, 6(1): 53–64.

Williams, B. (1999) *Working with Victims of Crime*, London: Jessica Kingsley.

Wilmott, P. (1987) 'Introduction', in P. Wilmott (ed.) *Policing and the Community*, London: PSI.

Wilson, J.Q. and Kelling, G.L. (1982, March) 'Broken windows', *Atlantic Monthly*, pp. 29–38.

Wilson, J.Q. and Herrnstein, R. (1985) *Crime and Human Nature*, New York: Simon and Schuster.

Winlow, S. and Hall, S. (2006) *Violent Night*, London: Berg.

Wright, M. (1982) *Making Good*, London: Burnett.

Wright, M. (1991) *Justice for Victims and Offenders*, Philadelphia, PA: Open University Press.

Young, J. (1986) 'The failure of radical criminology', in R. Matthews and J. Young (eds) *Confronting Crime*, London: Sage.

Young, J. (1992) 'Ten points of realism', in J. Young and R. Matthews (eds) *Rethinking Criminology: Realist Debates*, London: Sage.

Young, J. (1997) *The Criminology of Intolerance*, London: Centre for Criminology, Middlesex University.

Young, J. (1999) *The Exclusive Society*, London: Sage.

Young, J. (2001) 'Identity, community and social exclusion', in R. Matthews and J. Pitts (eds) *Crime, Disorder and Community Safety*, London: Routledge.

Young, J. (2007) *The Vertigo of Late Modernity*, London: Sage.

INDEX

Note: Page numbers for illustrations appear in **bold**.

www.routledge.com/sociology

The Ideal Companion to
Criminology: The Basics, 2nd Edition

Fifty Key Thinkers in Criminology

Edited by **Keith Hayward, Shadd Maruna**, and **Jayne Mooney**

Fifty Key Thinkers in Criminology brings the history of criminological thought alive through a collection of fascinating life stories. The book covers a range of historical and contemporary thinkers from around the world, offering a stimulating combination of biographical fact with historical and cultural context. A rich mix of life-and-times detail and theoretical reflection is designed to generate further discussion on some of the key contributions that have shaped the field of criminology.

Featured profiles include:

- Cesare Beccaria
- Nils Christie
- Albert Cohen
- Carol Smart
- W. E. B. DuBois
- John Braithwaite

Fifty Key Thinkers in Criminology is an accessible and informative guide that includes helpful cross-referencing and suggestions for further reading. It is of value to all students of criminology and of interest to those in related disciplines, such as sociology and criminal justice.

Pb: 978-0-415-42911-5
Hb: 978-0-415-42910-8
eBook: 978-0-203-86503-3

For more information and to order a copy visit
www.routledge.com/9780415429115

Available from all good bookshops

www.routledge.com/sociology

ROUTLEDGE

The Ideal Companion to
Criminology: The Basics, 2nd Edition

Crime and
Criminal Justice

By **Ian Marsh, Gaynor Melville,
Keith Morgan, Gareth Norris,**
and **John Cochrane**

Crime and Criminal Justice provides students with a comprehensive
and engaging introduction to the study of criminology by taking an
interdisciplinary approach to explaining criminal behaviour and
criminal justice.

The book is divided into two parts, which address the two essential
bases that form the discipline of criminology. Part One describes,
discusses and evaluates a range of theoretical approaches that have
offered explanations for crime, drawing upon contributions from
the disciplines of sociology, psychology, and biology. It then goes on
to apply these theories to specific forms of criminality. Part Two
offers an accessible but detailed review of the major philosophical
aims and sociological theories of punishment, and examines the
main areas of the contemporary criminal justice system – including
the police, the courts and judiciary, prisons, and more recent
approaches to punishment.

Presenting a clear and thorough review of theoretical thinking on
crime, and of the context and current workings of the criminal
justice system, this book provides students with an excellent
grounding in the study of criminology.

Pb: 978-0-415-58152-3
Hb: 978-0-415-58151-6
eBook: 978-0-203-83378-0

For more information and to order a copy visit
www.routledge.com/9780415581523

Available from all good bookshops

www.routledge.com/law

ROUTLEDGE

The Ideal Companion to
Criminology: The Basics, 2nd Edition

Criminology: The
Key Concepts

Martin O'Brien, University of
Chester, UK

Majid Yar, University of Kent, UK

Criminology: The Key Concepts is an authoritative and comprehensive
study guide and reference resource that will take you through all
the concepts, approaches, issues and institutions central to the
study of crime in contemporary society.

Topics covered in this easy-to-use, A-Z guide include:

- policing, sentencing and the justice system;
- types of crime, including corporate crime, cybercrime,
  sex and hate crimes;
- feminist, Marxist and cultural approaches to criminology,
  terrorism, state crime, war crimes and human rights;
- social issues such as antisocial behaviour, domestic
  violence and pornography;
- criminal psychology and deviance.

Fully cross-referenced, with extensive suggestions for further
reading and in-depth study of the topics discussed, this is an
essential reference guide for students of criminology at all levels.

> **Pb:** 978-0-415-42794-4
> **Hb:** 978-0-415-42793-7
> eBook: 978-0-203-89518-4

For more information and to order a copy visit
www.routledge.com/9780415427944

Available from all good bookshops

Taylor & Francis

eBOOKS
ORDER YOUR
FREE 30 DAY
INSTITUTIONAL
TRIAL TODAY!

FOR LIBRARIES

Over 23,000 eBook titles in the Humanities,
Social Sciences, STM and Law from some of the
world's leading imprints.

Choose from a range of subject packages or create your own!

Benefits for you
▶ Free MARC records
▶ COUNTER-compliant usage statistics
▶ Flexible purchase and pricing options

Benefits for your user
▶ Off-site, anytime access via Athens or referring URL
▶ Print or copy pages or chapters
▶ Full content search
▶ Bookmark, highlight and annotate text
▶ Access to thousands of pages of quality research
at the click of a button

For more information, pricing enquiries or to order
a free trial, contact your local online sales team.

UK and Rest of World: online.sales@tandf.co.uk
US, Canada and Latin America:
e-reference@taylorandfrancis.com

www.ebooksubscriptions.com

Taylor & Francis eBooks
Taylor & Francis Group

A flexible and dynamic resource for teaching, learning and research.